'This is an exceptional and painstaking work of rare dedication that is structurally expansive and conceptually rigorous. Most significantly, the editors and the team of translators, interviewers and critical essayists have elegantly woven a complex tapestry of aesthetics, politics and ethics that marks one of the most involved, committed and intricate authors of our time. The book radiantly brings to light the myriad trajectories through which Nabarun Bhattacharya was able to catch and express the deepest undertones of our overwrought times.

Beneath that tale lies another layer—that, like all true political prophets, Bhattacharya could presciently prefigure and predict—an ominous and macabre sublunar future, the contours of which continue to remain spectral and contingent.'

—Professor Prasanta Chakravarty,
Department of English, University of Delhi

'This is a timely introduction to Nabarun, a major activist writer of minor literature, inhabiting the borderlands of the ubiquitous modern order of capital, in the space-time of contemporary Kolkata. The book contains short stories, poems, an interview with the writer and essays on him—a well-curated collection, offering a rounded representation of Nabarun. As the book highlights, the deep subaltern denizens of Nabarun's world may be voided of agency and use but can't be voided of the imagination of freedom. Through the intervention of this text, Nabarun's radical insight and technologies of posthuman praxis will be available widely, inspiring many versions of another kind of life, a plural participatory anarchy of friendship.'

—Debashish Banerji,
Haridas Chaudhuri Professor of Indian Philosophies and Cultures and Doshi Professor of Asian Art, California Institute of Integral Studies (CIIS), San Francisco, CA

Nabarun Bhattacharya

Nabarun Bhattacharya

Aesthetics and Politics in a World after Ethics

Edited by

Sourit Bhattacharya, Arka Chattopadhyay and Samrat Sengupta

BLOOMSBURY
NEW DELHI • LONDON • OXFORD • NEW YORK • SYDNEY

BLOOMSBURY INDIA
Bloomsbury Publishing India Pvt. Ltd
Second Floor, LSC Building No. 4, DDA Complex, Pocket C – 6 & 7,
Vasant Kunj, New Delhi 110070

BLOOMSBURY, BLOOMSBURY ACADEMIC INDIA and the Diana logo are trademarks of Bloomsbury Publishing Plc

First published in India 2020
This Paperback edition published 2025

Bloomsbury Academic
An imprint of Bloomsbury Publishing Plc

ISBN: PB: 978-93-69525-55-3 ; eBook: 978-93-88630-51-1

2 4 6 8 10 9 7 5 3 1

Typeset in Minion Pro by Manipal Technologies Limited
Printed and bound in India

Contents

Interview with Nabarun Bhattacharya

Part II: Critical Essays on Nabarun Bhattacharya

Foreword

This book on the aesthetics and politics of Nabarun Bhattacharya comes at a critical moment in global politics as in Indian history, one that might have drawn a savage, satirical response from Nabarun himself. Much of his work is haunted by a darkly prescient foreshadowing of postmodern apocalypse. Despite the cult status and devoted following Nabarun Bhattacharya enjoys in contemporary Bengali literary circles, this is to my knowledge the first extended study of his work in English, offering translations of primary sources (an interview with the author and several of his poems and stories) and eleven long critical essays, as well as an editorial introduction. The editors are to be congratulated on their devotion to a difficult task and the critical intelligence with which they have focused on the key features of Nabarun Bhattacharya's revolutionary aesthetics. These include his fierce dismantling of the illusions that sustain the capitalist culture; the black humour with which he subverts the conventions of realism while focusing on marginal existences, the lives of the underclass; his linguistic and generic inventiveness and, above all, his dissolution of the boundaries between human, non-human animal and thing.

The radical power of Nabarun Bhattacharya's vision, 'in a world after ethics', lies precisely in his moral interrogation of contemporary society, politics and art: in his awareness that a world founded on violence and exploitation is ultimately self-destructive, and that the oppressed will rise. In some ways this is figured by a recurrent image in his work, that of the explosion—whether of the human bomb or of a hidden stockpile of weapons. Yet, in a richly absurdist oeuvre, such explosions are rarely the product of conscious intention, of a revolutionary enterprise dedicated to the destruction of class enemies. Rather, they occur by accident or oversight, through the self-conflagration of incendiary material that has, we realise, accumulated over time. Thus, instead of a narrative of revolutionary progress, of the kind that preoccupied his Communist forebears, Nabarun Bhattacharya's poetics are imbricated in a far bleaker landscape of waste, decay and death—in which we sense, as he writes in one of his poems, that:

> Something's burning
> In front of everyone, right before your eyes,
> Amidst all the people
> Homeland!

For a Marxist poet, novelist and political commentator, writing in a dystopian world, one that has abandoned both the principles of social justice and the pretence of benign power, such a vision is compounded equally of melancholy and anarchic humour. Whether in the volume of poems with which he burst on the Bengali literary scene, *Ei Mrityu Upatyaka Amar Desh Noy* (*This Valley of Death Is Not My Country*, 1973), or in his first two novels, *Harbart* (1993) and *Kangal Malsat* (2003), Nabarun Bhattacharya sought to subvert the conventions of social realism that had ruled left-wing Bengali literary representation, replacing them by a rich medley of motifs taken from popular culture and occult practise, a language that freely employed slang and obscenity, and a vision of subaltern actors ascending to take their place in the sky as a tribe of Fyatarus, winged offenders against social propriety and complacency. The subversive task of the radical writer, as Nabarun sees it, is, thus, not to preach revolution, but to employ his aesthetics as a form of politics: to upset hierarchy by elevating the downtrodden, to unsettle bhadralok sensibility by scatological humour and to disenchant our technological urban utopias by imagining fantastic weapons of mass destruction.

In its choice of literary material as well as of critical themes, this book explores the many aspects of Nabarun's vision: its obsession with waste, filth and detritus, its focus on destruction and death, its vision of a dystopic city, its critique of class and caste and its use of language to subvert literary propriety. What is particularly striking, however, is its attention to a distinctive but little-explored aspect of his work, its post-humanist dissatisfaction with an anthropocentric universe, as expressed in a deep concern with the lives of non-human animals and of objects. Nabarun, always a cerebral and self-conscious writer, himself reflected on this concern, seeing it—at least sometimes—as a way of escape from the greed and rapacity of the human race that appears to have appointed itself the task of destroying our planet. In the novella *Lubdhak* (2000), a human proposal to commit animal genocide (in order to rid the city of stray cats and dogs) requires its animal protagonists, faced with the threat of extinction, to organise themselves for the purpose of resistance. In the end, they do indeed evacuate the city, but only because they realise—as humans have failed to do—that it is doomed. That sense of an ending—a catastrophe compounded by human obtuseness, cruelty and folly on the one hand, and environmental disaster on the other—is everywhere in Nabarun's fiction. It is what makes his writing most relevant today. I congratulate the contributors to this volume for a remarkable and timely undertaking.

—Supriya Chaudhuri

Preface

I am possibly not the best person to write a preface to a book dedicated to the analyses and criticisms of Nabarun Bhattacharya's works. One reason is that I do not have formal training in literary theories, and my education has been essentially in the realm of social sciences. But then, an understanding of cultural anthropology and sociological changes is actually a great enabler while trying to understand a writer like him. But again, Nabarun never took literary criticism seriously. When his first novel, *Harbart*, came out as a book in the 1990s, the biggest critic of the Bengali cultural establishment of the day wrote in his review in a leading Bengali newspaper, 'Such language and imagery have no place in Bengali literature. This book will also fade from the memory of readers in a few years.' Notwithstanding, *Harbart* went on to win the highest literary award given by the Government of India (Sahitya Akademi), despite the fact that Nabarun had little regard for awards and prizes; a fresh English translation of the novel has been brought out by Seagull Books and then by New Directions, both of which are known for publishing serious writers. *Harbart* has also come out in German. Translations of a lot of his works other than *Harbart* are now available in French, Italian and Czech. An Italian translation of *Kangal Malshat* has come out recently. Today, five years after his death, Nabarun is threatening to just not being limited to a cult Bengali writer. Rather, the tilapia from Calcutta's fish tank is hitting faraway shores. Nabarun was very clear about his views on literary criticism. 'I write. They critique. Not the other way around. I do not write keeping in mind what they will appreciate' was his clear thought.

Nabarun was a complex writer, not least because he was interested in so many things in this world and beyond. His voracious appetite for reading was rarely satiated. From the geography of witchcraft to Mughal gardening, the nitty-gritty of the Russian Revolution to the economics of the Space Race, his knowledge was encyclopaedic. His literary universe spanned nearly all continents of this world as well as many languages of India. There were some recurring themes and beliefs that fascinated him. 'Death' and 'The Buddha' were constants here. While he believed in Communism, its anthropocentrism, doctrinal rigidity and historical cruelties disturbed him. There were questions in his mind. For example, if Bukharin and Preobrazhensky were right on the incompatibility of religion and communism, then how the number of Russian Orthodox churches had multiplied by eighty times in the 1942–1945 period when Stalin, the architect of the Atheist Five Year Plan, was still very much in the saddle? One can go on and on. It is not possible to sum up a person who was so involved in his work, used words as 'Molotov cocktail' and deliberately created characters to subvert the placid waters of Bengali literature and gave political literature possibly a new hope in the times of despair. I think Nabarun will be remembered as someone who grasped and painted a changing society in all his honest ruthlessness, and for his utter rejection of anthropocentrism that is possibly going to destroy the planet we inhabit and wipe out every species in the coming future.

—Tathagata Bhattacharya

Acknowledgements

An edited collection is a product of teamwork. It demands good communication between editors and contributors as well as between the editors themselves, and patience and thorough editing skills. For a collection that introduces a relatively lesser-known Bengali author, Nabarun Bhattacharya, to a global audience by including not only critical essays on him but also translations of his creative work, the element of understanding, patience and teamwork becomes vital. We would like to thank all our contributors for their insightful work, timely submission, rigorous revision and genuine understanding and warmth. It has been both challenging and exciting to work with a team of translators and academics which gives the book its unique demeanour and appeal.

We would also like to thank Tathagata Bhattacharya for giving us the copyright permission to translate from Nabarun Bhattacharya's stories, poems and interview. Our sincere thanks to Prof. Supriya Chaudhuri for writing a 'Foreword' to this book.

Finally, this book would not have been possible without the support from Bloomsbury. Our heartfelt thanks to Chandra Sekhar, who believed in the project from the beginning and guided us throughout with his prompt responses, practical suggestions and production-related support.

Nabarun Bhattacharya and His World: An Introduction

Sourit Bhattacharya, Arka Chattopadhyay and Samrat Sengupta

I

'This very moment of the cruel sovereign demonstrates the need for a new clock and time'

—Nabarun Bhattacharya (2016: 107)

Nabarun Bhattacharya: Aesthetics and Politics in a World after Ethics aims to introduce the Bengali writer (1948–2014) to a pan-Indian and global audience by presenting some of his short stories and poems in English translation and offering a series of critical readings of his works. As the above quote from one of his pieces on the contemporary post-millennial moment suggests, his literary imagination is geared towards a time which is unborn and which departs from the order of things at present, which he calls the 'moment of the cruel sovereign'. His aesthetics is informed by the politics of resistance and transcendence from the order of world capitalism as well as the shape it takes in a postcolonial nation-state like India, and more particularly in the state of West Bengal. Yet Nabarun's literary world does not remain confined solely to the 'local'. It traverses the local and stretches along spaces of suffering such as the war-damaged zones of Iraq or Afghanistan, the victims of neo-liberal politics like in rural China or the Indian state of Bihar and even the authoritarian communist regime of Russia. He portrays such suffering alongside the neo-liberal consumerist vision of a happy life and a seamless, easily accessible enjoyment. This latter vision invisibilises and justifies the lateral damage done to the expendable 'other', who often needs to be sacrificed for the maintenance of the consumerist world order. Nabarun's works, while critiquing this 'moment' of the capital, also thinks of a transcendence which is not always equivalent to the programmatic and the possible modes of resistance.

A deeply political writer, Nabarun's career could be roughly divided into three segments which often overlap, both temporally and ideationally. His first short story 'Bhashan' ('Immersion') was published in the literary magazine *Parichay* in 1968, a year that indicates an epochal moment both in Indian and world politics. While, on the one hand, there was the May 1968 uprising in France, the Scandinavian countries and most of Europe as well as in the US and parts of South America, the Indian radical left peasant movement of Naxalbari, on the other hand, was in full swing after its 'official' eruption on 24 May 1967. Nabarun's most celebrated poem, and most likely his first published poem, 'Ei Mrityu Upatyaka Amar Desh Na' ('This Valley of Death Is Not My Country') came out in 1972, first in a collection of revolutionary poems, and then in 1973, re-published in Nabarun's own anthology based on the name of the poem (Bhattacharya 2004 [1973]: 11–15). It was written in response to a mass-murder of youth activists of the Naxalbari movement. Being a committed Marxist and a visionary, Nabarun's writing in this period, roughly from 1968 to early 1980s, engages with issues such as state-sponsored violence, revolutionary sacrifice, social conditions of urban destitution, the trauma of the failure of the revolution ruthlessly massacred by state machinery, etc. The second phase of his writing (roughly from 1980s to the end of 1990s) involves a moment of post-revolutionary crisis and the existential condition of humans in an emergent consumerist world order that eventually culminates into the fall of Soviet Russia as well as that of the long-sustained dream of a communist future. This period focuses more on the crisis of making sense of the rapidly changing world. Shaped by these world-historical transitions, Nabarun's writing now delves into a planetary consciousness about man, animal and nature, especially when there appears to be a profound absurdity of considering humanist post-Enlightenment thinking as pivotal to the world order. Short stories like 'Andho Beral' ('The Blind Cat', 1997) or novels such as *Herbert*[1] (1993),

---

1 The title of the novel has been spelled differently in different English translations. While two of the three English translations have spelled the title 'Herbert', Arunava Sinha's translation, however, is titled 'Harbart'. Authors in this collection have used the spelling of the title as 'Herbert' and the character in the novel as 'Harbart' to retain the Bengali idiosyncrasies in pronunciation. Only in cases where Arunava Sinha's English translation has been used, the novel and the character are spelled as 'Harbart'.

which won him numerous awards and has been translated several times into English, were written in this period. The third phase of Nabarun's writing (in the 21st century) contains a strong challenge of the realistic within reality with the literary creation of the flying miscreants, Fyatarus; and the occult-empowered black magicians, Choktars, who together hatch a revolutionary armed violence in the city; or of the figure of the 'whore', Baby K, who drinks petrol and is highly inflammable, and, in one of the stories, uses her petrol-induced inflammability to explode the American soldiers involved in the Iraq war. These figures emerge from the margins of the mainstream society and could only transcend their existential conditions by resorting to the unreal and the undecidable damages to the system. The disenfranchised suffering 'other' of mainstream civilisation and society, therefore, does not remain determined only by the real time of capitalist civilisation but, through such narratives, imagines an alternative frame of imagined time–space where apparently impossible things can take place.

The popularity of Nabarun as a literary figure was confined to Bengali *avant-garde* literary circles till the 1990s. It expanded further only after this third phase of his writing which allowed a mixing of the serious with the trivial, bordering on radical populism. His claim to fame was the publication of *Kangal Malshat* (*The War Cry of the Vagabonds*, 2003) which introduces, more compellingly, the characters of Fyatarus and Choktars; and the first collection of Fyataru stories—*Fyatarur Bombachak* (2004). By the early years of 2000, performances of Fyataru stories in theatrical forms (under the direction of Debesh Chattopadhyay), especially with the hilarious and obscene expletives from the Fyataru poet Purandar Bhat (whose name 'Purandar' literally means the one who destroys the city) and the general anti-establishment spirit of the works, caught the imagination widely of the students and the youth in the postcolonial city of Kolkata. On the other hand, such fame, confined only to one kind of his writing, often relegated other important works to a margin. In this book, while we engage with Nabarun's more popular works, we also focus on his other writings and the numerous important issues, simultaneously global and local, that his writings have touched upon, alongside the phenomenon of populism in his writings and cultism around his figure. His use of the popular, the trivial and the mundane, as some essays in the collection will show, also questions the separation and reification of the intellectual class from the so-called 'masses', who are considered unimportant and stupid by people with social capital and cultural empowerment.

Another particular factor that has contributed to Nabarun's popularity is the cinematic adaptation of his novel, *Herbert*, by Suman Mukhopadhyay in 2005. The mundane world of the half-crazed clairvoyant commoner, Harbart was pitted against the moment of Naxalbari movement in which he got accidentally involved. The film, following the novel, brings back the dream of revolutionary resistance into the neo-liberal world order. The explosion of bombs stuffed and planted by Harbart's Naxalite nephew Binu, inside his uncle's quilt after the suicidal death of the eponymous protagonist, points at resistance as the sphere of the unanticipated, lying beyond the horizons of pragmatic comprehension. Moreover, in the world of 'serious' Bengali cinema occupied by the topics of drawing-room drama and crisis of relationship among upwardly mobile people, *Herbert* was a fresh lease of life for an audience waiting for the re-emergence of the 'political' in the public. Though the film was not a huge box-office success, it received considerable critical attention and the Silver Lotus National award for the best feature film in Bengali in 2006, building up a fresh readership for Nabarun. Suman Mukhopadhyay then also adapted *Kangal Malshat* to screen in 2015 amidst challenges from state authorities regarding the film's deeply political, anti-establishment rhetoric. More recently, film-maker Qaushiq (or Q as he is popularly known by) has made a documentary on Nabarun, available on YouTube. As we put together this volume, an English translation of Nabarun's *Kangal Malshat* is under way while an Italian translation of the novel is already published. Along with an open access journal issue on Nabarun compiled by two of the editors involved in the book for *Sanglap: Journal of Literary and Cultural Inquiry* (2.1 supplement), which involves English translations of some of his works and with translated works in this volume, Nabarun's works are available for a global readership. This volume, which comes after a critically acclaimed and popular Bengali critical compendium on his work by one of the editors included here, is a way to extend his readership and to point at the world literary nature of his work.

II

A writer like Nabarun writes on an international scale. His stories travel frequently from India to Russia and China, from Germany and France to Australia, in search of the 'world's last communist' (the title of one of his stories). Emboldened by a Communist idea of the international, Nabarun performs a scale-switching from the regional to the cosmic, as he shifts from the city of Kolkata to earth as a planet, about to be destroyed by the clash of a meteorite, in the novel *Lubdhak* (*Sirius*, 2006). Thus, he needs to be established beyond the boundaries of the Indian vernacular, as an important figure in the pantheon of contemporary world literature. The Sahitya-Akademi-award-winning novel *Herbert* (1993) has been translated into English, thrice by three different translators, the third being a new 2019 international edition from the New York-based press, New Directions. Reviews of this international edition have come out in important literary magazines like *The Paris Review*. The trend of international recognition continues with a German translation of *Herbert* and an Italian translation of *Kangal Malshat* (*War Cry of the Vagabonds*; 2003).

We can see how a political commitment to literature frames Nabarun Bhattacharya's aesthetic project, and the volume wishes to tease out various perspectives on this meeting of politics and aesthetics. Nabarun was a life-long Marxist whose political views veered from the ultra-left to a mature eco-Marxist position. He is the son of Bengali leftist playwright Bijan Bhattacharya and novelist-activist Mahasweta Devi, whose works have been translated and written on by several scholars, including Gayatri Chakravorty Spivak. Nabarun draws on this leftist lineage but stands unique as a writer, departing significantly from the run-of-the-mill Bengali Marxist literary tradition. A strong commitment to representing the oppressive urban conditions within which the downtrodden live and a revolutionary belief that the status-quo will be overthrown by the poor often orient his early to middle-period writings. Later, Nabarun shows further interest in questions of the non-human animal and the environment at large, asking us to understand the proportion and the nature of capitalist/anthropocentric violence, inflicted on human and nonhuman beings/objects in everyday life. Be it the novel on dogs, *Lubdhak* (*Sirius*), or on petro-capitalism and dystopia (*KhelnaNagar/Toy City*) and the machine (*Auto*), the political question in Nabarun echoes significant contemporary issues, such as animal rights, global warming and techno-capitalism. This opens up the possibility of questioning the traditional paradigm of humanist values in a world of catastrophic and violent encounters, such as nuclear war or holocaust, which keeps returning in Nabarun's works. It makes his work relevant to readers interested in the field of critical humanism and posthumanism.

His texts give voice to the marginal figures in the lowest stratum of the society, damaged variously by forces of capitalism, globalisation or ecological change, in a language which follows the everyday use of cuss-words in what can be called a major literary breakthrough in the Bengali language. This aspect of Nabarun demands a reading through the subaltern framework—another important practise in contemporary political historiography. In our day, when Dalit studies is getting widely acknowledged as a crucial field in South Asian politics, Nabarun's unrelenting engagement with the downtrodden and the oppressed deserves a serious critical excursus both at the level of his language and his content. On another note, the relative lack of strong female characters in his work calls for a feminist critique that takes into consideration his complex portrayal of revolutionary masculinity.

While Nabarun's content is unmistakably political, he is one writer whose form remains aesthetically experimental. *Kangal Malshat*'s playful language and a literary form that incorporates diverse discursive components like images, newspaper ads, etc. is a case in point. As contemporary political thought centralises the dialogue of politics and aesthetics (consider, for example, the French philosopher Jacques Rancière's book, *The Politics of Aesthetics*, 2003), Nabarun's fusion of revolutionary content with seemingly postmodern form needs to be unpacked, not only in terms of the art-politics encounter but also through other critical lenses, like the conjunction of Marxism and modernity and/or postmodernism and postcolonialism. The extended history of Kolkata's colonial past that Nabarun's novels trace, for example, makes a situated historical reading necessary. This is not to say that he does not transcend local colours. On the other hand, like a truly international author, he navigates seamlessly between a Kolkata genocide, during the Naxalite movement in the 1970s Bengal, and the famished dying children in Gaza during the Israel–Palestine conflict. And yet, his texts also stage a complex socio-political critique of globalisation, for example, in a series of stories on Soviet Russia. His consistent yet unconventional engagement with the question of terror in various short stories like 'Terrorist' or 'Fyataru and the Global Terror' makes him contemporary and relevant. He equally draws upon the question of violence at various levels and refers to revolutionary violence of Naxalbari, police encounters and custodial torture or mass extermination in concentration camp in his fictional and poetic renderings. Nabarun's works are, thus, transnational in the proper sense of the term.

If we consider his literary lineage, he fruitfully brings the Russian novelist Mikhail Bulgakov and 19th-century Bengali satirists like Troilokyanath Mukhopadhyay in the same bracket by pursuing an international tradition that breaks boundaries of canonical literature. The rich repository of various indigenous occult practises is widely utilised in Nabarun's works, in a way that it shows how the rise of 19th-century oral and literary tantric 'occult' traditions impacted 'local' art or more globally makes him into a silent partner to the philosopher Jacques Derrida who considers ghosts to be pivotal to Marxian politics (*Spectres of Marx*, 1993). A large corpus of postcolonial Latin American and African writings have used the trope of ghosts for revolutionary politics (e.g. Isabella Allende's *The House of the Spirits*, Juan Rulfo's *Pedro Paramo*, Pepetela's *The Return of the Water Spirit*, Ngugi wa Thiong'o's *Matigari*, Ivan Vadislavic's *Portrait with Keys*, etc.). This would place Nabarun in the map of contemporary world literature of Marxism and resistance. From a different point of view, Nabarun's manifold references to the occult from necromancy to seance are representative of an Indian *episteme*, vastly different from the western knowledge-system, colonially imposed on the sub-continent.

Nabarun's simultaneously internationalist and local use of avant-gardism has been a matter of much debate within the Bengali literary sphere. To cite one recent example (from an English essay), Supriya Chaudhuri notes that the growth and development of the 'novel' as a literary form in Bengal was related with the region's own aesthetic forms as well as its critical engagements with 'western' modernity (Chaudhuri 2012: 101–123). The two legacies of Bengali literary modernity, she mentions in the first part of her essay, are very much alive in Nabarun's works. The auto-critical humor in the early prose writings of Kaliprasanna Singha or Tekchand Thakur on the emergent colonial upper-middle class and the astute critique of the same class by Bankimchandra and his successors are repeatedly featured in Nabarun's prose which he mixes with the other legacy of *battala sahitya* (*battala* literally means 'beneath the banyan tree' and suggests something akin to what the railway novels in Victorian England meant for popular consumption). Characters like Nabani Dhar in the Fyataru stories (an author of bawdy pornographic novels) or Purandar Bhat (a poet who first appeared in *Kangal Malshat* and who writes using expletives and street language) in Nabarun challenges the refined discourse of middle-class bhadraloks. They are an obvious reference to the 'other' legacy of Bengali modernity, which is more democratic, everyday and multicultural and goes beyond the narrow sphere of educated elites possessing cultural and social capital in a postcolonial society. Here it is important to note that the cultural hiatus between the elite and the proletariat has been a critical focus from 1930 onwards in Bengali modernist writings which were deeply influenced by Marxist literary circles such as the Progressive Writers' Association or journals such as *Parichay* (Das 2003: 8–12). While celebrated novelists like Tarashankar Bandyopadhyay, Manik Bandyopadhyay, Adwaita Mallabarman or, at a later stage, Mahasweta Devi represented lives of farmers, fishermen, tribals or the urban proletariat, their representations were 'largely', albeit critically and heterogeneously, realist. Nabarun's primary engagement with city life brings the worlds of the underprivileged and the downtrodden together with the worlds of the socially secure to induce irony and dark humour. His portrayal of class-struggle both draws from and challenges 'realism' in its content and form. There, he breaks from earlier modernists and moves towards the world of 'fantasy, surreal farce and linguistic and narrative experiment' (Chaudhuri 2012: 122), forcing the portrayal of the struggle towards a classless future into an 'undecidable' form. Here, he follows the legacy and influence of other literary avant-garde figures of 1970s and 1980s like Subimal Mishra or movements such as the *Hungry Generation*, which wanted to break away from the derivative use of the realist form of Bengali literary modernity.

Nabarun's experimentalism as a formally sophisticated writer does not undercut the political conviction of his corpus. On the contrary, it enhances the political. Herein lies the meeting point of aesthetics and politics for him. His works espouse an ethic that bonds aesthetics with politics by combining avant-garde form (one may remember the palimpsest-like form of *Kangal Malshat* or the intertextual cut-ups in *Harbart* and *Lubdhak*) with explicit political content. Quite unlike the European avant-garde tradition that primarily approached the political through the decay of the aesthetic, in Nabarun, the politics of the avant-garde is not just about an anti-representational politics of eclectic forms. In his writings, political discontent as a thematic content breaks into a linear realistic form to wreak havoc with it. As a result, what we have in Nabarun is an intense politicisation of avant-grade forms. This avant-gardism is so endemic to Nabarun's politics, vision, and writing and so widely discussed in critical endeavours on him (both in Bengali and English; for English see specifically the special issue on Nabarun in *Sanglap: Journal of Literary and Cultural Inquiry* (2015) as well as works by Sourit Bhattacharya, Dibyakusum Ray and Madhuja Mukherjee, among others) that we chose not to devote a full essay on this area. On the other hand, because Nabarun's aesthetics and politics are inseparable, none of the essays in this book are able to bypass this aspect.

As the crisis of parliamentary democracy becomes a major global discussion, Nabarun's works, which have shown an abiding faith in non-doctrinaire forms of Marxism and Leftism, and which have always raised critical questions about the democratic practise in India, can be instructive in more ways than one. His works, expectedly, have equally drawn upon the crisis of the back-footing of Marxist ideology in the 1990s across the globe, as he portrays the crisis of Communism and brings in the complex question of counter-revolution in the globalised world. Instead of solely following the traditional Marxist narratives of programmatic class-struggle, his works are intercepted heavily with populist modes of narration, humour, irony, absurdity or the irrational. Yet, his works frequently talk about rupture and radical opening towards a future to come. His writings are strongly futuristic and future-oriented.

This book, as an introductory volume on Nabarun, collects critical essays and translations of some of his poems and short stories, not to mention an interview that will familiarise readers with his visions and imaginings, his thoughts and readings and his beliefs and ideologies as a writer. The essays largely aim at presenting Nabarun's works in the light of ethical and political crisis in a world where no simple, monochromatic idea of doing justice to all, irrespective of experiences of marginality and various forms of subjugations, can be sustained. Ethics is conceptualised here as an approximation of the impossible task of addressing the 'other' (such as the animal, the thing, the economical or gendered subaltern) without co-opting with or subjugating its alterity to a hegemonic political order—a task which has the tendency to remain incomplete. The editors believe that Nabarun's oeuvre depicts such a world of ethical dilemma and a lack of unquestionable faith in a preordained idea of justice. It can also chronologically trace (as his creative world changes from 1970s to the current post-millennium world) the transition into such a supposed 'post-ethical world'. Ranging from state repression of India's Naxalbari revolution in the 1960s and 1970s when anti-state, anti-institutional radical political movements were rampant until the present crisis of global terror, this volume will show how Nabarun's works have not only captured the major moments of crisis plaguing postcolonial India or a global world order but have also consistently problematised questions of ethics, politics and aesthetics. From the moral intellectual crisis of both the traditional and the radical Left, up to the spread of consumerist economy and the birth of the new global middle-classes (who, even now, often shelve the question of justice in lieu of a life of seamless individual success and material gratification), it is difficult to find any easy explanation to the question of right politics, ethics and justice. The essays in this volume attempt to show how Nabarun's aesthetic world encounters this crisis and yet his aesthetic politics makes us feel the desire and necessity for taking up an ethical position.

III

The poems and stories translated here are selected from different phases of Nabarun's career and can, thus, ably point at his thoughts and radical transition in style and politics. Translated attentively by Rijula Das, V Ramaswamy, Debadrita Bose, Arka Chattopadhyay, Samrat Sengupta, Atindriya Chakraborty, Malini Bhattacharya, Supriya Chaudhuri, Partha Pratim Roy Chowdhury and Sourit Bhattacharya, these stories, poems and interviews include his first published story 'Bhashan' ('Immersion') as well as important late stories like 'American Petromax' or 'Nuclear Winter'. There are stories that directly engage with politics, such as 'Leopard-Man' and 'Scarecrow', and those that capture the political through indirect psychological questions of everyday, insignificant criminality as in 'Toy' or by way of a Kafkaesque parable in '4+1'. To represent Nabarun at his critical best, we also have a Fyataru story and the iconic poem, 'This Valley of Death Is Not My Country'. The themes of the poems and the stories range from early 1970s' state-violence on revolutionaries of the Naxalbari Movement to the crisis of Marxism under the rule of the democratic left, the aftermath of consumerism and the flow of neo-liberal capital, the shocking nature within the mundane, mysterious and occult practises in a postcolonial city, critique of war, nuclear fallout and many others. His literary forms include radical left revolutionary realist narratives as well as non-realist modes that have ghosts, flying humans or petrol-drinking whores in a dystopic, neo-liberal world order. These translations, we believe, will provide a solid entry point into Nabarun's charismatic imaginary for scholars interested in related fields. The essays include topics ranging from animality, language and resistance (Aritra Chakraborti), the animal and cosmic logic (Dibyakusum Ray), machine and biopolitics (Arka Chattopadhyay) and objects and commodities (Samrat Sengupta) to subaltern resistance and postcolonial politics (Anindya Sekhar Purakayastha), postcolonial city space (Anuparna Mukherjee), counter-history and counter-memory (Anustup Basu), Indian occult and radical aesthetics (Carola Erika Lorea), gendered violence (Priyanka Basu), toxic ecologies and eco-gothic (Sourit Bhattacharya) and adaptation of his work on stage and screen (Arnab Banerji). These essays, compiled with care and thought, wish to not only bring Nabarun's engagement with diverse but significant local and world-historical topics to a wider public attention but also to situate and suggest his compelling world literary style and appeal.

As we pass through a difficult historical present when the economic logic of neoliberalism and the disturbing rise of fascism and authoritarianism attempt to regularly stifle the characteristically 'human' practice of critical thinking, and put humanities and humanistic work as a field of study and activism under serious threat, Nabarun's anti-establishment writings and his unstinting faith and lifelong work in empowering the marginal and the downtrodden through art remain a beacon of hope. At the same time, the rise of social movements on a global scale, based on class, caste, race, gender and ecology as well as about rising poverty, hunger, fundamentalism, corruption, unprecedented disparity in wealth possession and the dire effects of climate change remind us that people are relentlessly agitated against the current world order and have taken to the street to demand social justice. As we type the final words, we face the global repercussions of the Covid-19 outbreak. We fear not only about our own race and its survival against a series of viral outbreaks, but also of a socio-economically harsher world that awaits us. Along with this, we see images of cleaner cities and waters, of nature beginning to come back in an otherwise busy and non-natural urban life. Some of these materials and emotional contradictions at a simultaneously local and global scale permeate Nabarun's critical and creative imaginary. Never before, it seems to us, were Nabarun's writings and thoughts more timely and suggestive.

References

Bhattacharya, Nabarun (2004 [1973]), 'Ei Mrityu Upatyaka Amar Desh Na'. In *Ei Mrityu Upotyoka Amar Desh Na*, 11–15. Kolkata: Saptarshi.

Bhattacharya, Nabarun (2016), 'Bortoman Somoyer Bhabna'. In *Aro Kathabarta*, 107–114. Kolkata: Bhashabandhan.

Chaudhuri, Supriya (2012), 'The Bengali Novel'. In *The Cambridge Companion to Modern Indian Culture*, edited by Vasudha Dalmia and Reshmi Sadana, 101–123. New York: Cambridge University Press.

Das, Dhanonjay (2003), 'Sampadoker Nibedon'. In *Marxbaadi Sahitya Bitarka*, edited by Dhananjay Das, 8–12. Kolkata: Karuna Prakashani.

Part I

Nabarun Bhattacharya's Works in Translation

Short Stories

Immersion

'The time has come', the Walrus said,
'To talk of many things.'
—*Alice in Wonderland*

Unexpectedly, I died unnoticed. That night, the streets were maddeningly chaotic. Ma Durga and her children—one more than the family-control regulations allowed—were leaving in a truck, reducing her many toiling worshippers to tears. The same trucks in which ghostly sacks of rice travel at night through the city. They cannot appear in daylight. Only in the darkness of night can they be moved from one godown to another. Ma Durga also travelled at night. Drums, brass bands and fireworks created a strange symphony. From time to time, her worshippers were chanting her name. I, too, died at exactly this moment.

The madwoman I have never loved was sitting next to me, crying uncontrollably and singing softly. I didn't hear her entire song. Even though I wanted to, I couldn't. The park where I was dying was right in front of the road. Big buses, trams—everything goes by the park. In the last war, even a convoy went through that road. I heard this from mad old Radhanath; Radhanath has now been reborn after being squashed under a bus last year. Cheers and sounds of joyous celebration were coming from the road, preventing me from hearing the madwoman's song. I never loved the madwoman, not even at the moment of my death. I was feeling sorry for her.

My strength was waning slowly. The red fire ants that lived in the park climbed up my body and danced with joy. I then received divine perception. I understood that the fire ants had not tasted human eyes in a long time. 'What Joy! What Joy!' Some of the more intelligent ants were calling out to the rest of their clan amidst their dancing atop my body. A long time ago, I saw a meeting in this park. A sickle and hammer symbol was drawn across a red flag. The speaker said strange things—that everyone has a right to eat. Suddenly, a strange species called 'police' ran out of black cars and surrounded the park. And then, it was all death and disaster. I won't describe all of it. But I found a red turban. Sometimes, I would wear it at the dead of night and march around the park or stand in front of the toilet. Last year, on the day of Radhanath's death, that turban was stolen. This year, two parties came and had a meeting in the park. Both their flags were red. One party had their flag festooned with a sickle-hammer-star symbol, and the other had a sickle and a blade of grass on their's. And then it was all death and disaster. I won't describe all of it. That time, I did not find anything. I am saying all these things for only one reason; I remembered what that man said in the first meeting. He would have been happy. At least, the fire ants are doing what he wanted.

At this time, I heard the band from the road; someone was taking their goddess away. The madwoman started crying very loudly, brought her ear to my nose trying to hear the sound of my breath, a bomb went off on the road, the iron railings around the park shook violently and I died. I died with my eyes open, thirsty and watching all the stars in the sky. I watched with my dead eyes, how beautiful the world was—like me.

The fire ants conveyed the news to the field rats, the rats relayed it to the dogs and a few cats followed the dogs. The madwoman held me close all night. All night, the dogs did not let the cats come near me. The madwoman kept the dogs away, screaming at them and waving a stick. The dogs were not letting go easily. At the end of the night, a one-eyed black bitch circumvented the madwoman's barricade and bit my stomach. Even though the bitch had to run away because of the madwoman, she tore the clothes off my body. I remained naked. What did I have to care about? Before dying, I was a madman; after death, I was happy. I wasn't ashamed anymore. It felt like I had become a sage—a hermit. Like the fire ants, I also said, 'What joy! What Joy!' The fire ants had begun their work in the meantime. I didn't know there was a secret passage between my right eye and my left. A line of red ants entered through one eye and left through the other. This secret pathway became old to them in no time, and they started to find new ways though my nose and ears, and then my ears and eyes. The madwoman did not see them. Otherwise, she would have killed them. In the light of dawn, the madwoman brought her mouth next to mine, asked me if I wanted water. What could I say? She saw my open mouth and thought I wanted some water. She took a tin can and went away.

I was thinking about another night then. The madwoman would return and resume her lullaby—that monotonous, languid tune didn't allow any memories to surface. It was a long time ago. The madwoman had not yet come to this park then. Radhanath was still alive. It was a winter's night. I was sitting, wearing the same thing I wore even in the summer heat—my overcoat. I found it lying somewhere, and I still haven't lost that coat. It is laying next to my head. Whatever it may be, I was sitting in the park that night. A big, black car stopped outside. The car was very good; it made no sound even when the engine was on. Two men came out of the car with a sack. They threw the sack into the park and went back to the car. The car soundlessly drove away in seconds. I was scared. Why were they in such a hurry? After a while, I found enough courage to go and open the sack. A little baby was in it. Small eyes, small nose, a tiny head like a potato—I felt moved. Like the madwoman, I stayed beside the child all night, staving off dogs with a stick. I thought those men who left it there may still come back. They didn't. I don't know why but I felt I was the father of the child; I wouldn't let the dogs feed on it. In the morning, people came, the police came, another black car with a white cross came. Two men in khaki uniforms came with a long stretcher. That little baby looked so alone in such a large stretcher. They didn't let me go with them. I answered all their questions. They looked at each other in surprise, and then they let me go. I found my way back to the park. I don't know why, after all this time, I thought about that night again.

The madwoman came back with water; she poured it into my mouth, on my head and ran her fingers through my hair. The day grew harsher; the sun began to blaze overhead. The water in my hair and my mouth began to dry. The madwoman stopped her song and stared at my face. Slowly, one and then two people came to the park. When they left, other passersby came and filled their spots. The crowd kept growing, with different kinds of people joining. One bearded, bespectacled young man pointed to the madwoman and told his friend,

'See, an abstract Behula.'[1] I didn't understand what he meant. Many of them looked at me and made a sound, just like dogs make when they drink from a saucer. I didn't understand why they did that either.

Time passed. The police came. They asked the madwoman questions, but she didn't reply. She simply stared at my face, unblinking. That black car with the white cross came then. Two men brought out a stretcher; I recognised them. They had aged. Trouble struck when they tried to take me away. The madwoman wouldn't let me go. The two old men didn't dare approach because of the madwoman's brandished stick. One policeman asked the madwoman to go away. The madwoman hurled abuse at him. The policeman went to hit her with his baton. At this, the madwoman suddenly lifted her clothes and told him to see her 'ma'—her cunt. The policeman shielded his eyes with his hands and ran away, chanting, 'Ram Ram'. The crowd began to shoo the madwoman away. The two old men picked me up on the stretcher. I was put down unceremoniously inside the black car. They slammed the door shut. It was dark all around. I could hear the madwoman wail outside. I suddenly thought, those two old coots did not bring my overcoat. Then I thought, let it be. Durga puja was already over and winter was approaching. The madwoman would wear it.

I could still hear the madwoman crying. The car was shaking as it moved. I thought—this is me; I'm going away. I also thought that I really do love that madwoman. The black car kept moving on.

—Translated by Rijula Das

(Translated from Nabarun Bhattacharya (2006), 'Bhashan'. In *Shrestho Golpo*, 21–24. Kolkata: Dey's Publication.)

1 Folk heroine of *Manasamangal.* When Manasa, the snake goddess, kills Behula's husband, Lakhinder, on their wedding night, Behula sets sail for the home of the Gods with her husband's corpse. Moved by Behula's love and perseverance, Manasa resurrects Lakhinder and his dead brothers.

Scarecrow

This incident took place on 15 August 1979. In some cases, the names of people and places have been changed. The names of Gambhira, Ganpat Ram, Nirbhoy Pasowan and Bharat Bindh will be found here. They are among the many field labourers, farmers and Harijan leaders who were killed by Bihar's landowners and policemen. No part of this writing is fictitious.

The scarecrow was sleepy because the stuffy, hot day was letting out the heat from the earth, but later, at around two in the morning, a bark of cloud fell off and the moon was visible again. A gentle breeze from the jungle blew the scraps and rags of cloth around the scarecrow's body, undulating in the wind. The road was right in front of him and beyond the road, the Harijan slum. Two dogs were lying on the road. But behind them, in the pigsty where last year the flooding river rotted the dead carcasses, jackals hovered. The two dogs ran that way. When they left, a jeep stopped on the road.

The jeep had been waiting a long time for the moon to come out. There were three men inside it. Among them, only Nepali, who was behind the steering wheel, was mildly intoxicated; Gangotri and Daulat weren't. When the jeep started, Daulat was still urinating. He ran, jumped into the jeep, put the stock of the rifle on the floor and held the barrel with his sweaty hands. Once upon a time, the stock had some polish on it, but having rested anywhere and everywhere, it had now become rough-edged. Foregoing the headlights, the jeep moved past Parakochula Block office, through the rundown, sleeping Sarai Bajar road and on to the national highway, navigating by moonlight. As it turned slightly leftward, only a little, the jeep jumped on the dirt road, blowing dust as it moved. The three of them wrapped *gamchas* around their faces. The simple geography of the locale was this—Thakur Dharmanath lived in Bishanpur. From where they stood, one corner of Parakochula would lead to Sarai Bajar, the national highway. And from there, towards the left, lay the Bishanpur Saraiya village and, beyond that, Ojha Bigana. The jeep was old but sturdy. Only the chained door in the back squeaked.

Nirbhoy Pasowan's home was near the road, and beyond the road the scarecrow stood. Nirbhoy went out in the morning, like he did every day, came back late at night. He had two sons. He was arrested in November 1969 and, in the April of 1978, he was released. After his release, he sat outside his house on the verandah for a few hours, and then went out again. Since then, the Harijan field labourers had gone on strikes four times demanding minimum labour wage (eight rupees and ten paise). They were joined by the Bindh field workers, and the situation got steadily worse. On his way back from the jail after his release, Nirbhoy bought a khaki shirt from Sarai Bajar. He was wearing that same shirt now. Nirbhoy Pasowan was sleeping with his mouth open and even though his half-muddled eyes were enveloped in darkness, the moonlight invaded him later.

Even when the scarecrow screamed, they didn't wake up. Nirbhoy's wife, two sons (a fourteen and a twelve-year-old) and his old father were sleeping in the rooms inside and on the verandah. The jeep made a low growling sound as it stood outside, because Nepali did not stop the engine. Daulat and Gangotri went ahead. They stood still for about seven seconds. And then they both walked silently, and stood next to a charpoy. Under the charpoy, an enameled saucer covering a pot was kept. Nirbhoy was sleeping on the charpoy. Daulat pointed the gun inside the sleeping man's open mouth, the sound was so muffled and soft that it didn't sound like gunfire. The bullet went through his gums, the roof of his mouth and out through the back of his head, shattering it, and hit the ground, ricocheted and ascended a little way towards the moon. Nirbhoy's body jerked and his hands went up as his hands didn't realise yet that they would never be needed again. The dogs stopped barking suddenly; in the darkness, in the rooms, in the verandah and in the slums, a few screams broke out. Daulat shot aimlessly at them; Gangotri dragged Nirbhoy's dead head by its hair outside the charpoy and hacked his head off with two swings of his long billhook; the severed head hung from his hand. Gangotri was splattered in blood. Nirbhoy's eldest son, still sleepy, saw his father's head hacked off. Daulat and Gangotri ran back to the moving jeep. Gangotri threw the severed head into the jeep, shooting out at the torches in the distant darkness as they lit up the land, balancing himself in the shaking jeep. When the jeep turned the corner and lit up the grotesque, round face of the scarecrow, Daulat shot at it in fear, piercing the scarecrow's left eye.

The scarecrow saw the jeep move on, blowing its cloud of dust, with his one eye. When the jeep had moved on, the three of them turned their heads to see dots of burning torches getting smaller and smaller in the billowing clouds of dust. The scarecrow heard waves of crying, settling down like wares in a bazaar. The dust was settling. Burning torches ran through the fields. The Harijans were relaying the news to one another. A lot of blood seeped out of Nirbhoy's neck. At first, it spilled in big jerking gusts, then it thinned out, dripping in droplets. The blood seeped through the charpoy's ropes, the charpoy's wood and soaked the khaki shirt. Old blood coagulated to block the path of new blood seeping into its territory. Clutches of brain and splintered skull were scattered everywhere.

The smell of spilled brain and blood are different. When the jeep was moving, Gangotri borrowed the battery-torch from Nepali and directed it on the jeep's floor. The jeep was from Muzzaffarpur. Transporting heavy luggage, like iron trunks, must have caved in part of its floor. By the light of the torch, they saw that Nirbhoy's head had fallen into that crater, moving side to side as the jeep jerked, eyes half-open, staring into the darkness. They could see the dead man's teeth. When Ganogtri moved the torch's lens, he saw a rag cloth lying on the floor, a mobil-grease-wiping dirty rag. He pushed that rag towards Nirbhoy's severed head with his foot. Nirbhoy's head was deformed, elongated sideways from the sudden trauma of the bullet. The back of his head was almost missing. In the gust of wind, Nirbhoy's hair was rearranging itself, sometimes parting in the middle. They took the same road to go back. The jeep didn't take the right-hand side road from Bishanpur level-crossing, that leads to Dharmanath Thakur's two-and-a-half-storeyed house. Instead, the jeep took the gravel road that went behind the rather rustic-looking house, and stopped. All three of them sat in the jeep. The Thakur—a fat man with arthritis ringing through every joint—was helped by three men to the jeep, accompanied by Thakur's eldest son. The son wore sleeping pyjamas and a shirt, with a revolver in his pocket—licensed, of course. The three men in the jeep were told beforehand that a Harijan head could not lie on Bishanpur's land. So, they lit the flashlight to lead the Thakur to the back of the jeep. At first, Daulat and Gangotri shone the light on the jeep's floor. Then Gangotri held up the severed head by the hair. As it turned in the motion, they saw the bones in the neck and the hole where the windpipe would have been. Gangotri lowered the severed head. Then, the whole business was that of simple give and take. That's why Thakur's eldest son placed his hand on the revolver's trigger. Nepali turned his neck to look back from his seat behind the wheel and noticed him. On the left side of the jeep, behind a mud wall, two men sat on their haunches with shotguns. From the top of Thakur's house, another man had his rifle trained on Nepali's head. Two five-cell flashlights shone on Daulat's and Gangotri's faces, but they showed no sign of fear. Two men held Dharmanath Thakur under his arms, and he put his hand in the bag hanging around his neck, taking out 1,000-rupee bundles in 10 rupee notes, one by one, and throwing them towards the men in the jeep. The state-stamped, bank-owned bands around the bundles were already torn off. In the blinding light of the two torches, the bundles flew past them like large insects, and the men in the jeep grabbed them in the air. One … two … three … six bundles flew through the air, followed by a light, bent 100-rupee note. 'Have some sweets,' Thakur said. All the flashlights went away almost at the same time. The jeep, with Nirbhoy's head, started its engine, on its way now to Muzzaffarpur. It stopped in front of Khakpaheli jungle; they threw the lopped head into the bushes. It was almost dawn. The same head was sleeping in Bishanpur Saraiya some hours ago. The jackals would eat the skin, the meat, but they would leave the hair. That lopped head was so tired, it wasn't dreaming when it slept on the charpoy. The road again was exploding with dust, the three men in the jeep draped their *gamchas* around their faces once more. They washed the jeep in the pond, they washed the head-lopping billhook. Nepali started the jeep again. The dust still blew, and Gangotri and Daulat slept in the back, their heads lolling with the jeep. Under their seats, they had their guns and the billhook. Nepali bit the dead bidi between his teeth and sang—'this is the public, they know everything, this is the public'. The jeep was a Jonga, bought off the military and fitted with a diesel engine.

The scarecrow noticed that the Harijans did not go to the police. The reason was simple—the police would not take their report. And even if they did, the case would be buried with the report. Three years ago, when the slum was set on fire, twenty-four houses and two people were burned alive and there were also some rapes. The police did not make a case or a report; even though they squashed a three-month old baby under their feet. Instead, the villagers gathered, children and old folks alike, around the headless body of Nirbhoy Pasowan. In the underdeveloped areas of rural, agrarian India, when the man of the family dies, his illiterate wife and other village women cry in a particular way. The same was happening for Nirbhoy Pasowan. They were slapping their chests, pulling on their hair and falling repeatedly on the ground. Nirbhoy's father, old Pasowan, sat on his haunches staring at his son's headless body on the ground. People from neighbouring villages and further afield were milling in, the place was overflowing with people. Two boys went out on their cycles. They came back to say even more people are coming in, and they couldn't leave with Nirbhoy's body just yet. Even those that would not go with Nirbhoy to the cremation were coming in to be there as long as possible. Some people from quite a long way away came wearing stilts, with bows and arrows on their back. Some conventional weapons had also come by then. When the headcount had gone beyond 10,000, Nirbhoy's eldest son took off the khaki shirt from his father's body with the help of others. They were not gathering there specially to do something—that was rumoured later. They were going to Sarai Bajar, and from there to the river ghat. But when Ramasriya and Bharosa Bindh stood on top of joined bicycles and said only Dharmanath Thakur could have killed their leader, Nirbhoy Pasowan, the situation changed. They picked up the charpoy with Nirbhoy's body on it. Even though it was daytime, they brought with them as many fire torches and as much kerosene as they could find. People were streaming in from both sides of the road. They knew Nirbhoy Pasowan's body would travel this way. More than 10,000 people waited a little before Sarai Bajar. A speeding jeep came towards them; but this was a different kind of jeep—a red flag was streaming from atop. The jeep came to a stop. It was going in a different direction, but Ramasriya and Bharosa Bindh knew the riders. The jeep was going towards Sarsawan but they turned it around, putting Nirbhoy Pasowan's charpoy on it horizontally. The jeep crawled on. They did not cover Nirbhoy's headless body, the red flag cast its shadow on him. Let everyone see that the landowner, Thakur Dharmanath, had murdered the Harijan leader, Nirbhoy Pasowan. The killers were outsiders, hired. The men who had driven the jeep with the red flag walked next to it. Among them, the muffler-wrapped, half-crazed, middle-aged man was Dr Kathiar; originally from Madhya Pradesh, Kathiyar had spent the last twenty years in this area.

In the empty village, the women were crying. The scarecrow was watching them; tears seeping out of his holed-out left eye. Destitute scarecrows do this when destitute men are killed. So what if the scarecrow stands with his hands spread apart, he is entirely unable to prevent these wrongs. And the news does not travel far. Even in Calcutta, where everyone knows everything, the news of murder and arson in a remote village of Bihar comes out in a small corner of a large paper, and who can decipher what that really means, what really happens. First, no one wants to read that news. And even if they do, the magic of news reporting and writing is such that the reader thinks that abruptly in some unknown, uncivilised part of remote Bihar, a great gang of criminal mobsters committed arson and killed one shopkeeper. Now if the police had to fire a few rounds just to control this great army of criminals, and if in those rounds one or two nameless thugs were shot, who would care? Our heroic press is fighting for freedom twenty-four hours daily but, in August 1979, Bihar landowners' armed assault and death of field labourers and Harijan leaders like Ganapat Ram, Nirbhoy Pasowan, Bharat Bindh and others did not merit even one millimetre of space in their newspapers. However, agrarian economists know about these things; the general public is not supposed to know these things. It would astound the public to know the complexity of thought spent on mere field labourers and farmers. We can come to that later. For now, let us look into the murder and arson.

In Sarai Bajar, this convoy of people set fire to Thakur Dharmanath's grain warehouse, grocery store and clothing shop. A truck with Thakur's grain arrived, and they set fire to that too. They also set fire to an Ambassador car. Thakur's eldest son had come to survey his father's business; he fired his revolver and, in turn, was shot. Bolts of cloths were set on fire. Their own clothes were rags and scraps like the scarecrow's, but they didn't steal even a yard of cloth from Thakur's shops. Two pillars of black smoke went up to the sky; at that time, Thakur's pet sub-inspector, Mishra, was cycling to Parakochula block office to telephone Sarai Bajar police thana that the five rifles in the thana would do nothing against an armed mob of more than 10,000. They came with a headless corpse on their back, and no one could tell where they would go from there. Most probably, they would move towards Bishanpur. Bihar's landowners were special and powerful people. Over the telephone, Mishra could hear orders being issued, the sound of running boots and moving trucks. When the landowners killed Gambhira, they tied him to a tractor. But what if these Harijan villagers now went to Bishanpur with their batons, spears and bows and arrows? They were saying Nirbhoy Pasowan was murdered. They even brought a decapitated body with them. Nirbhoy had a scar on his forehead; there was a picture of it. But who did the body really belong to? This was where the state's strategy became interesting. A man released in April 1978, orchestrated four big labour strikes just by walking around and talking to people. Everyone knew this but no more than this would ever be recorded. Because the authority did not recognise a decapitated body. So far as the state was concerned, Nirbhoy Pasowan was not dead. Anyone could bring a headless corpse, and they did it all the time. The irony of this was that the Harijans, even the mute scarecrow, agreed—Nirbhoy Pasowan was not dead. The jackals in Khakpaheli jungle had by then eaten Nirbhoy's cheeks, his lips and were brawling over the rest of his head.

The scarecrow, sometimes known as a monster in other places, knew this—no Harijan ever went to Bishanpur. When they did, they went alone, heads bowed to the ground.

Where the scarecrow sat, heard the hurled abuses, there they purified the land with holy Ganga water. So, when more than 10,000 Harijans and assorted lower castes were marching with a decapitated corpse on their back, their path was blocked to save Bishanpur. Two trucks were blocking the road, horizontally standing next to one another; next to them, on the road, behind the trucks, above the trucks, behind the trees and bushes were special armed forces. They had semi-automatic guns and were, in the real sense, the para-military forces. Their commanding officer yelled into a portable microphone—'Back off, go back, I will shoot'. They walked forward. The police waved a red rag (not to be confused with the jeep's red flag) at them. Then bullets rained on the jeep, perforating it entirely; as a mark of respect, one bullet ricocheted off of the jeep's metal body and went through Nirbhoy's headless, dead feet. It must have been divine intervention that even in a shower of bullets, only three farmers died. Since the Harijans moved away, the para-military targeted the jeep. Nirbhoy Pasowan's corpse and the three other dead farmers' bodies were released three days later. The town morgue did not have ice; the bodies were beginning to smell. The armed guards had already camped in Bishanpur.

The sky, the sun and the stars were visible through the scarecrow's holed-out left eye. That same sky was now quiet, breathless in terror and fear. The field labourers' rage was contagious. Blazing embers from Nirbhoy Pasowan's pyre—burnt wood, bone and flesh devouring coal—were starting fires in Sarsawan, Alaoli, Choutham, even villages as far away as Guharpur, disregarding the heavy footfalls of curfew, of surveillance. Nirbhoy's wife screamed for three days, and then went entirely quiet. His father, old Pasowan, sat on the verandah and opened his mouth from time to time when he ran out of breath. Nirbhoy's eldest son went out every morning. The police came by twice a day and once at night. As a war strategy, they were leaving Nirbhoy Pasowan's home untouched. But thirty-six Harijans and Bindhs had been arrested, most of them were fugitives now. And yet, a new school had started in Sarai Bajar, *Nirbhoy Pasowan Bidyamandir*; two new teachers joined, even in that chaos. They wore dirty pyjama-punjabi and dusty shoes; they slept on top of the school benches. Sub-inspector Sharma tried to intimidate them, but they talked to each other quietly in English. That scared Sharma. Children came to the school in the day and adults came in the night. Both the teachers also went out to them.

Two very different castes and social strata came together in mutual needs and alliances across the locality, solidifying the caste war of opposing poles vying with each other. When small flapping wings grew larger and larger till the red flag and the opposing faction's retributive war and march of power had coalesced in an unending struggle, only then, an agricultural economist, with a degree from New Delhi's Jawaharlal Nehru University, visited. He believed in deploying Marxist thought and American sociological practices simultaneously. He brought back recorded interviews with the half-mad Dr Kathiar, Ramasriya and the two schoolteachers in his tape-recorder. He had observed the situation. Old Pasowan and the scarecrow's pictures were printed in a famous journal, but neither of them knew that. Through a number of variables, environmental specifics, native and foreign paradigms, the economist's essay came to the conclusion that the nature of this struggle was very pessimistic. Because of the myth-making surrounding, Nirbhoy Pasowan would only give birth to another unsung, unnoticed epic, but not to another revolution. An old revisionist was misleading these people, and if this went on—he predicted—Indian revolutionary struggle would be obliterated. In reality, Dr Kathiar talked about Gandhi in his interview, which enraged the agricultural economist—*a stupid old fool*—but the Harijans stared at the tape recorder. He opined that the Nirbhoy Pasowan school was another way to stop revolution in its track. The two schoolteachers did not have much time for the agricultural economist; so, he called them parasites. His essay, 'The Slaughter of Agricultural Labourers in Bihar—Reality and Myth', was lauded in learned, academic circles.

Small voices float out of the school, as they recite with their teachers—

Enough with your reign of capital
This is your time of ruination
Long live the revolution
Long live, long live

Another teacher is going to join the school, the rumour says. The Harijan slum is literate now. There's graffiti on their wall…

> The one who carries the plough
> Is the one who owns the land

... *minimum wage* ... Dr Kathiar mumbles, wipes his face with his muffler ... Nirbhoy's sons, and everyone else, call him Doctor baba ... the shattered jeep was tied to a cow cart and taken to Muzzaffarpur to be repaired ... it will be back soon…

> …Those who fight against us
> Will be reduced to smithereens…

Nirbhoy Pasowan's son has put the khaki shirt on the scarecrow's shoulders. The shirt moves in the wind. The big, bloody mark still remains on the shirt's back. In a few months there will be an election. The police trucks and jeeps patrol the streets daily; so, the Harijan children and dogs don't go on to the streets anymore. In a few months, voting booths will be hijacked, guns will be fired, ballot papers will be forcibly stamped on gunpoint. After two in the morning, the dogs on the street stare at the sky and whine. Sometimes, they are joined by women and old men. It has been heard that Thakur Dharmanath is contesting this election. When the police trucks and jeeps turn from Bishanpur Saraiya, their headlights shine on the one-eyed scarecrow, wearing his blood-soaked khaki shirt, smiling at them. His shirt moves in the wind. The scarecrow does not have a vote.

—Translated by Rijula Das

(Translated from Nabarun Bhattacharya (2006), 'Kaktarua'. In *Shrestho Golpo*, 61–68. Kolkata: Dey's Publication.)

Fyataru in Spring Festival

Miss Piu, Miss Jhinuk and…

In the beginning, when only starters like lemon and salt are served, our readers are already made aware that the most popular writer of our times, Nabani Dhar, and his ex-model wife, Meghamala Dhar, live on the ninth floor of the Himgiri Apartments in South Kolkata. Today, everyone is familiar with Nabani's 543 odd novels like *Im-Fragile-Potent*, *Shadow in Petticoat*, *Senility of the Saint*, etc. Who hasn't read them? Who? How is that even possible?

Whatever it might be, what happened was, just the day before Holi, a short, obese, dark man in a dirty terry-lined shirt and similar pants, clutching a discoloured, disfigured briefcase between his legs, was spotted at the Muchipara Bus Stop. He was having a go, one by one, at the groundnuts from a shabby looking packet. Suddenly, Miss Piu and Miss Jhinuk appeared in jeans and fashionable tees to board a taxi. They were friends; got bit roles in new TV serials. They were busy with their smartphones. Amused by the appearance of this dork, they started giggling while sending messages on their phones. The man happened to fart. So, they giggled even more.

Finishing the nuts, the short one turned to them. In his gruff voice he asked—

How much?

They were scared and confused. What did he mean? Again, with more gruffness, he asked—

How much?

Miss Piu at last said limply—

What?

The man removed the briefcase from between his legs and holding it high with his right hand started drumming it with his left and sang in a horrific voice—

How long do I spend my nights alone?[1]

Not wasting another moment, getting flustered and frightened, Miss Piu and Miss Jhinuk started walking.

DS had just finished that one line when he noticed Madan and Purandar Bhat. Madan bellowed at him—

I have told you repeatedly that you cannot remain a Fyataru anymore. You had never paid heed before. Now, you will be expelled from the clan. I am not ready to hear any argument. What say, Purandar?

I have been in revolutionary politics; have seen more people getting expelled from the party than joining.

'His name is DS
A bottle of liquor
Murdered on mademoiselle
For being a frivoler.'

DS started whimpering and blowing his nose. Madan started, somewhat tenderly this time—

See. You had elbowed that Anglo woman near Metro cinema. Did I say anything? When your wife was pregnant, you ogled the young nurses. How long can you be excused?

Startling them, all of a sudden, DS started howling. People started to stare.

Will you stop? Why have you started mourning?

Purandar said—

Mayhem! Pure mayhem it is.

DS subsided to whimpers from the howls, and started—

I never did anything. I was watching the road and munching the nuts while those two bitches…

Shame on you DS, they are celebrities, they both come on TV!

Madan is furious.

Don't tell me about the cheap shows they do. Celebrity my foot! The red-light areas of Harkata demand more respect.

DS stopped whimpering and said—

1 A popular and sensuous Bengali film song.

They were laughing at me. I farted and they giggled even more. When I could not control, I asked them their rates twice and sang that song of Kumar Sanu.[2]

Purandar said—

Madan-da, had I been in DS's place, I would have done the same thing. He sang, I would have pelted poems...

DS became more composed.

What poems?

'Looking at the poet
You laugh and nod
Soon shall I
Perch you on my rod.'

That's cool. But boss, the meaning of the word 'rod' here…

Leave it. You don't need to know the meaning. So, Purandar, for this time DS is excused.

Seems so.

Forget those coquettes. Now then, Nabani-da's prestige is at stake. Yesterday he was dead drunk and kept crying. He said repeatedly, 'Even with you three as my brothers, I have to succumb to this insult; I would rather take some Folidol and die.'

What happened? Has Meghu boudi[3] eloped?

No, it's not her. Those fuckers who stay at Himgiri Apartments will be celebrating Holi in the compound tomorrow evening. It is called the spring festival. Do you know what it is, DS?

Spring brings pox, and the Goddess of pox will be worshipped.

No. Such lack of knowledge in a big fat head is a spectacle! The spring festival is celebrated on the day of Holi—girls tie flowers and sing like cats, and some alpha-males throw colours from the backside. Pure whoring.

So what the fuck is it to Nabani-da? If they want to act like whores, let them.

---

2 A popular Bengali singer

3 A common Bengali term for married women with kids.

No. One hundred and twenty filthy rich families stay in the apartment. But, there is only one as popular as the writer Nabani Dhar, and they never called him. They did not even put his name in the card. Instead, they have called some whooping old procurator as chief guest. Five hundred and forty-three bestsellers and he was struck out.

So, let us fly and charge bombs from the terrace. Let's screw the celebration.

Not that I have not thought of that. First thing is that they have covered the top. Number two, Nabani-da lives on the ninth floor. If something falls from above, they will take it as Nabani-da's doing. Once a plate and a bottle had slipped from his hands. Thank God there was no one around or he would have been framed for murder!

Purandar was quiet for some time. Finally, he said—

But why did they leave Nabani-da out? Nabani-da is expected in all the functions.

You too are becoming a dickhead just like DS. Nabani-da is writing his autobiography, *Split Wide Open.*

So what?

That is the blunder! Along with his own scandals, he is exposing everyone else's—whose wife is going around with whom and all that. They have filed at least four or five defamation cases against him. They have also threatened him. All of them at Himgiri have decided in a meeting that there will be no entry for Nabani-da.

So what will we do?

Nothing is decided as yet. Let's have some tea and biscuits at the tea stall. Then, the brain will clear up.

With that, Madan took out his dentures from the side pocket of his kurta and wore them straight away.

Madan's Brain Opens Up…

The three lit a *Charminar* after the tea and biscuits. A woman was standing by the roadside waiting for her kid's school bus. DS and Purandar were smoking and throwing glances. So, they did not realise that Madan was not smoking. Eyes closed, he was swaying a little. They got startled when suddenly he laughed out loud.

This is what Madan is. No rumpus with me.

What happened?

What? Solid, liquid, smoke, all three went in and the plan came up.

What? Of fucking up the function?

Father of all fucks. But in a new style. Oh! What a brain I have up here! Everything will happen without me moving a finger! With legs dangling from the terrace, we'll watch the show.

Okay, tell us the plan.

Not the whole plan. The Telipara slum is just outside the Himgiri Apartment. Right?

Right.

Good.

There is a country liquor shanty inside the slum.

Yes.

There live the thugs, old and young.

Though you won't get those who are in jail.

Okay, the rest will do. Tomorrow we three will go to the shanty around 3 pm. We shall share one bottle. Both of you will keep quiet, appear depressed. On my signal, DS will cry out loud. I'll take care of the rest.

In the Liquor Shanty At Telipara

Many fellows smeared with tar, colours from the press, silver and brown, are boozing. There is a song playing. They are throwing colours in between stray slangs and moves. Suddenly, DS cried out loud. Madan rose.

We are poor, hungry. The old are having fun with ripe whores at hotels. There is no one to hear our cries.

The crowd gathered around. DS went on. Madan said—

Will they allow us if you just cry? They are rich people. They will listen to songs, but if we do, they will be kicking our asses.

Some cried out amidst the crowd—

Who the fuck dares kick the asses of the poor?

Madan now wore his dentures.

There on the other side is Himgiri Apartments. There is a big show going on. We too went but they drove us away.

DS wailed.

Yes, they have been testing mics since morning.

Madan's voice rose.

He is our younger brother. He said singers like Kumar Sanu will be coming. Abhijit as well; so he planned to go. We thought this is a day of festivities and there won't be much traffic. We thought we could go too but they did not allow us.

Kumar Sanu. Abhijit. The news spread like wildfire.

Get them! Fuck them!

A big crowd consisting of tipsy people, women and children went towards Himgiri. The chief guest, the famous procurator, Gojendranath Porel, had just arrived. The mic testing was on. Using the influence of one promoter resident, Miss Piu and Miss Jhinuk had arrived with their boyfriends. The evening was waning. Girls with flower bands, boys in designer kurtas, colours and food and hidden business of booze were ready. A sudden noise came from outside.

The doormen had closed the doors in fear. People came crashing on the gate. Amid this chaos, no one noticed three sample Fyatarus' take-off and soft landing on the terrace of Himgiri. They sat there with their legs dangling.

The clamour turned into howls. Stones came pelting by, along with bottles and containers. Instead of waking up to the vernal door of festivities, they trembled at the car park. Who knew what was happening? Roars came from outside.

Beat them up! Beat the fuckers!

On everyone's request, the secretary had made an attempt to reach the gate but, at that very moment, a mini bomb exploded at the gate. Crashing sounds. The secretary called the police—

I am calling from Himgiri Apartments. Please send police force immediately.

What do you mean? Force on a day of festivity? Are you crazy?

We are being attacked.

What did you say?

Attack.

Brawls do happen on such days. Manage it.

Manage, how? These are thugs of Telipara slum attacking.

Okay. Hang up. Holy shit, who is on duty now?

Another socket bomb exploded. The police arrived. The elections were on the cards. Even the police did not want to bother the parties; so a meeting was called. It was a peace meeting. It took some time. It's a difficult thing to make the boozers see reason. The spring festival was fucked. The ambience of terror lingered on. With food packets in hand, Mr Porel, Miss Piu and Miss Jhinuk went home with police protection.

Further into the Night…

The three dived to Nabani Dhar's flat. Nabani was wearing a pair of half pants, with Sai Baba's lockets and beads on his bare chest.

Oh brothers, come to my arms. Black Dog. Ice Cubes. Soda. Nabani called out—

Meghu, Meghu … Just see who is here!

Meghamala Dhar came out, wearing a housecoat over her transparent nightdress. She was holding a tray with fish fries in it.

It's okay, no need to call. I know my brothers have come.

Nabani said—

Up its arse with the spring festival! It has been a complete flop! Fucked right left and centre! My bum is on fire!

DS said—

Meghu boudi?

Yes dear, say!

I'll take four and four, total of eight fries home. Today is Holi after all. I have a wife and a son. They never had this stuff.

—Translated by Debadrita Bose

(Translated from Nabarun Bhattacharya (2006), 'Basanta Utsabe Fyataru'. In *Shrestho Golpo*, 256–262. Kolkata: Dey's Publication.)

4+1

One

It was a day of incessant rain. Though it wasn't torrential enough to cause waterlogging. The wind was shivering cold. Daylight was weak. The tram driver could have been more cautious but not that he didn't press the brake. The tram had just taken a turn and wasn't even running that fast. In spite of the brake, when it bit the tracks before coming to a stop, the accident had already happened. The two at the front suffered minor injuries but the other two at the back got away with it. One of them had a crack on his forehead. Another hurt his nose and gums and teeth too. They were bleeding. This was hearsay from the crowd which gathered immediately on the spot. Apart from the four men, there was one more who was dead. He hadn't died in the accident. He had become an unmistakable corpse before all that could happen. They had been carrying him on a cot; his body bound to it with ropes and covered by a black plastic sheet. Generally, we see flower and incense sticks around these cots in which corpses are carried. This one had nothing. It was known later that there were a broken pair of black rimmed glasses, a few pieces of chalk, some torn papers and a half-eaten thin arrowroot biscuit—all tied up in a dirty piece of cloth near the head of the dead man. It was hoped that the papers would offer some clue about his identity. They didn't. There was nothing on the papers barring some meaningless doodles. Perhaps, one could draw a far-fetched meaning from them. But, there was no meaning to that meaning.

The tram driver was most frightened. There was no reason for him not to be frightened. The moment he had taken the turn, he could see them coming. The four men with the corpse. They were coming straight towards the tram. He was stunned and stood motionless in his driver's cage. There weren't too many pedestrians that day. But, a crowd gathered quite quickly. Everyone was shocked to find things as they were. The police were called in soon.

After colliding head-on with the tram, the four carriers of the corpse had stopped and didn't move a bone. Until the police came and took them away, they hadn't given room for the tram to pass. Two of them at the front were bleeding. Everyone asked them to stand clear. Some excited young men thought, they were deafened by heavy drinking. It was a cloudy and blurry day of rains after all. Though the houses in this part of the city were old and quite high, they did have bright new shops on their ground floors. The shadows creep in quickly in the afternoon. That day, they were getting thicker by the minute. The intelligent citizens, who can always smell a rat or two, had said that it was just a stunt, a spectacle. According to them, the corpse was fake, the man was still alive, and all these were actors. For them, everything was planned. Perhaps, it was an ad for an upcoming play or some unwanted idiot's dumb joke. The policemen, who had come first, guessed something similar. And yet, the four men didn't look like lumpens who have a great time decking up a corpse during Dolyatra[1]. Perhaps, they were high on heroin. Ordinary men and ordinary policemen think alike. Over them, we have the extraordinary thoughts of extraordinary men and extraordinary policemen. The newly appointed IPS officer had thought alike. Not that there was a lot of trouble. A few trams had stopped one after the other in a line. There was a crowd, four dead silent carriers of a corpse and the corpse itself, covered in a black plastic sheet. The corpse was that of a sinewy middle-aged man with a cracked black rimmed glass, covered in a dirty piece of cloth near his head. The frame of the glass had an old thread attached to it. It looked like one of the glasses distributed in the free cataract operation camps that are set up in localities from time to time. Beside it lay some remnants of chalks. One could barely write with them. There were doodled papers with plus signs, dots and number five written on them, according to the claims made. But, all this is the result of fruitlessly speculative research on almost illegible pencil scribbles. No one had any idea who had eaten half of the shabby-looking biscuit. One could say with some certitude that it wasn't the dead man; at least as nothing like that was informed after the post-mortem. When trams stop after one another in a cue, the naked street children, with festering wounds on their

1 The Indian festival of colours.

bodies, rush in like blowflies to play their little games of climbing up and down. In the meantime, the young IPS officer had instructed the cops to arrest the four men along with the corpse. He used his resources to make sure that the corpse was immediately transferred to a mortuary where it could be preserved. The corpse could well be a booby trap. The four men were handcuffed and taken for investigations. The police report said that though they were holding on to the four legs of the cot tightly, when they were handcuffed, they had lost their stubbornness. They always looked straight ahead with eyes wide open. They wouldn't drop their eyelid, not even during the investigations, it is said.

The IPS officer was well within his rights to be suspicious. There were explosions in Bombay, Kolkata[2] and southern India. Speculations about a Pak[3]-fed terrorism were in the air. In such horrible times, there was no taking risk, either in central or at state level. From his Lenin, he knew how the ultra-left and the ultra-right have joined hands. They needed to know who these thin, slimy and experienced-looking men were. It's true that Carlos[4] had been caught, but so what? Where's Tiger Memon[5]? What about the mystery of the actress falling to her death from a skyscraper[6] or Nargis's son[7]? RDX, AK-47, drug, Uranium and Plutonium smuggling. Does India have an atom bomb? Whether they have it or not, under these circumstances, nothing is negligible. Real life isn't a *Roja*[8] or a *1942: A Love Story*[9].

---

2 Bombay (present-day Mumbai) and Kolkata are names of metropolitan cities in India.

3 'Pak' refers to Pakistan, one of India's neighbouring countries with whom it has always had a fraught relationship.

4 Carlos is the pseudonym of an Indian terrorist who was in the news in mid-1990s when the story was written.

5 Tiger Memon was another Indian terrorist who was allegedly behind the 1993 Bombay bomb blast case.

6 This is an allusion to the Bollywood actress Vidya Bharti who fell to death from her five-storey apartment on 5 April 1993.

7 Nargis (1929–1981) was a popular Hindi film actress whose son, Sanjay Dutt (1959–present), also a film actor, was accused of being involved in the Bombay blasts of 1993 with charges of illegal possession of arms.

8 *Roja* (1992) was a Tamil film directed by Mani Ratnam which tackled issues like border terrorism.

9 *1942: A Love Story* (1994) was a Hindi film, directed by Vidhu Vinod Chopra. It dealt with the pre-independence years and the violent struggles and counter-struggles of Indian independence.

Two

Before the investigations began, the forensics informed that it was the corpse of a weak and thin old man who had everything in his body that a body generally has but in an 'insulted' form. When a body part gets injured, or becomes weak due to a disease, the doctors say, it's 'insulted'. For example, if one has had jaundice twice, once he gets well, the doctors would say, his liver has faced 'insult' twice. The corpse tied to the cot with ropes under the cover of a black plastic sheet had 'insults' written into most of its vital organs—liver, kidney, bladder, penis, eye, scrotum and so on. Recently, in the United States, experiments have shown that things like religion, poetry, love, violence, justice, theft, hunger, sexuality, wifely feelings, consciousness of having children, silence, desire to rape and love of music are all properties belonging to the different lobes of the human skull. This corpse hadn't been subjected to such experiments but there is hope in the fact that the government has decided to preserve it. It still remains in peace haven, entirely on governmental expense. Therefore, it's ready for those experiments.

The interrogations started gently so that information could be extracted from them by using gentleness as a strategy. In investigations, there are always these twists and turns which eventually bamboozle the interrogated person and force him to speak the truth. But, in this case, it didn't work because they didn't utter a single word. Those who interrogate are not always masters of speech. Occasionally, they resort to violence. Some say, they do that deliberately while others believe it happens in the heat of the moment. Whatever it is, this second type of interrogation started with the two at the back who were unharmed by the accident. Slaps made no impression. They were dangled and kicked but that didn't work either. Things could have become lethal, had the young IPS not intervened. He stopped the violent interrogation. After treatment for a couple of days, they once again stood up on their feet. Then all four were sent to doctors.

Three

Let's not get into the mundane details of experiments like flashing light on eyes or knocking knee joints with small hammers. Multiple electrodes were inserted in their brains. Let's make one thing clear to the readers here that they mustn't take this as a third variety of investigation. Science isn't torture though torture uses science. The eminent doctors called a meeting after observing the lines of light on the monitoring machine. After this, they gave the head of the police a detailed report in English. He kept a photocopy of it and forwarded the original to the Ministry of Home Affairs where they too preserved a photocopy and sent the original to higher officials. The report used complicated technical expressions like 'no evoked potential in auditory/visual cortex on peripheral sensory stimulation' or 'sensory aphasia' or 'sensorial deficit', etc. What all that came down to in simple language was that all four of them were blind, deaf and dumb. If someone is blind and deaf, they have to be dumb. If that's the case, it's impossible to establish any communication with them. All efforts failed. When you supplied food to them by making them hold the plate or the glass, they would respond. You can't know if they can smell. The expression doesn't change at all. Eyelids don't fall. They don't hear. They don't see. They don't speak. They would never hear, see or speak. There is no way you can ever know anything from them. They have been imprisoned in one particular place. On the other hand, the original document continues to get transferred from one place to another with the number of photocopies on the increase with every movement. But, even that journey will eventually come to a stop with the president. Even then, there is no chance of knowing anything about the four blind, deaf and dumb carriers of the corpse.

Four

The corpse is in an ultra-modern preservatory now. Only a few American billionaires have kept their bodies intact in preservatories more sophisticated than this. They are hoping that science in near future will be able to bring them back to life with its newest discovery. If that happens, they will wake up after a few hundred years, skipping two or three generations, and resume their businesses and recreations. We cannot say that our corpse has similar thoughts and desires. Though, if he can be revived, perhaps the veil of mystery will lift. The young IPS officer, of course, didn't think on these lines.

As we have already said, the four men are locked up elsewhere. The doors of their chamber are as strong as they can get. They are always locked with security guards sitting outside all the time. There is a little square opening with net on the ceiling through which the sun and moon light perform their diagonal scribbles across the room. When the sun and the moon change positions in the sky, the light flees in a moment like a magical cat, as if never there. Sometimes, there are sparrows isolated from their flocks that come and sit on the net and peck on it. Occasionally, the gay wind glides into the chamber and, looking at the four prisoners, stumbles into stillness. Their eyelids don't move. They sit silently on the floor. The security guards don't like to do their work, especially at night. Some of them have made claims of hearing murmurs and chuckles from inside the chamber. The young IPS officer still visits the place from time to time. But, it wouldn't be fair to call him young because time is passing as relentlessly as ever. Only inside the corpse-carriers' chamber, time has come to a stop.

Whose corpse is it? What's his name? Does he have a friend or a relation in this world? How did he die? What's the identity of the four carriers? Which burning ghat were they going to that day? How could they ever reach the burning ghat? How could something like this ever happen?

If anyone knows anything about this, he or she is requested to come forward and inform the concerned authority. The authorities are lying in wait.

—Translated by Arka Chattopadhyay

(Translated from Nabarun Bhattacharya (2006), '4+1'. In *Shrestho Golpo*, 146–150. Kolkata: Dey's Publication.)

Toy

Mithil and Mimi never left Toy alone at home. Not for a long time at least. There wasn't even a plan as such. But, Mithil called Mimi from the office to tell her that Mahendra was screening Tarkovsky's *Nostalgia* at his place on VCR. They asked Amita-di[1] to look after Toy. No one lived in the top floor of their remote three-storeyed apartment. In their frugal-looking apartment, there was only one flat on every floor. Toy and his family lived on the first floor, and Amita-di on the ground floor. Before going any further, let's get to know the aquarium.

Last year, there was trouble at Mithil's workplace. The boss of Mithil's division retired. Someone came from Bombay to replace him. He was in a Tata Concern there. The moment he joined, a whole series of ego-tussles began. There were disagreements over trifles all the time. Mithil became increasingly anxious about all this pettiness. He started doing Yoga—Pranayam[2] and Shavashan[3]. Mithil's Yoga teacher asked him to buy an aquarium. He was a devotee of Aurobindo[4] and Mother Teresa[5]. He told Mithil that Mother had observed somewhere in her writings about the calming effect of watching fishes in an aquarium. He also said that this had really worked for a lot of people. This is how an aquarium made its way into their home for a therapeutic reason of sorts. It wasn't huge. It didn't contain a great number of fishes. Swordtail, Guppy, Angel, Black Molly, Gourami and so on.[6] The catfish came later. The earthworms were kept in the bathroom under drops of water. It was a difficult arrangement. So, in came dry foods for the fish. Toy had joined Mithil in his obsession with the aquarium even at the cost of watching television. Mithil and Mimi bought Toy the book

---

1 Di is a Bengali honorific for women.

2 An exercise involving inhaling and exhaling.

3 Another yoga exercise that involves a supine position respectively.

4 Aurobindo (1872–1950) was an Indian nationalist leader, yogi and poet.

5 Mother Teresa (1910–1997) was a Roman Catholic religious sister and missionary who spent most of her days in India.

6 The names of various tropical fishes.

Multicolored Fins from the book fair. One day, after reading the book, Toy asked—

Papa, why isn't there a fighter in our aquarium?

No point. They'll fight each other to death.

But the book says, they don't kill each other; they only tear each other's wings. The wings grow back.

Have you read that right?

Yes. Do you know what Angel's real name is?

No.

Terofilus amikei.

That evening, Mimi had explained clearly what Toy was supposed to do hour by hour: Complan[7] at seven, fruit custard at night; there could even be a surprise gift waiting for Toy. It would have been good to have a children's programme on TV that evening but there wasn't. Toy was expected to do his studies after drinking Complan. Amita-di would come and see him at eight. The apartment security guard would be cautious. Unless it was a known person, he would ask all others to come later though no one was scheduled to come. Mimi and Mithil would be back by nine-fifteen. Toy was so quiet and well behaved that there was no reason to worry about him. Mimi boarded the minibus from the nearest stop. Toy waved at her from the veranda. Mahendra's place was just a matter of four stops.

Toy counted the cars from the veranda for quite some time. He played his favourite game of predicting cars. The winter hadn't set in at the time although the sun was setting early. There was a faint trace of fog around the light. The game of predicting cars was Toy's own invention. No one else knew about it. It's time for an ambassador now. And there it came. One nil. Now Maruti. In came a police van instead. The score was one-all now. Another Maruti. Now it was two to one in favour of Maruti. Cycles, two-wheelers, minibuses—they were not counted in this game. All the three rooms in the flat were well lit. After winning 45–37, when Toy had his Complan, it was five minutes past seven. Mithil and Mimi called at seven-fifteen. Everything all right? Yes. Are you afraid? No. The home-task of five sums must be done. You can

---

7 Complan is a popular energy drink for boys and girls in India.

do the handwriting exercise tomorrow morning. Toy disconnected the phone and sat with the sums. The last of them was big and difficult. There were so many multiplications and divisions! And just as Toy geared up for that one, the doorbell rang. It was Amita-di!

What are you doing, Mr Toy?

I am doing my homework. Maths.

Such a good boy! Are you afraid?

No. Not at all.

Amita-di gave Toy four Hajmolas[8]. He kept two of them on the table for himself and the other two on the bedside of his parents. Toy couldn't quite solve the final sum. It was ten minutes past eight then.

Toy went to the bathroom to pee. After he was done, he stood up on the commode and opened the box fixed on the opposite wall which was deliberately kept out of Toy's reach. The moment he opened it, a beautiful aroma combining the Eau de Cologne and aftershave filled the air. When Mithil went on tours, he took a cute miniature immersion heater with him. He used it for shaving. Toy silently brought it down.

Mithil and Mimi came back exactly at nine-thirty and Toy was watching TV with rapt attention. It was Pink Floyd live from Australia on cable TV. Psychedelic and smoky light everywhere; waves of long hair in slow motion; flashing lights like lightning on the cords of the blue guitar. They had brought ice cream for Toy. So, Toy didn't have fruit custard after dinner. He went to bed. Mimi had fallen asleep telling him stories. Mithil was still awake. The candlelights of 'Nostalgia' were all around him. He felt that familiar restlessness returning in his head, as if to save the lonely candle's only light. Sitting with a cigarette in front of the aquarium sounded like a good idea.

The light in the aquarium was on. The lid was open, and a pencil was placed horizontally to maintain the gap between the lid and the glass wall. The small immersion heater was hanging from it. All the fishes were dead. Because the heater was on, there was an invisible wave inside and an up-and-down of hot and cold water. The dead fishes were afloat within that invisible wave, flipping back and forth and constantly skidding from one end to another. The water was still

8 A popular brand of digestive candies.

quite warm. The silver bubbles were coming out from the diver's half-open mouth. Tiny bubbles were also coming out from the surface of the immersion heater.

Toy didn't go to school the next day. His parents took him to the psychiatrist Dibyendu Mukherjee. Mimi's maternal uncle knew him well. Mithil and Mimi were sitting outside. Dr Mukherjee talked to him for almost an hour before they came out with an Amul chocolate in Toy's hands and smiles on both faces.

Mr Toy, you sit and read this picture book. Let me have a little talk with papa and mamma.

Toy nodded gently. Dr Mukherjee said, oh what a great chat we had!

In his clinic, Dr Mukherjee had said this to Toy's parents—

I don't think the incident is as serious and macabre as you think. What impressed me the most in the conversation with your son is that he doesn't have a bone of aggression in him. He is such a soft-hearted boy. I'd simply ask you to ignore what happened. It's not a problem. He is perfectly normal. Sort of curiosity, you can say; it's almost scientific…

Sometime after the incident, Mithil read an article on children with criminal propensities from England and France in an overseas journal. An interesting debate had emerged from the discussions. One French psychologist said that these children had described their crimes in such a calm and cold-blooded manner that one could almost detect a scientific attitude in it. Mithil read it out to Mimi.

Toy's parents stopped being concerned about him after that.

—Translated by Arka Chattopadhyay

(Translated from Nabarun Bhattacharya (2006), 'Toy'. In *Shrestho Golpo*, 143–145. Kolkata: Dey's Publication.)

Leopard-Man

If work comes up, or one's out on a holiday, or a close relative is undergoing complicated treatment at AIIMS[1], or one goes to wangle a favour through some political fixer—there could well be many reasons for a person to need to go to Delhi. Of course, at the very outset one should accept that there are many more people who don't go to Delhi and will never go there or anywhere else for that matter. These folks who don't go anywhere and will never go, if they ever do, they would at best be crammed like cattle in a lorry and then queue up, beside NH 34 or any other highway along which buses and trucks ply, to dig earth. It's near them—although the areas are shrinking—that leopards exist. Whatever we know or pretend to know about what people, in general, do, we certainly don't know a quarter of a quarter of that as far as leopards are concerned. So, adding the two together, leopard-man and what he is all about is something whose particulars never reach the general public, or even the intelligentsia. But not for a moment should anyone think that the leopard-man is a wolf-child or something like the lovely, white-skinned Tarzan on a black-skinned mother's bosom. Neither does this leopard-man have any connection to the monkey-man[2] who was dancing on the heads of the media a few months back. And so, without any further fanfare, we can ask the writer of the story, or the ox of the story, to advance directly towards presenting the leopard-man.

So, the main point thus far is: if you want to closely observe the leopard-man, mister, you have to go to Delhi.

No, just going to Delhi won't do. Because the leopard-man can't be found in places like the Red Fort or the Parliament, Connaught Circus or Appu Ghar, Pragati Maidan or Jantar Mantar. You have to venture

---

1 All India Institute of Medical Science, New Delhi, India.

2 Name of a monster resembling monkey reported to be roaming in the streets of Delhi and attacking people in mid-2001, the same year the current story was first published. It has been read as an effect of mass hysteria.

across the Yamuna, towards Noida, in the direction where Delhi is expanding rapidly. And once you cross the checkpost at Noida, you are in Uttar Pradesh. The easiest way to locate the place is the Buddha statue which is right in the middle of the road where the Delhi–Uttar Pradesh border lies. Once there, you should ask which way 'Atta' is. If you have a car, it's three minutes. If you don't, you can go by rickshaw or auto too. But it's best not to attempt walking. You'll be exhausted. Your legs will fall off. Whatever else Delhi might be, it's not a city like Kolkata; here, the distance has to be seen from a whale's perspective and not from that of a tilapia fish.

This 'Atta' is a sensational plaza, although of modest size. What can't one find there! There's food and drink, of course, catering to every possible taste. The foreign brands of clothes and garments on display here are enough to make one's eyes weary, and besides, TVs, CD systems, DVDs, imported CDs, cassettes, ice cream, Kenwood, cakes, JVC, fancy local and foreign cookies, Reebok, Kolkata-style roll shops, Indigo Nation, snacks, machines churning out popcorn in a minute and machines to prepare coffee directly from coffee seeds in just a little more time, fruit juices, jewellery, Sony handy-cams as well as faux handicrafts and exhibitions of pirated books. After walking around for a bit, just as you're beginning to feel a bit tired, you'll see a huge and grotesque red-and-black building of steel and glass facing a vast, parched field that stretches to the very horizon. Maybe it's this field that's comparable to an ocean because the abominable building is named 'Ocean View Hotel'. The scorched earth of this ocean is also littered with construction waste and regular daily garbage and even if there's grass hidden somewhere there's no way of knowing that, the hot wind laden with petrol and diesel fumes sends waves of thousands of discarded plastic bags flying, with pan masala sachets making up its foam, and in some places, like torpedoed vessels, a few shanties scattered here and there, in which, of course, dwell people who don't go anywhere and won't ever go anywhere either. The ground floor of this building is like a massive glass case within which you can see orchids hanging, light streaming in from outside, suit-clad waiters walking around and lots of people eating. Looking at the cars parked outside, you'll realise that it's simply impossible for the hoi polloi to eat there.

This is a famous restaurant called 'Hot Breads'. Apparently, they have a branch in Kolkata too. It's good if you can go there, and even better if there's a little child with you. Because right away you'll be astonished and your child too will be stunned into disbelief—the leopard-man will advance towards you. He'll come walking on two legs. Following behind him, swinging this way and that, his long tail. And in a very human voice, he'll say 'hello' to your child and hold out his hand. Although it seems to be a full-fledged leopard, it walks and talks like a man. And it wears a pair of goggles. That wasn't there earlier. It was the proprietors' idea. It's only the proprietors who have such an artistic mind. I can bet that if I were to make you, or if you had made me, into a leopard-man, the detail of the pair of goggles wouldn't even have entered any of our heads. Capital is so far ahead in such thinking. People like us can't even imagine how far thinking has advanced beyond that archaic volume called, *Das Kapital.*

Leopard-man's job is to keep the children who come to Atta's 'Hot Breads' in good cheer and to perform his role of entertainer in such a way that the children never get scared. It's in order to make sure that they aren't frightened that he says 'hello' softly and extends his paw, which has no claws. Children, especially the shrewd, clever and savvy children nowadays, immediately get over any fear. They then get enthralled playing games with the leopard-man, one of which is to pull his tail from behind. Very often, many naughty children also get together and form a group that's so rowdy that it becomes difficult for the waiters carrying things to move about. Adult guests get inconvenienced too. Leopard-man then takes the band of children through the glass door, to the hotel compound outside. There's a huge synthetic carpet laid there. No chance of any child scraping its arms or legs there. Large swings made of plastic are placed on the carpet, and steps going up, also of plastic, which one climbs to come down a slide, again of plastic. Sometimes the goggles-clad leopard-man plays koo-chug-chug with the children. Leopard-man is the engine in front and behind him, arms-on-shoulders, are the tiny wagons. During this playtime, the adults inside can eat whatever they like in peace. And finally, at the very end, when, after paying the bill and the tip, the children get inside their cars together with the accompanying adults, leopard-man stands at the door and waves his hand. If you come here, leopard-man will also wave at the kid you come with.

The name of this leopard-man of three hours every day—from five in the evening till eight at night—is Dipaiya. His home, that is to say, their original home, was in a place called Sarsonwa near Benares. Dipaiya was only a child when his father brought him to Delhi. He stays some eight kilometres away from 'Atta' in a densely-populated shanty town called Ashok Nagar, where there is also a large Bangladeshi community, most of whose menfolk pull rickshaws while the women work as maidservants in the various housing complexes. There are also people from around Delhi, whose farmlands have been gobbled up by the government, and people from Bihar, Punjab and Rajasthan, who can no longer remember how they arrived here, whether it was by train or lorry; people who don't go anywhere else or won't ever go.

Dipaiya is over forty. His wife's name is Bharbuti. They have four children. The eldest is a skinny fourteen-year-old boy, Vikram. A canal cuts through Ashok Nagar, its water is a black admixture that emanates odours of all kinds of chemicals. These are toxic effluents flowing from factories. There are also various kinds and sizes of waste materials, within which the bodies of murder victims can also be found. The most astonishing thing is the amazing capacity of the fish. Because there are fish even in that toxic water, and one or two cranes come to prey on them. Sometimes, a skinny peacock can also be spotted on the bank of the canal. Boys jump naked into the water. Dipaiya's son, Vikram, is also part of that band. None of them will ever go anywhere from here. The Yamuna's waters have a foul, stagnant smell. But the odour of this canal is different. There's a bridge across it and, standing on that, one can see plastic bags slung on the columns, looking like clinging snails. It's on that bridge that at night three girls with tight blouses stand, one of them completely stupid. The other two doll her up and bring her there. They stand on the bridge and dance, twirling their arms, illuminated by the headlights of every kind of car. When Dipaiya returns by bicycle, he too has to suffer the beams of those headlights. On his way back, Dipaiya halts and goes behind the Primary Model School to have his quota of hooch. Rickshaw-pullers drink there, those who lay stones on the banks of the Yamuna and work on roads also drink there, as do workers from various small factories, those who don't have any union.

Leopard-man's leopard costume is imported and synthetic. Although made for Dipaiyas from cold countries, it has to be worn by a Dipaiya from a hot land. There are no holes near the nose. There were two holes for the eyes but on account of wearing the goggles, not much air gets in through that. He perspires inside the leopard costume; it becomes sticky and begins to steam and the pungent odour makes him suffocate. Every day, Dipaiya gets fifty rupees for dressing up as leopard-man. Sometimes, the waiters give him stale cream-rolls or sandwiches gone sour. Some good-hearted parents offer money too. This job, meaning the leopard-man job, is not all that Dipaiya does. He works all day in a fan-manufacturing factory, where table-fans are made. Dipaiya arrives at the factory at nine in the morning. He carries with him rotis and *tarkari*[3], *alu-karela*[4] or *alu-bengan*[5]. Six people work there. When the owner bought a small TV set so that he could watch one-day cricket matches, everyone was very happy. For fear of it getting stolen, the owner took it home with him before a Sunday, carrying it in the rear of his scooter. He brought it back again the following Monday. Perhaps, Dipaiya too will buy a black-and-white TV set some day. There was also the matter of a job for his son.

One can't be sure about the TV purchase though. Dipaiya already had a pain in his chest, although no one knows the reason for that. Getting some sundry ailment was not something to worry too much about but it was also true that given the paints, primer and the metal parts he constantly handled in the fan-manufacturing factory, it could well be something resulting from that. Besides, he smoked bidis, he drank hooch, all these were much-needed things, but they could also hurt you so badly that maybe, soon, you wouldn't need them anymore. We don't think about the dangerous consequences but just like that drain of black effluent they are ever present. And like the magical fish which survive in that, millions and millions of people survive in an

3 Any preparation with vegetables.

4 A preparation with potatoes and bitter gourd.

5 A preparation with potatoes and eggplant.

immense toxic black drain, one of whom is Dipaiya, whom we already know as leopard-man.

The children who are delighted every day, like the child accompanying you was delighted seeing the leopard-man, they'll all grow up to become very big one day; they'll learn and know a lot, but they'll never know the real name of the leopard-man. Coming to think about it, you aren't supposed to know that either. If Dipaiya dies, it won't make any difference to the leopard-man slough. Rather, someone else will wear it and become the leopard-man. He'll play with the children. There shouldn't be any dearth of people who'll dress up as a leopard-man for three hours every day. And it's not as if the wage will always be fifty rupees. It will increase.

But although I grasped everything, I am still confused about something. Even after knowing everything, I can't digest the fact that although Dipaiya is dead, leopard-man continues to wave his hand. The arithmetic is alright, but a black, flowing fissure remains, over which lies a bridge, on which, at night, illuminated by car headlights, one can see three girls twirling their arms and dancing, while leopard-man returns home on his bicycle.

—Translated by V. Ramaswamy

(Translated from Nabarun Bhattacharya (2006), 'Chitamanush'. In *Shrestho Golpo*, 221–225. Kolkata: Dey's Publication.)

Terrorist

1

I arrived in this city from another big city almost 1,500 miles away. There's always a reason for us to travel from one city to another, which is never true. We have to perform that job as well. So I'm visiting hospitals here. I have with me various kinds of equipment and catalogues of several models of X-ray machines. In the hotel where I'm putting up, there's my daily diary, with notes regarding the hospitals or clinics that I've visited each day and the expense incurred on travel, and there are a few magazines as well as my visiting cards. If they suddenly conduct a search, they wouldn't find anything suspicious. There's nothing suspicious in my briefcase either. There's a mobile phone with roaming facility. Nothing will be found in the mobile phone. Because everything about the job I've really come for lies buried within the rear of my mind. The frontal part of the mind is still and completely tranquil like a clear, transparent aquarium—without any fish or air bubbles, rising up like pearls. In order to initiate this system in my mind, I had to learn 'thought stoppage'. Tomorrow I'll meet the person, the one who'll dial a number on a mobile phone to detonate an explosion of a bomb that's fitted with a timer. I'll collect the bomb this evening. I have to place the bomb today itself.

2

After changing taxis twice, I arrived at a place beside the city's suburban railway, where there's a discarded concrete buffer and, just a little distance away, a level-crossing which was supposed to be closed now. It was. Bicycles lined up on both sides, as well as motorcycles, van-rickshaws and lorries. The man was dressed just the way he was supposed to be.

What time's the next train?

I knew he would say that.

The next train's after ten minutes.

That was what my reply ought to have been. He lit a cigarette. That too matched. The cigarette was not filter-tipped.

Do you smoke?

No.

Do you know, Barbie dolls have become more expensive?

I know that.

'Barbie dolls' meant that no one was watching. If he had said 'Dunhill' instead, that would mean someone was watching. If he said 'candles', it would mean we were surrounded.

It's almost evening.

After that we crossed the railtrack and walked ahead. We took a rickshaw, that is to say, a cycle-rickshaw. After going for a bit, we got off at a slum locality. Children's cries. Smoke. Sounds of cooking. The acrid smell of rubber burning. There, a woman gave me the box, placed within a plastic bag. Looking at it from outside, one would think it contained a doll or chocolates. A three or four-storeyed building could be blown up with this. All the air around where it would explode would be ejected. And when it returned, the place would be engulfed in flames.

3

Oh, I forgot to mention that two of my X-ray machines were booked today. That too was intimated to me by fax. The market for our machines is growing by the day. That's how it's supposed to be. The private healthcare sector is a giant global enterprise now. If things continued like this, I could well expect a special performance reward after I returned. I most definitely could. But that's if I return. Many like me go to unknown cities far away and never return.

4

I had seen a photograph of the building. The image was committed to memory too. That's what was important.

I had seen the photo of the minister as well. Also, of the girl that he used to visit. It wouldn't matter if I hadn't seen either of those.

Everything was as had been explained to me. There was an abandoned warehouse behind the building and in between was a sliver of space, it would be wrong to even call it an alley.

It was drizzling. The door, that is to say the ancient door with a rusted lock, was very sturdy. It took a little while to open it. With the light of the mobile-phone torch, I saw that the room was empty. Only on one side were there lots of large drainpipes. In one of those, I had placed the box kept within a plastic bag, which, as I said earlier, could, to all appearances, be taken to contain a doll or chocolates.

There was one hitch though. I couldn't lock the door afterwards. But looking at it, one couldn't really discern that the lock was open. Another cause for unease was that the room was larger than what I had anticipated. It would have been better if the bomb exploded in a smaller space. Of course, this was not something one needed to worry about. Even if the result did not match the plan, after all, the girl's flat was directly above. The girl worked in the office of a foreign airline. The minister came to her house at eight-thirty. After that, the white fluorescent light would be turned off. A blue light would burn. Which was so dim that only if one looked carefully could one catch the mild blue haze.

5

We met exactly the way it had been planned. Calling him Rowdy would perhaps be the best description of the man's appearance. We met at a bar. He was sitting at the table in front of the door of the toilet. After I sat a little while at the table, opposite him, he took out a packet of cigarettes from his shirt pocket. I knew the brand. The waiter arrived. I ordered a beer. He took out a cigarette, held it in his lips and asked—

Do you have a light?

I held out my Zippo lighter.

Zippo! Fine! I used to have one. Lost it.

But it's quite easily available now.

I didn't buy it. I know it's available. It was a present.

Oh.

The waiter came with the beer. Rowdy offered me a cigarette. I sipped the beer. A cold mist was forming on the beer glass, making it cloudy. I absent-mindedly drew a cross on that with my finger. That meant the bomb had been placed in the correct spot.

A little later, Rowdy left. I picked up the beer glass and emptied it. The waiter filled up the glass again.

6

One didn't always remember the rule of thought stoppage. And not at all while asleep. After all, can dreams be stopped? That same night, that is to say, the night before the explosion, I saw Rowdy sitting and looking at a whole lot of photos strewn on the floor in the room where I had placed the bomb. The minister's face. The girl's face. But I knew this girl! Knew her intimately. I was perspiring, trying to think why her face appeared in the photo. I was standing right in front of Rowdy. Yet, he couldn't see me. So, was I invisible? My clothes, shoes, watch, Zippo lighter—were these not visible too? After all, Rowdy was one of our team. So why was I worried so much about whether he could see me or not? And in place of the girl was someone else, where on earth did the photo of that particular girl, the one who my whole body knew intimately, come from? Rowdy looked in my direction and smiled. Why? Had he seen me then? Had he recognised me? I went to pick up the girl's photo from the floor. But I couldn't. The photo lay under a dirty sheet of glass. Rowdy took out a mobile phone. He was pressing the buttons. Rowdy was dialling someone. I looked towards the drainpipes. That's where the explosion would take place. But neither Rowdy nor I were suicide-squad guys. I wasn't supposed to be anywhere near the explosion site. Why did it turn out this way? Our plan was entirely different. So, was the plan changed subsequently! And Rowdy had found out about that, but I hadn't been informed! What would happen if the bomb exploded now? Rowdy now put the mobile phone to his ear, he didn't say anything, he was listening to something. There was an explosion, but somewhere far away. Rowdy had heard the sound of the blast. I heard it too. Suddenly, Rowdy, the photos lying on the floor, all the drainpipes stacked there—everything was transformed into an X-ray plate.

I woke up with a start in my hotel room. I was perspiring. My chest was heaving. I removed my vest. It was ten past two at night. The explosion was to take place at ten past ten the coming night. The time shown in watch advertisements. I turned up the fan and drank some water. I turned on the light at the dressing table. There were X-ray machine catalogues there. There was a wonderful place to sit on the verandah of the first floor of the hotel where I had an appointment tomorrow night at a quarter to ten with the purchase officer of the biggest nursing home in this city. That's where we would sit. It was the favourite spot of the purchase officer. Apparently, he struck lucky deals there. When I fell asleep again, there were no more dreams. I was relaxed after smoking a cigarette. I slept beautifully.

7

I was in a little bit of stress. It was almost five to ten when the man arrived. He was fat; looking at him one would surmise he was always stammering nervously; there was always sweat on his brow. He said he had got stuck in a traffic jam. That the traffic was worse than usual because of the new flyover being constructed.

We sat at the first-floor verandah. There was a bluish light. Probably a light like this one was burning in that girl's room too. And Rowdy knew about that. Rowdy also knew that the minister had arrived. The purchase officer said he would have whiskey. I had what I always did, beer. I ordered two plates of fish fingers. Car horns, city sounds, the instrumental music playing inside, our conversation ... The purchase officer dipped fish fingers in mustard and ate; he perspired as he drank whiskey.

I gulp the first peg very quickly. The second one too. After that, little by little, slowly ... By the way, do you only drink beer?

Yes.

Strange!

I looked at my watch. It was eight past ten.

Actually, I've found that nothing other than beer agrees with my system.

You're right, you know. It's best to stick to one's own poison. Don't you agree!

It was nine past ten. I would definitely hear the sound of the explosion from here. The flash would probably be visible too. Just ten seconds to go now. I lit a cigarette. I offered him one.

Thank you, I don't smoke.

8

There was no explosion at ten past ten.

There was no reason for that to happen. Yes, it's true that I go around from one city to another selling X-ray machines. But I am not a terrorist. There's no minister or bomb, no stacked drainpipes or girl in blue light, any Rowdy or thought stoppage—none of that is true. But it's true that I had a dream. This had got into my head after I saw a Hollywood movie on Star Movies. After seeing the film, whichever city I go to, in parallel, I keep devising a plan for a terrorist strike. That's how I push the dull routine of my job of peddling X-ray machines into a corner. My livelihood is like a side business now. I don't have words to thank Hollywood. After 9/11, they keep supplying me with means for terrorist plots.

The purchase officer placed an order for three machines. So, five machines in all. In our trade, this wasn't something to sneer at. Fatty also said that they were going to open more branches in medium-sized towns. He also grunted about many other things. In sum, I probably have to come again to this city after a few months.

A new terrorist plot would also be needed then.

—Translated by V. Ramaswamy

(Translated from Nabarun Bhattacharya (2006), 'Terrorist'. In *Shrestho Golpo*, 268–272. Kolkata: Dey's Publication.)

American Petromax

Visible from the side were cars of various sizes and makes going over the flyover; hearse-vans and police-vans too went by occasionally. In the course of watching this non-stop movement, suddenly a moped went by, making a moaning sound. Obviously, it was slow compared to the other vehicles. The colour on the rider's helmet was peeling off; his windcheater was flapping in the wind, he was plump—one couldn't say, maybe it was Parijat. Parijat had left his wife and family and was living together with Baby K, that is to say Baby *Khanki*[1]. The counsel of Fireman, his friend from the country liquor bar in Garcha, could not dissuade him. Petrol had seeped into all of Parijat's veins, nerves, tubes and tendons, thick and thin. He had a burning sensation in his body and limbs. The doctor had said, be careful, living together shouldn't become dying together. Parijat did not heed that. Carrying a jerrycan with him, he bought petrol from the pump. It was becoming expensive. Baby K drank five litres of petrol in one go, three or four times a day. Parijat was reduced to eating in pice-hotels[2] or surviving on *tarka-roti*[3]. The air in the room where they lived together was laden with petrol fumes. Lighting a flame was out of the question.

The last time Parijat had sat on the *taktaposh*[4] and drunk with Fireman at the bar in Garcha, it was evening, and suddenly there was load-shedding[5]. Just before the lights went off, Fireman was saying—

You destroyed your home, wife and child and even my pet tomcat for your Baby K! I told you in no uncertain terms. But you didn't listen to me.

---

1 Vulgar term for a prostitute such as whore or (in short form) ho in English.

2 A roadside restaurant serving cheap Bengali meals.

3 Lentils with bread (cooked on a griddle), a staple item in roadside Punjabi restaurants, also known as *dhabas*.

4 A plain rectangular platform or wooden cot.

5 A commonly used term in parts of India for power cuts, owing to power shortage.

Parijat was silent. There was a tragic shadow on his mug. He sat shrivelled up and hunched over; when Fireman lit his cigarette, he became alarmed.

Don't be afraid! I am Fireman. Putting fires out is my job, not lighting one.

I know, but I'm scared. Just observe in most matchsticks, burning bits fly out. Suppose a flame landed here. It'll ignite as soon as it catches my breath.

That's why the angle at which I struck the match was outwards. But I was thinking about something else.

What's that?

I forgot. Want to have some more? Shall I get a pint?

Get it. There's something amazing happening inside. There's a clamour inside my head.

Petrol and alcohol in the head at the same time. There's bound to be clamour.

Load-shedding. When one's eyes adjusted to the darkness, one could see at a distance a Nepali boy lighting a lamp. That's what Parijat had been looking at. As soon as one pumped, the flame sprang out of the mantle and then retracted. Fireman returned with a pint. He was big to begin with. In the light and shadow, he appeared even bigger. When the flame in the pressurised lamp became steady, Fireman saw in its light that Parijat was weeping, with occasional sobs. Parijat thought Fireman would say something. Fireman poured from the pint bottle till both glasses were half full. He added water. He put two peanuts into his mouth. And all the while, he looked repeatedly at the flame hissing inside the lamp.

What happened? You turned silent.

Fireman looked at Parijat. There was a faint smile on his otherwise relaxed face.

You know, seeing the lamp, I remembered something. In my childhood, I used to attend the Kali Pujo in the courtyard of my mother's house. My uncle would squat and light the lamp, and my grandfather, alcohol in his breath, would dandle me on his lap and say, 'This lamp is US Army stuff. Not any ordinary one. It had arrived for the wartime market. It's a genuine American Petromax. Can you see how bright the light is!'

But the story of Parijat and Baby K became a historic re-enactment of an almost unknown incident in Calcutta during the Second World War and, thus, came to be put into writing. There's no opinion expressed about which among these was tragedy and which one was farce. The final outcomes of the two incidents weren't the same either. The first incident was this—on an evening of black-marketing during the Second World War, a slender Bengali poet was walking on the pavement in Chowringhee with his wife. The wife was tiny. Just then, a few American soldiers, it's not known whether they were white or black, lifted up the wife on their outstretched hands and slipped into some alley. The Bengali poet was crying aloud about what had happened; he was fortunate; he spotted some MPs, that is to say, the US Army's own military police, and it was they who went and rescued the benumbed wife. Capable commentators have no doubt that the history of Bengali poetry would have been different if the incident had been otherwise. The same kind of incident, even if wasn't exactly like the other one, happened on the 9 August 2007. On the way to Iraq and North Korea, some soldiers of the US Army were in Kolkata for a few days. Naturally, the bars and other fun-spots in the Chowringhee area were taken over for their revelry.

On that evening of caprice, the whole Chowringhee area was abuzz with a sexy throb. And Parijat and Baby K were walking cheerfully in front of Metro cinema, in the direction of Tiger, having just eaten momos[6] at the shop of a one-eyed Chinaman who wore a singlet and a pair of shorts. The vendors on the pavement were selling khaki boxers of the US Army, dildos, small oh-so-cute baby dinosaurs and bunches of rhododendrons tied together in bouquets. The clouds in the sky were like nets to catch the moon, the drone of military transport planes and the erratic flight of aged bats. Parijat said to Baby K—

How was the momo?

Tasty!

Like to have some tea?

No.

I'll have tea.

---

6 An East and South-Asian preparation of meat-filled dumplings popular across India.

Go ahead. I'm going to have petrol.

There was a violent break in the dialogue because just then 3 GIs—two black and one white, all giant-sized—made a basketball-style feint; Parijat fell for that and landed simpering on the road, and then they lifted up Baby K on their outstretched hands and vanished into a side alley, entering a very seedy bar. As soon as they entered, the door shut behind them with a loud retort. Parijat banged on the door. One can't say whether the sound of his banging penetrated through the heavy door. Parijat cried and called out to people. No one paid the slightest heed. The distressed cries emitted by Parijat were drowned by the hum of the US Army Humvees.

Inside the bar, right then, the three GIs plus another thirty-four US Army soldiers plied Baby Whore with whiskey and lifted her atop a table. Crazy music. Baby Ho was dancing on top of the table, and below her the thirty-seven soldiers too danced; they clapped. Fuck her! Fuck her! They cried—a lot like the scene in the *Jumma Chumma De De, Jumma Chumma De De Chumma* song[7]. It would have carried on like that, but suddenly a soldier jumped up on Baby Ho's table and planted a king-size Marlboro cigarette between her lips. Bluish petrol fumes were already emanating with a hissing sound from the seven orifices of the dance-rapt Baby Ho. The air around her was laden with petrol fumes. The soldier took out a lighter and lit the cigarette on Baby Ho's lips.

Later, thirty-seven soldiers, three waiters and the body of a female midget, shrunken after burning, were found in that burnt out bar. After examining all the forty-one tandoori corpses, it was stated in the report of the US Army's military forensic bureau that the explosion was like something caused by four or five Molotov cocktails.

The whole building was in flames. Parijat, momo in his breath, stood gaping on the pavement along with many others. He looked, through eyes blurred with tears, at the leaping flames of the deadly fire.

A fire-engine had arrived with its bell clanging. Alighting from the vehicle, Fireman spotted Parijat in the light cast by the flames and advanced … Parijat had wailed—

7 A popular song from a song-and-dance sequence in the Hindi film *Hum* (1991), starring Amitabh Bachchan and Kimi Katkar. The lyrics mean, 'Kiss me Jumma'.

Baby K, she's gone!

Fireman had expressed his sympathy by patting Parijat twice on his shoulder, and then, looking at the fire, he had said to himself—

American Petromax!

—Translated by V. Ramaswamy

(Translated from Nabarun Bhattacharya (2010), 'American Petromax'. In *Shrestho Golpo*, 7–9. Kolkata: Bhashabandhan Prakashani.)

Nuclear Winter[1]

That winter will be terrifying. Temperature will drop thousands of degrees below the freezing point. There will be no trace of sunlight anywhere. A protracted and opaque darkness will descend upon the earth. Rains will have the taste of acid. Amidst all this, humans will be awaiting anxiously, gasping for breath, trudging along and trembling in cold darkness, an imminent, inevitable end. That nuclear winter will arrive after a nuclear world war. Six hundred fifty million years ago, a winter like this caused the extinction of dinosaurs from the earth. It was known as an impact winter. The crashing of a giant meteorite or maybe an asteroid in Mexico had caused a cloud of dust so dense that it concealed the sun for ages, beckoning the ice age. Or it could have happened from the rage of volcanoes. That would be known as a volcanic winter. An impact winter or a volcanic winter is not produced by humans, but the credit for a nuclear winter will go entirely to them. The explosion, radiation, fire and pollution from a nuclear fallout will annihilate millions of people, and then there will be a cloud full of smoke and dust ascending to a height of six to nine miles. This will be the beginning of a nuclear winter. An increasing uncertainty, a growing anxiety plagues us today. Thousands of nuclear weapons and missiles are lying in wait in hundreds of underground silos, underwater submarines and long-distance fighter jets. Waiting patiently for the command. We're not very far from the midnight hours on doomsday clock. Certainly not very far from a nuclear winter. Dinosaurs existed on this planet far longer than humans have lived here. They would have continued to live had there not be an impact winter. Do humans have anything to learn, to understand from this? Or will they finally take that terrible decision? With those frozen, fatal fingers press the eject buttons. Is a nuclear winter only biding its time?

1 Many thanks to Arka Chattopadhyay and Samrat Sengupta for their suggestions and comments. Special thanks to Arunima Bhattacharya for her patient and thorough readings and her helpful suggestions and edits. I owe her a great deal for this one.

Like every other day, in the wintry chill of that December Sunday too, Jyotish ate his lunch routinely seated on his low wooden seat after removing the flynet from his rice plate. Mangala's job is to cook, feed his mother and then cover food for Jytoish and leave. Jyotish saw that, like every other day, that same cat, a rusty old tomcat, was sitting at the door sill. A crow was hopping around on the unwashed utensils, making a clatter. A dead cockroach, lying upside down in the kitchen corner, was undergoing some tiny movement. It was because an army of red ants was dragging at it. While eating his lunch, it occurred to Jyotish that there was no food for the tomcat as there was no fish for lunch today.

There is nothing for you here today. Go, get lost, try your luck at the neighbours'. It's a Sunday, people are hogging meat and poultry today. Go, shoo...

The tomcat heard but did not move. A chilly wind crawled along the courtyard through to the kitchen but then did not pass through the window to the alleyway. Riding on the wind came the smell of piss, of wet rags, burned incense and some muffled sound of a TV playing nearby. Even while having lunch, Jyotish felt like singing Shyamal's 'Sediner Sonajhora Sandhya'[2]. He had heard him sing that while seated at the very front row during their Kali puja annual event. What a song! Could it happen again? Would such a song be made again? And add to it Radhakanta's sublime tabla. Our own Sisir-da rushed forth to Mitra to get his signature on a newly minted hundred-rupee note. And later that night, Akhilbandhu[3] joined us too. Could it happen again? Could anyone sing like him now? Do we have such talent today? There's just loud and uncontrolled screaming everywhere. Is there anything worthwhile left? Everything good and rich is gone. Could one dribble like Chuni or dash around like P.K.? The last of the great was Sourav. Even he was trapped, rallied against and then plucked out of profession. We have seen how a captain

2 Shyamal Mitra (1929–1987) was a versatile playback singer and music producer from Bengal who composed and sang songs for the Bengali and Hindi film industries. 'Sediner Sonajhora Sandhya' (That Gold-bedecked Evening) is one of his most popular songs.

3 Akhilbandhu Ghosh (1920–1988) is considered one of the finest modern classical singers from Bengal. Many of his songs remain popular even today.

looks like. Like Pataudi. A one-eyed man. Could anyone be like him? Have such pomp and style? Everything's messed up now. Everything. Even Sourav too. Or Uttam Kumar. Completely messed up. Manu-da as well. Has anyone seen the bloody face of Suchitra, like ever?[4] Everything is messed up. Priya-da, what a leader! Would run like a horse as he administered meetings. All messed up now. Would it happen again? Ever? Just what needs to happen is happening routinely. Full of shit!

That Sunday, Jyotish did not anticipate that the case would get so messed up that whatever local social gathering or adda he would visit afterwards, even for a minute, someone or the other, without even giving the slightest hint that they would, and without ever being able to guess who would, would suddenly say—

Leave alone Sourav and whosoever; tell us now what happened on the roof?

What happened on the roof? With several missing teeth, shrunken cheeks full of prickly white beard and a cigarette in hand, a shocked Jyotish would feel sucked out. Turning back, he would walk in a hurry, dragging his left foot a bit because of the aching pain in that knee. The hem of his trousers, having brushed against the road, was ripped here and there and caught some dried mud on them; he would hear laughter behind his back, a few claps and a cackle, and that voice resounding like the blinking flash of a camera—

What happened on the roof, Jyotish-da?

---

4 Chuni Goswami and P. K. Banerjee were two of the most talented football players from Bengal who represented India at international tournaments including the Olympics and Asian Games in the late 1950s and 1960s. Sourav Ganguly is a world-known cricketer from Bengal who represented and captained the Indian cricket team at various international stages such as the World Cup. Mansoor Ali Khan Pataudi is one of the finest cricketers to have played for India who captained the Indian cricket team in the 1960s and 1970s. He was married to Sharmila Tagore, a renowned Bengali actress who worked for Bengali and Hindi film industries. Uttam Kumar is one of the finest and most admired film actors in the Bengali film industry. Suchitra Sen, another fine actress, was often paired against Uttam Kumar in popular Bengali films, and together they are often considered Bengali film's golden couple. Manna Dey was an excellent classical singer from Bengal. Priya Ranjan Dasmunsi was a noted political leader from the Congress Party, a union minister and a member of the Indian Lok Sabha who was well known for his managerial and administrative skills.

Passing off the crowd, Jyotish would sneak into a nearby alleyway or in an empty-looking lane. He would light his twelve-and-a-half-rupee bullet cigarette again, drag hard as if ripping off his ribs and then run again. A small, *Charminar* filter cigarette. The huff and puff would be over now. But he would be panting fast for swallowing the smoke. Or because he ran fast, he had swallowed the smoke. That bitter smoke. Ragged cloths coloured to look like football jerseys of Brazil and Argentina were tied across the lane. He would stagger as he would attempt a brisk walk.

Of course, there are other kinds of cold too. A wet cold from beneath the earth. Cold feels different in a temperate country. In those countries, 22,000 military officers, murdered and inhumed in freezing cold, had turned into corpses—part frozen earth and part skeleton. Before they would have been discovered and dug out ages later, they seemed to have a cozy life in their dark and frozen winter of death. In countries with sultry climate, dead bodies buried in earth rot quickly. It may be raining torrentially. There can be a suffocating cold from it too spreading out into the earth. We have no clue as to how many different kinds of cold there can be. In the messy mohallas on the fringes of our capital, Delhi, old people, in order to hide from the cold, wrap their bodies with discarded polybags collected from the waste and fastened with nylon threads. They believe it is possible to ward off the cold by wearing the warmth emanating from the headlights of thousands of cars plying in the city. In the suburbs of Chicago, a twelve-year-old boy used to jump from one roof to another all day wearing a Batman cape. One day, he locked himself out inside the freezer of a refrigerator in an abandoned house. That refrigerator model did not have a mechanism to unlock the freezer drawers from inside, which actually makes sense. Why will it open from inside? It's natural that people will open it from outside; and then lock it after putting their food items, such as meat, fish, etc., from inside. This is precisely what needs to happen. What happened on the roof, Jyotish-da? What happened, boss? What? Ogling at somebody else's wife on the roof, eh? So many scams happen on roofs. While drying clothes or taking them off the lines, scams may always happen. What happened on the roof, Jyotish-da? What? Would it happen again?

Everything's messed up. Everything. Such a beauty that Suchitra Sen was, and now vanished from sight. You still did not tell us what had happened on the roof!

On that fateful December Sunday, after finishing his lunch, Jyotish kept all his soiled utensils, plates, bowls, etc. at one side of the courtyard and used a mug to pour water on them. Only for this reason, Jyotish liked winters; in winters there were no centipedes or millipedes anywhere, no God-knows-where-they-come-from slimy round snails climbing everything. On that Sunday, Jyotish did not shower. After lunch, like every other day, he put his wrapper on and went out, fastening the leash on the main door from outside. A few steps through the alleyway led to the road. The road then fell onto the main bus station road. There was a cricket match today on the bus road. Because it was a Sunday, Jyotish had a spicy, cardamom-flavoured white paan. He bought a packet of *Charminar* cigarettes and hurriedly lit one. And then went back to watch the match. The guest team from the rival neighbourhood were fielding. It was clear that they were like more hotshots in the tennis-ball cricket; a lanky, dark-featured quickie with a slightly offish delivery style suddenly released a toxic beamer almost chest high. Our boys are an impotent bunch; where they needed to fucking swing their bat and smash fours and sixes, they are taking useless singles. Twenty-seven for five. No, nothing could happen. What a career we saw from Chandi Ganguly's son, Sourav! Could you rotten lot learn anything from him? It made sense if some of them were pinch hitters. Defence was nonsense. You see a ball and just hit it out of the park. If you have good luck, you'll connect with some, and if not, get the fuck out. Simple. Jyotish felt a bit drowsy. Was there something in the paan? Could one get drowsy from cardamom? It never happened before. The boy who was umpiring for the match was talking on his mobile phone. Jyotish's brother, Palton, also has a mobile phone. Who cares if he lives elsewhere? He's after all his own brother. His mobile was, of course, Jyotish's too. It played songs, and had a camera as well. He never told him the price. Why would he? Everything's messed up now. Nobody knows what led to this muddle. Everything's messed up. All this CPI(M) hullaballoo, everything will be a mess soon. They will then see the prowess of Didi[5]. You fuckers will feel it when she beats you with a broom. Every game has a dead end. A dead game has no result. Wasn't there a song, everything's a mistake, a mistake? A canter in a song. And then the falling note. On the other hand, see Sandhya remained with us, Utpala remained and so did Pratima too.[6] And in between, there was some forgetting, everything's a mistake. What was the name of that song? Fucking shit! Can't remember anything these days. Everything's messed up. Another wicket fell. Thirty-one for six. The rival boys were clamouring, screaming. Rough noise. Jyotish had just come out of the Roxie movie theatre after watching *Junglee*[7], and noticed some crass scuffles on the street. Movie ticket smugglers had a fight with some rowdy boys from Malanga lane. Fiery soda bottles were flying in the sky in quick succession, and so were bricks. Jyotish yawned as he walked back home. What happened on the roof, would you come out clean please? It is a cold winter in Calcutta this year, but nothing compared to that of a nuclear winter. The winter that is coming. The winter that is the title of our story.

Coming back home, Jyotish threw himself on his plank bed and, wrapping around his quilt, fell asleep. Jyotish did not have much of a difference between a Sunday and the rest of the days in a week, but it was only on Sundays that the post-lunch nap almost absorbed him. The clamour of the cricket match did not reach Jyotish's house. But a vague, muffled song playing either on a TV or an FM radio floated around. What song was this? Who sang it? Nothing was clear. Jyotish remembered of that Kali puja event again in which Pannalal began singing at two-thirty in the morning. He first sang 'Boshon Poro Ma';

---

5 While didi is how Bengalis address their elder sisters, here Didi stands for Mamata Benerjee who came from grassroot politics and fought hard with the CPI(M) to eventually become the Chief Minister of Bengal. Bengalis affectionately call her Didi.

6 Sandhya Mukhopadhyay, Utpala Sen and Pratima Bandyopadhyay are all renowned trained classical singers from Bengal and contributed widely to playback music in the 1950s till the 1970s for the popular Bengali film industry.

7 *Junglee* was a 1961 Hindi (Bollywood) film starring Shami Kapoor and Lalita Power which was a blockbuster hit and had the iconic Shami Kapoor song, 'Chahe Koyi Mujhe Junglee Kahe' (Let someone call me wild).

and then, 'Sokoli Tomar Ichcha'.[8] And then he hanged himself. Would it happen again? In that mess all around, Jyotish felt sleepy. The songs, the cawing of crows, the noise from washing utensils—everything seemed to die out. Like that expressionless face with which a suicide bomber carried explosives, Jyotish's deepening sleep carried dreams, lightweight, fragmented, ripped apart and, like cropped, unwanted hair, scattered out on the floor in a barber shop—meaningless. Unknown faces talked to him. Why did they talk? Although Jyotish was not the only person who had dreams like these. Everyone in this world has had such dreams. This has been a matter of widespread academic debate and writing; experts who trade in sleep and dreams have been able to capture the exact levels of sleep when dreams seize us. But nothing of these will remain after the nuclear winter. No one will be alive to dream or to talk of dreams. There will be a sleep without a break.

Dada, hello, elder brother, wake up.

Jyotish woke up after being pushed around by Palton. It's already dark outside, how?

Mum's room is empty. Where is maa?

Jyotish screamed—

Maa-a-a-a...

Tell me what happened. I brought some massage oil for maa's knee-pain. But I could not find her in her room.

I sat her on the roof. She said, son, would you seat me on the roof in the sun? My knee is hurting badly today.

The two brothers then saw her on the roof. Lying still on one side, dead. The sunlight had gone out of the roof. Afternoon had been over. Scared, the old woman had called out Jyotish a number of times, and getting no response back from him she had tried to get to the stairs herself, dragging her feet in pain. She could not. She had peed herself. Her body had gotten wet from the cold pee. It had been getting colder around. She had died then. Her wet body had become hard. Jyotish

8 Pannalal Bhattacharya (1930–1966) is considered to have developed and popularised the Shayama Sangeet genre, a Bengali devotional music genre dedicated to the Goddess Shyama or Kali. 'Boson Poro Maa' (Mother, Please Dress Up) and 'Sokoli Tomari Ichha' (Everything's Your Wish) are two of his most popular songs.

entirely forgot that he had sat his mother on the roof. She died counting her sacred beads.

Jyotish howled. Saliva dripped from his mouth. Palton cried too, and then screamed—

You just killed mother! How could you kill her? How could you leave her in the cold to die?

Nuclear winter has not come upon us as yet. But it will. Without a shadow of a doubt. And until it comes, we will continue to hear the question—

What happened on the roof, Jyotish-da?

—Translated by Sourit Bhattacharya

(Translated from Nabarun Bhattacharya (2014), 'Nuclear Winter'. In *Angshik Chandragrahan*, 9–16. Kolkata: Bhashabandhan Prakashani.)

Poems

This Valley of Death Is Not My Country

I spit on the father who fears to point at his child's corpse
I spit on the brother and his shameless sanity despite everything
I spit on the teacher, the intellectual, the poet and the clerk
who do not seek to avenge this bloodbath out in the open
Eight corpses
lie stretched across the pathway of reckoning
I am losing my senses bit by bit
Eight open pairs of eyes look at me in sleep
I scream out
I will turn insane
I will kill myself
I will do whatever I want to do
I will eat the sun, the moon and the stars
I will smash all bridges between the viewer and the viewed
This is the exact time for poetry
Through stenciled manifestos on naked walls
A collage crafted of own blood, tears and bones—
now is the time for poetry
in the torn face of severest pain
right now is the time to hurl poetry
face to face with real terror—
keeping eyes fixed at the blinding headlight of the vans
at the three naught three and whatever else the killers have
It is time to face them with poetry
Through stone-cold lock-up chambers
Shattering the yellow lamps of crime investigation cells
In courthouses run by murderers
In seats of learning that teach lies and spew venoms of hatred
In the state machine churning abuse and terror
In the heartless chest of gunmen who serve that machine—
Let the anger of poetry echo out in fury
Let the poets of the world prepare themselves, like Lorca,

strange strong hammers made of iron
A thousand hands raised against bleary skies of dockyards, jute mills, against boiling pits of furnaces,
tons of coal fuming in acid vendetta, blazing in the life-maddened gall
to reclaim all that there was
and all that there shall ever be.
No, there's nothing to fear anymore.
The pale face of fear belongs to some stranger
when I know that Death is nothing but Love.
If I am killed, I shall become a million tiny flames
and spread across all the earthen lamps of the world
I am eternal
I shall return each season, each year, each aeon
as the green hope of soil
I am eternal
I shall stay in joy, I shall stay in sorrow
I shall live through each new birth and cremation
As long as the world is alive
As long as human beings are alive.

—Translated by Atindriya Chakrabarty

(Translated from Nabarun Bhattachaya (2004 [1973]), 'Ei Mrityu Upatyoka Amar Desh Na'. In *Ei Mrityu Upatyoka Amar Desh Na*, 11–14. Kolkata: Saptarshi Prakashan.)

Who in the Moonlight, with Rifles on Shoulders…

Some whale dives out into the moon's beams
Some people sit to scrawl lines of greed
Some girl casts her underthings off
Who are they—walking in the moonlight—
with rifles on their shoulders?
The yellow saplings are shaded by skyscrapers
Overhead, some are counting their profits
Lose yourself not to love yet
Some are walking through the woods—
with rifles on their shoulders
What poet is one who writes no forest fire?
Beggar-kids lick empty leaves
Handles of water-pumps stay hoisted—by thirsty hands
Who walks through such midnights?
with rifles on their shoulders?
All the shit spewed in the name of literature
Media-traders busy sticking them all along the brain's body
The kite of reckoning—its string is cut—it drifts down the empty skies
In such hours, who are they, walking,
with rifles on their shoulders?
Words bring life to poetry
So are the poets just sifting through words?
Kilns are but burning pyres for cowardly eyes
Tell me, who are they, walking through the nights—
with rifles on their shoulders?
You—who buy iPhones on midnights—
tell me how nights of hunger are spent
either you fight, or you surrender
Some forget fear to walk—
with rifles on their shoulders

Not in rhythm, seeking conquest
Buds of dreams blast like mines
The seven stars of the northern skies—they form a question mark—and stare
in interrogation—at they who walk, so deep into the night,
with rifles on their shoulders

Who are they who walk—with rifles on their shoulders?
They walk all night—with rifles on their shoulders
Their feet are hurting and yet they walk—with rifles on their shoulders
They walk in moonlight—with rifles on their shoulders

—Translated by Atindriya Chakrabarty and Malini Bhattacharya

(Translated from Nabarun Bhattacharya (2009), 'Jyotsnay Kara Rifle Kandhe Hatchhe'. In *Raater Circus*, 86–87. Kolkata: Bhasabandhan Prakashani.)

What Kind of City Is This

What kind of city is this
That forgets its sparrows
What kind of city is this
That forgets its warriors, whores and poets
What kind of city is this
Where multistoreyed crematoriums rise into the sky
What kind of city is this
Where dogs and trams are about to be banned
What kind of city is this
Where trees shut their eyes in fear
What kind of city is this
Where one can't hear drumbeats any more
What kind of city is this
Where fake eunuchs dance in the newspapers every day
What kind of city is this
Where one, licking his fingers to count banknotes, turns out to have no tongue
What kind of city is this
Where plastic bags can vote
What kind of city is this
Where writers burn out like cigarettes
What kind of city is this
Where students blind from birth are battered to death on blackboards

This city is dead
My last wish for it—a grenade.

—Translated by Supriya Chaudhuri

(Translated from Nabarun Bhattacharya (2009), 'E Kemon Shohor'. In *Raater Circus*, 45. Kolkata: Bhasabandhan Prakashani.)

Tram

I too am dying out from Calcutta, tram.
Written off because I'm too slow, obstinate, unprofitable:
Dark when untouched by electricity,
I too become night-blind, stupid:
Like a beached dolphin, nose down, motionless.
No one will put up with these old crocks anymore;
Now it's all fast food, debentures, shares, smart money.
Better for both of us to get out of it all,
Isn't that so, tram?

No one will take you on the second Hooghly Bridge, tram.
No one will take you to Salt Lake, to the Taj Bengal,
To the marshes of Greater Calcutta, the reckless curves of the Bypass.
Does Madonna's wild tempo ever
Make its way into a sonorous *alap* or *jod*?

Many years from now, indeed,
Your lights slipping away at night on the Maidan
While here and there, strung around temple or church,
Bells ring out a message;
Each ticket like a page of poetry,
The conductor-librarian,
The ancient driver—
all this will become antique Egypt,
The vanquished will be lost in the depths.

Yet, tram, with you
the protest march held step;
And sitting in your second-class carriage
the poet of rallies
Sang untunefully,

songs of revolt and freedom.
With your three eyes and rain-soaked lights you were
the unearthly transport of lovers.

I too am being written off in Calcutta, tram.
I too from networks overhead
visible or invisible, draw no dreams.
Tram, I too am being taken off
because I'm too slow, awkward, unprofitable.

In the end, tram, the people of Calcutta
Will lack the word 'outline';
Nothing but set hymns; no one
will so much as sing a song of rejection.
Like a patient refused entry at hospital after hospital,
Like an injured boxer or football player,
In hurt pride, insult, neglect,
scrapped by the profit principle,
We too are dying out from Calcutta, tram.

—Translated by Supriya Chaudhuri

(Translated from Nabarun Bhattacharya (2004), 'Tram'. In *Mukhe Megher Rumal Badha*, 74–75. Kolkata: Saptarshi Prakashan, 2004.)

Something's Burning

Something's burning
In a corner, untimely, under the mattress, in the crematorium,
Something's definitely burning
I can smell the smoke
Someone's lit a cheap tobacco twist
Someone's squatting over a clay stove, blowing on the coals
Someone's put a shrivelled baby
Dead of enteritis, on a funeral pyre
Flaming birds tumble from the sky
Somewhere, a gas cylinder has exploded
There's a fire in a coal mine, in a fireworks factory
Something is burning
All four corners have caught fire
The burning mosquito net will descend on you as you sleep
Something's burning
The stars burn, the spacecraft with its crew is on fire
Entrails, gut are afire with hunger
The youth's afire with love
The body of desire burns, chaff, cotton soaked in machine oil
Something's definitely burning
You're hit by a blast of heat
Buildings, moral values, huge portrait hanging somewhere
Promises, television, rare books
Something's burning
I'm rummaging through everything to find
What's burning, where
What's causing the blisters on my hands
Something's burning, something's caught fire
Burning quietly, burning in silence
But if a storm comes it'll suddenly burst into flame
I'm telling you, something's burning

Fire engine, umbilical cavity, sun
Something's burning
In front of everyone, right before your eyes,
Amidst all the people
Homeland!

—Translated by Supriya Chaudhuri

(Translated from Nabarun Bhattacharya (2004), 'Kichu Ekta Purchhe'. In *Ei Mrityu Upatyoka Amar Desh Na*, 63. Kolkata: Saptarshi Prakashan.)

Type

A choked sky crematorium
The city's blue funeral
mounting stairs of meaningless days
A night-time hollow cough, a drunkard's face
erupts coughs and verses
words while floating
on the road
in drizzle a typewriter's verses wake up
A blind typist who sits in the dark

—Translated by Samrat Sengupta

(Translated from Nabarun Bhattacharya (2015), 'Type'. In *Agronthito Kobita*, 14. Kolkata: Bhashabandhan Prakashani.)

Disabled Three

(1)

Raincoat of sky
Covered the Diamond Harbour Road
That noon
A dumb boy and a deaf girl
Crossing the road
That love was speechless

(2)

Touching with my fingers
I felt them all—face, nose, throat
Holding the railings, I realised it was a jail
Cold weight of manacles around the neck
Wind and rain came searching for me
Felt philosophy is brail

(3)

An undivided party worker's leg
Was struck in a firing inside the Dumdum jail
Since then for both the sides he has used crutches
A child watches and wonders
If this is what is stilt?

—Translated by Samrat Sengupta

(Translated from Nabarun Bhattacharya (2015), 'Pratibandhi Tin'. In *Agronthito Kobita*, 46. Kolkata: Bhashabandhan Prakashani.)

A Family Poem

Our family of three
My son Tathagata, wife Pranati and me
Three mirrors gazing back at us
In gloomy light like a fish's eyeball
The gleam that never sleeps
Perhaps a half shadow of luminance stays
A gas oven burning in the darkened home kitchen
Phosphorus touch on cheeks of sand and rock
Wiped again and again by the murky sea

But it may not be my family
Perhaps my wife and son were
Stripped, and walked in the Auschwitz Gas Chamber
Me a tailor or a cobbler half skilled
Shot in the head by a bullet near the icy pit
With an infected chest I used to come up from the mines of Natal or Spain
Laid upon wooden shelves they coughed as well
Smoky sunlight spreads
Hoofing incessantly the sun vomits blood
Sooty lungs in the moon

In every blowing wind the last gasping of ours
So many times my family got erased
At homeland
Diseases, Bullets, Hospital corridors, Malnutrition, Fear
Everywhere, in all places, every time we had been

We three could have been Nikolai Bukharin's family
We three could have been in that brass country, Chile
It is so common to see
Someone who claims to be a writer, someone who teaches,

Someone who is a student mad for sports
Perhaps captivated in Leningrad, coffinless and starved,
From Stalingrad my last postcard
Reached the destination where nothing remained but a shell hole
Buchenwald, Bergen-Belsen, Karaganda
Somewhere falling flat on my face, specs broken
Hated Hitler heart and soul
Yet no allegation against comrade Stalin
At Dresden, Warsaw, Prague
Our pianos, wall clocks, toys charred along with us
Perhaps just now we gathered at Chechnya for prayer
After a while Russian bombs shall descend from sky
At Vietnam, Japanese day, Iraq, Rwanda—
Many many families of three
Disenfranchised of even a photograph

However apart from all these there are so many unnamed families
Those who collectively commit suicide
Or murdered for reasons unknown
Some families vacate rooms as well
Without prior information
Mirrors eroded of mercury are not mirrors any more
They turn into transparent glass,
In every blowing wind the last gasp of us

Across countries and continents quiver, assassins'
Numbing Hypnoses
In this open-eyed neon, the executioner shall arrive for sure
All three of us witnessing spider nets hugging constellations
Terrorised by absurd inexorable brutal meteors
The Mediterranean assumes silence

—Translated by Samrat Sengupta

(Translated from Nabarun Bhattacharya (2015), 'Ekti Paribarik Kobita'. In *Agronthito Kobita*, 150–151. Kolkata: Bhashabandhan Prakashani.)

Interview with Nabarun Bhattacharya

There Is an Uncanny Pluralism in Marxism

Goutam: Nabarun-da, let's start with the use of slang in fiction. Usually, slang in literature is either complimented or condemned, but always for wrong reasons. Nobody bothers to consider the author's rationale for using slang, its scope as an instrument of social criticism or the trauma that gives rise to it. The mainstream doesn't accommodate slang as well. For a long time, you too have been criticised for this, isn't it?

Nabarun: I am still criticised. I remember when I received the Bankim Purashkar, someone said to me that I won such an award because I extensively used cuss words. I feel that this criticism of slang—or the lack of real constructive criticism thereof—points at our sheer immaturity. Secondly, since we have long exiled Tekchand, Bhabani Charan or *Hutom* from our literary canon, their legacy hasn't found continuity in our literature. Had there been a steady transmission from thereon, these censures regarding slang wouldn't have occurred at all. Today there is no taboo on using slang in American or Russian literature. Slang is just a part of the living language there. I approach slang from a similar perspective. Speaking on the uses of slang is, therefore, not a sign of maturity, I feel.

Rajib: But the entire middle-class Bengali readers do not view slang from that lens. Apparently, their mindset is still somewhat limited.

Nabarun: Not that; their mindset has actually been kept in confines. Due to this, the general vocabulary of millions of people does not get reflected in their literature. Besides, swearing shouldn't just be viewed from this limiting scope of profanity. These elements add a different dimension to language. They are the ornaments of a language.

Goutam: Yes, indeed. It is a form of expression.

Nabarun: Yes, expression—an inevitable expression. People use such expressions, and I honour this; nothing more than that. In this context,

I must also mention that some of my writings do not contain slang at all. The anti-slang squad does not notice those writings. All their concerns are dedicated exclusively towards those that have swear words. To put it better using an analogy, no matter how high the proverbial vulture may choose to soar, it always has its eyes fixated on the dunghill.

(...)

Rajib: Perhaps, this is an expression of our reading habits. The taste of the so-called quintessential bhadralok controls the entire phenomenon.

Nabarun: Definitely.

Rajib: Who are these people? Who are these self-styled bhadraloks?

Nabarun: Jibanananda speaks of the bhadralok in his works. The bhadralok takes a bus from Ballygunge, and simply because a dirty-looking labourer comes and sits beside him, he gets off the bus, takes a cab instead and reaches his destination. I do not write keeping such laughable people in mind. Further, I'd like to add that I use slang very spontaneously when I am speaking. I didn't have much opportunity to socialise with the bhadraloks, and my unconstrained use of slang is a reflection of that lack of interaction. I feel that many expressions do not find their genuine shape unless they are expressed through slang. For example, everything can be absolutely nullified just by saying '*baal*'[1]. By actually not saying much, this simple word can express everything that's intended.

Rajib: I think that the social setting of old Calcutta where you grew up had no such taboo over slang.

Nabarun: Absolutely. Even afterwards, when my son was growing up, there was no class division in friendships. A taxi driver's son or the son of a female domestic help, all of them shared the same space; they played together. They too have used the same slang. Later, perhaps, these differences broadened more and more as the spaces for free

1 Loosely translates into the English slang 'shit'. The original in Bengali means public hair.

mixing started to get lost. The playground is an important space for friendships. Playgrounds too are becoming extinct.

Goutam: Yes. Physical connection is giving way to virtual connectivity.

Nabarun: Indeed.

Rajib: On another note, let's speak of one of your works that, perhaps, many are not aware of. You have translated a couple of science fictions which were compiled and published from the National Book Trust with the title *All This Happened Tomorrow.* We know that science fiction interests you. To what extent do you think has science fiction influenced your writings?

Nabarun: Science fiction…

Rajib: Not exactly science fiction; some strange mysterious events that didn't happen yet but could happen any day.

Nabarun: Both science and science fiction interest me. I had closely read the Strugatsky Brothers. Stanislaw Lem is one of my favourites, and that's not just because of *Solaris* or *Stalker.* Lem is not easily available here; while I was in England, in 2008, I collected some works of Lem. When National Book Trust approached me with the translation project, I figured that this was an area close to my heart. Some of these aspects have had an influence on my own writings as well. For example, some frontier theories, such as Taleb's *The Black Swan*, find a reflection in my work because I love reading and knowing about them.

Rajib: Like in *Khelna Nagar* (*Toy City*)…

Nabarun: Yes, *Khelna Nagar* contains elements of science fiction. Look at the character of Windcheater. The manner in which it functions as a double agent contains many interesting elements. Technology plays a huge role there in hiding its dreadfully cruel face. You see, technology is basically a double-edged sword—it plays an instrumental role both in the hands of terrorists and those who eliminate terrorists. Mere technology has rendered mankind so helpless and, that too, how! The fact that today man thinks of himself as omnipotent is nothing but a pure fallacy. Recently, I was watching something about the assassination of (Osama) Bin Laden, and I found that some blue-CDs have been recovered from his base camp. The CDs have coded instructions. As you can see, the world around us has actually moved to a very different space altogether; science fiction and science have intermingled so strongly that it is extremely hard to distinguish the two.

Rajib: Another important detail must be observed here. Even though in your writings you create an ambience of science fiction, you never refuse to acknowledge the politics of existence.

Nabarun: Yes; because, in reality, these things function in parallel. In the German concentration camps, technology reached at a terrifying height. Zyklon B was used to murder millions of people and, to me, it was a technological marvel. Nevertheless, through the lives and experiences of the people slaughtered there, for example, through the death of a poet like Robert Desnos or Ernest Hellmann, science and existential crisis interpenetrate. German concentration camps took the technique of murdering people to an altogether different level of sophistication. Stalin, in comparison, had a cruder technique for execution. Either people were deserted in the snow or bullets were lodged in the heads—two bullets per head—as was done for the execution of Issac Babel. Germans took this technique of instantaneously killing large numbers of people within a short span to a whole new level of expertise. Certainly, science fiction and life unmistakably merged in those concentration camps. Another interesting anecdote is that of a prisoner in the German concentration camp who was not executed because he was a highly skilled chemist. Instead, he was made to work for the Germans. He was the eminent author, Primo Levi. In the end, however, he committed suicide.

Rajib: In the introduction to the Hindi translation of *Khelna Nagar* and *Juddho Poristhiti*, you have mentioned that their central theme is cruelty. Cruelty is a distinctive trait applicable to *Auto*, *Herbert* and to some of your other works too. Have you been doing this consciously?

Goutam: But can you call *Herbert* a novel of cruelty? I think it's more of a novel of disillusionment.

Nabarun: Correct; but obliquely, *Harbart* too contains cruelty.

Goutam: Right.

Nabarun: The last century is, in fact, the cruelest century in the history of mankind. Twenty million lives in the First World War and another fifty-five million in the Second World War were decimated. Besides, there are wars going on in Iraq, Iran, Vietnam, Indo-China, Indo-Pakistan—innumerable wars. I cannot bring myself to move away from these world wars and the theatre of war zones. This, for me, is the site of contemporary history. Its impact is still visible in the 21st century.

Goutam: Does your concept of subversion take its roots here?

Nabarun: I have been eager to see a successful subversion for a long time now. In this process of subversion, I indict capitalism, imperialism and faulty social practises; I will not exonerate any of them because they are equal partners in cruelty.

Rajib: It means that even amidst this chaos, you fantasise about a hopeful solution somewhere down the line. Does this empower your Fyatarus to emerge in this crisis?

Nabarun: Hope is an intrinsic urge of all mankind and, naturally, I am not at all ready to surrender to negativity. Moreover, yielding is not a spontaneous human inclination. Had they not been hopeful, how did people in the concentration camps keep themselves alive, or keep their artistic sensibilities in order? Authors like Solzhenitsyn have published work after their horrible experiences of imprisonment and life in the concentration camps. Even people who did not live in the camps and experienced it from outside, Vasily Grossman for example, wrote extensively about the cruelty of these camps. Therefore, surrendering to this cruelty is out of question. Further, the history of applied Marxism clearly shows that it's a comparatively new phenomenon in the historical timescale. In comparison to capitalism, applied Marxism has come into being for a brief period. Scholars like Samir Amin through their research have traced the roots of capitalism back to the Song dynasty in China. Therefore, in respect of this timescale, the rise and fall of socialism should not be seen as decisively final. This being the case, we have a world to win. This is something I still believe in, and I write these thoughts because I believe in socialism. I am an out and out political person and an unrepentant radical—perhaps, this attitude won't be clearly explicable right now, courtesy the presence of a CPI(M) regime in West Bengal, however, to me, this is my cardinal truth.

Rajib: In the character of Ranajoy from *Juddho Poristhiti*, we witness a tragedy being concentrated around the event of him finding a weapon.

Nabarun: Ranajoy is not the only one; it is, in fact, the tragedy of an entire decade. I know of at least one such case, of people leaving a suicide note and having a heart attack at the impact of the fall of the USSR. People do not remember these things because they are very few in numbers. Nevertheless, the agony of disillusionment is a devastating torment.

Rajib: You have not weaponised the Fyatarus though.

Nabarun: No, I have not, and I will not.

Rajib: Despite this, weapons and attacks play an important role in *Kangal Malshat, Mausoleum* or *Mobologe Novel.*

Goutam: In fact, weapons become a character in these novels.

Nabarun: Right. However, I deal with this in an entirely sarcastic manner, and never have I ever given it a realistic shape. Take the salt cannon from *Kangal Malshat* as an example. When shots are fired from the salt cannon, the projectiles land on top of police vans and start dancing around. Absolutely nothing more than this happens. Not a single soul dies. This is more of a war cry of the impotent.

Rajib: There are many who try to arbitrarily generalise your entire equation with weapons and label it as an offshoot of contemporaneity, attaching it to the incessant use of weapons nowadays.

Nabarun: It is not at all fair, but having said that, I do have an active interest in weapons. While writing *Kangal Malshat*, I have read many works on AK-47. I believe that AK-47 is the most interesting military invention of the last century which still plays a major role. One AK-47 can do miracles. So, how this machine was manufactured, who created it and how it was made are the things which interest me. The origin and application of a weapon of this magnitude carry in it the realities of the past century and the present. That such an assault rifle which fires around twenty-five to twenty-six bullets per second is necessary reflects on the contemporary human condition.

Goutam: Insas Rifle too has an equally interesting mechanism. It makes the target visible even in darkness to the one armed with an Insas, whereas, the target cannot see the assailant.

Nabarun: Another intriguing aspect of the Insas rifles is that it's more of a weapon that disables and assaults its victims instead of killing them. At the most, Insas injures. Also, when one is shot and wounded, another two can be engaged in carrying the injured. You can basically neutralise three people at the same time. Such minute development in weapons of this sort is highly compelling.

Rajib: Your writings have also reflected lives that are placed at the further side of this bracket of weapons, war and blood thirst. For example, take *Lubdhak* or a more recent story like 'Mahajaaner Aayna', wherein I feel there is a profound influence of Buddhist religion and philosophy.

Nabarun: One can actually call me a sort of practising Buddhist. I have in the past practised Buddhist meditation and continue to do so. This has certainly left a profound impact on me. It can be traced in a number of my works like 'Mahajaaner Aayna' and others. However, in 'Mahajaaner Aayna', Buddha appears in a different context—at a particular moment within a specific time frame, Buddha identifies a person who is facing death and won't live long and strikes a conversation with him. I try to understand how Buddha perceives this human choice in this state of godless nothingness. Despite this, Buddha is not the most important character here. The most important character is Ujjwali; Buddha is there just to strengthen the argument. You see, this particular genre of writing was not very consciously conceived; instead, it dawned upon me while I was at it. Stories come to me from real, practical incidents. Honestly, I did notice a girl carrying a mirror on her head and this very girl later came to me and narrated her story. She explained how long she had to walk, how far she had to travel in a boat and various other things that she had to do—I was fascinated upon hearing these. Later, when I tried to structure this narrative into a short fiction, the conclusion came spontaneously. None of it is actually premeditated. To tell you the truth, much of the creative process actually takes place unconsciously. An alchemy functions within this unconscious who reveals the routes; provided the search is genuine.

(...)

Rajib: There has been a recent tendency in Bengali literature of becoming an author without having a substantial and regular reading habit. As your readers, we can understand that you are a remarkable exception to this trend. How does your reading habit influence your writings?

Nabarun: I have never studied in a systematic and planned manner, but I have always nurtured a tremendous curiosity towards acquiring knowledge. For example, when I am not reading something, I tune in to Discovery channel. There, recently, I watched a programme about the extinction of dinosaurs in the cretaceous boundary. I had a rough idea about the subject, but this made it clearer. I came to realise that had the meteorite not landed on Mexico, dinosaurs would have still continued to inhabit the earth and humans probably wouldn't have been here. None of these books, arts and paintings—none of these—would have been there, neither would elections have taken place. What is most interesting though is that after the extinction of dinosaurs, there was no trace of life on earth for a long period. After an immense gap, the whole thing again started from scratch, and life emerged from the level of single-celled organisms of amoeba. The net culminating result of this extensive process is human beings—those laughable human beings who are all too content and ecstatic about watching substandard commercial news channels. Often, I reflect upon the sheer precariousness of this process of creation; this uncertainty of existence which can come to a final destination any moment now. This precarity makes me wonder. My readings, however, are thoroughly unpredictable and they depend upon my whim. Some may find it very funny to know that currently I am reading P.G. Wodehouse, Buddhist philosophy, tantra and Nagarjuna's philosophy simultaneously. Three pages of one work, four pages of the other and so on; some I've been able to grasp and some I have not. Despite reading so much, I have not been able to read up on my favourite topic—football. There are many soccer novels—mostly written in Latin America and some in England. I wish to collect a few of them. Mati Nandi here tried to do something substantial with soccer novels, but football has been unable to emerge as an industry like cricket in Bengal or India.

Rajib: Nabarun-da, many of your works have been adapted for screen and stage. *Mahanagar@Kolkata* and *Herbert* were adapted into movies. *Fyataru*, *Kangal Malshat* and *Juddho Poristhiti* have been reconstructed for theatrical productions. They may be made into movies as well. In the introduction to your collected works, you have mentioned, 'Market almost has no bearing upon the impetus which drives me to write.' In spite of this, your writings are being co-opted by the market through movies and theatres. How would you respond to it?

Nabarun: Certainly, I am satisfied. Despite claiming that there is no connection between my work and the market, indeed there remains a trace of some equation somehow.

Rajib: Is it not then a compromise with the market?

Nabarun: Absolutely not. The market did not approach me, artists did. Suman (Mukherjee), Debesh (Chatterjee), Rangan (Chakrabarty), Santanu Basu, Ashok Mukherjee from the theatre workshop or Paramabrata Chatterjee—all of them are artists. I am connected to them in the same manner as an artist is related to another artist. There is definitely an intermediary monetary link involved, but it does not amount as much so as to initiate a compromise.

Goutam: Speaking of the market, we must bear in mind that the so-called commercial publishing houses that are now publishing Nabarun-da are actually collecting his works published in various little magazines, and the process is strictly executed in Nabarun-da's terms. His writings have a market of its own.

Nabarun: Anyone who writes ultimately wants to reach the reader. I consider myself fortunate because no matter how inconsequential it might be, I have been able to reach out to my readers.

(...)

Rajib: In *Herbert*, we come across a sudden surge of poetic vigour. Then, after quite a long break, we come across Purandar Bhat. Is there continuity at work here?

Nabarun: Ha! Everything you observe is nothing but me. A creature of my sort is able to take innumerable avatars.[2] Hence, every so often, I write for Harbart; and on many occasions, I become Purandar Bhat. Purandar Bhat's poems, however, function as rewarding avenues through which I channelise my earnest exasperations. I get massive satisfaction in writing them. I will write more in this timber in future.

(...)

Goutam: The man you wrote about in 'Korai'...

Nabarun: The character mentioned in 'Korai' was actually travelling with me in a bus with a *korai*[3]. I noticed in surprise that both his hands had an extra finger, and he was playing a tune with the *korai*. I knew it right away that I couldn't give this man a miss.

Goutam: Take, for instance, the auto-rickshaw driver from the novella *Auto* who actively discourages women wearing sleeveless shirts to sit in the front seat of the vehicle alongside the driver. Ultimately, an unblemished character is what he holds dearest. You have certainly met or heard about such people.

Nabarun: I have experienced them all personally. Not everything can be concocted.

---

2 In Bengali the analogy used here is of *Shatarupe Sarada*, a prominent anthology on the life and times of Sri Sarada Devi. The colloquial import is to refer to the innumerable forms through which one individual is capable to express himself/herself.

3 An Indian wok; a round-bottomed frying pan.

Goutam: When you are giving shape to all these incidents that you have experienced, you are also engaged in experimenting with the form of the novel itself. For instance, every chapter in *Kangal Malshat* ends with either 'to be continued' or 'not to be continued'.

Nabarun: I need to clarify that not everything is deliberate. There was only a consistent buzz in my head that a grand mischief had to be committed—an act of splendid transgression. I had the irresistible urge of muddying everyone into this practical joke. It all started to roll from there and went on.

Rajib: In this process, the real and the unreal intermeshed. The Dhuins, Lambodars, Nishapatis, Sridhars got assimilated into the Danrkaak, the Bonberal, Begum Johnson and so on.[4]

Nabarun: Yes, that may be. All of them can be easily connected by the fact that no one knows who they are, where they belong, the time they belong to, etc.—nothing is apparently known about them. Begum Johnson, however, has clear historical coordinates, but who is this Bonberal? No one. What is at best known of Danrkaak is that he is a father to Bhodi. But it is never disclosed what Danrkaak actually is. The narrative technique plays a significant role here. Why should I care to explain everything? I would deliberately baffle readers with something, forge some perplexing and mysterious images here and there, and so on. An author should keep some tricks up his sleeve like a magician. Such as in *Herbert*. I am not supposed to suggest as its author that the electric cremator would detonate in the end. My task as the author is to seek out the most unexpected and unlooked for elements in the narrative and situate them in a way that causes a short circuit. I'd have to leave the unanticipated as it is. The entire plan is solidly grounded in reality. It is a fact that in the past dead bodies in this part of the world were burned together with their mattresses. The practise was discontinued after a while. I had no connection, whatsoever, with either of the decisions. But in those years when mattresses were burned along with dead bodies, would it not be possible to imagine that kept

4 Two sets of characters in *Kangal Malshat*

hidden inside mattresses some dynamite sticks might have made their way into the electric stoves as well?

Goutam: Tell us the context for *Herbert.*

Nabarun: In 1991, I lost my job. I started reading about a lot of things and, while at it, I chanced upon a letter published in an English daily about an air hostess who communicated with her father after her death in a plane crash. I made a mental note of this. Besides, I worked at an NGO during this period for six or seven hundred rupees a month. On my way to the office, there was a tailoring shop whose signboard read 'Proprietor: Haru Sarkar'. I do not know for sure whether Harbart developed from Haru but all these factors were playing in my mind while writing.

Rajib: There was also a ruffian called Harbart.

Nabarun: Yes. There was a mobster called Harbart in our locality—a legendary one. Perhaps, the name evolved from there. However, I wouldn't have written a single line if not for the steady insistence of Surajit Ghosh (Editor of *Proma*). He requested a novel for the festive edition of his magazine. I had never written anything of that sort before; I did not know how to write one. Eventually, I realised that it is indeed possible to give a proper shape to my thoughts that had developed during this period. The entire thing didn't happen overnight though. Actually, I am fanatic about structure. I decided on the structuration beforehand. Before starting to write, I divided the narrative into several episodes. Some chapters I wrote well in advance; while others, I penned later. The entire thing was completed in fourteen days. I was obsessed at that time. I had a mild fever. I used to intoxicate myself mildly and set at writing *Herbert* in that intense daze.

(...)

Rajib: You suffered from depression when *Herbert* was sent to the press...

Nabarun: Tremendously depressed. I did not want *Herbert* to get published. Though it may seem strange, I became so intensely attached to *Herbert* that I did not want to let go of it; I did not want to give it to the public. I remember crying profusely after handing over the work to Surajit.

Rajib: Nabarun-da, you have always been intrigued by supernatural elements.

Goutam: Yes. You have developed connections with several people with supernatural abilities. You went to someone near Kalighat who was a fortune teller.

Rajib: Shankar-da.

(…)

Nabarun: Yes. I enjoy the company of such people. I do not think that this realistic world is everything. I do not think that my quest for the transcendental has any contention with Marxism because what is mystical is also real. Just because it does not respond to your sense organs, you cannot call it illusion. You cannot. Once I met a person on the street who knew absolutely nothing about me. He told me that I would go on to win the Sahitya Academy award, and I won the award that very year. Is there anything left to say after this?

Goutam: In the same sense Marxism too can be called an unreal utopia.

Nabarun: Definitely unreal. Civilisation has no precedence or tradition attached to Marxism. After the emergence of Marxism in theory, its practical establishment is nothing but a human project. In the present scenario, Marx is criminally underrated. The Left Front has maligned Marx exceptionally.

Goutam: People these days associate Marxism with Buddhadeb Bhattacharya (the CPI[M] leader and current Chief Minister of West Bengal).

Nabarun: Right. But that should not be the case. The profundity of Marxism cannot be compared to that of the Upanishad. *The more you have the less you are*—this Marxist insight is but comparable only to Rabindranath. There is no document more exceptional than the *Economic* *and Philosophic Manuscripts* in world literature. His greatest contribution is his insight into alienation and commodity fetishism. Any subject under the earth can be perfectly analysed with his alienation theory. It explains the mechanism of a serial killer, and, at the same time, it spells out the reasons behind the dismantling of a political party. One cannot move a step further without Marx. It is for this very reason that Sartre said that his philosophy was clearly founded but within certainties—that is to say, within Marxist horizons. I think of myself as belonging within the Marxist horizons. I do not think that it has any opposition with the supernatural. I remember an anecdote. Once his daughters asked Marx what according to him was the greatest virtue in women. He replied that it was a weakness. Many would get offended by this, but Marx is made up of all this and much more. I respect Marx as a human being, as a Renaissance human being. Since he was a Renaissance human being, Marx profusely used slang. After *The Poverty of Philosophy*, Marx says of Proudhon, 'I have put his theory between his buttocks'—I have busted his ass. This is Marx; and this is the temperament of the Renaissance. This is the very reason why Shakespeare or Rabelais brings into play such abundance of slang. Compare this with the Victorian orthodox morality where all curiosity is centred exclusively on the covered and coveted areas of the body, and where all the notoriety breaks loose in the dark. The poor are at least free from this hypocrisy. Who are the ones that actually nurture this real corruption and perversion? They are the multi-millionaires. They don't understand robust humour; all they have is camouflaged perversion. They are the perfect example of enemies that surround us in every nook and corner. Each and every television channel, sponsored by these multi-millionaires, has been invaded with a systematic takeover by cultural imperialism. As a result, you won't find any European movies telecast in any of the multiple channels they fund; and the select few channels that somehow televise European movies go on repeating the same films endlessly. Many classics like Tarkovsky's are never shown in these channels. Yet, in the past, broadcasters under the Government of India used to screen European movies such as Costa-Grava's *Z* or Tarkovsky every Saturday night. These are films that the state could show then. On the other hand, private channels cannot even show Bunuel.

Goutam: In this context what do you think is the prospect of Marxism? Do you think that a revival of Marxist politics is possible, keeping in view the state of affairs both regionally and internationally?

Nabarun: There is an uncanny pluralism in Marxism and, hence, according to me, its possibilities are endless. In this connection, I am reminded of Kondratiev—an economist, murdered by Stalin. He was the proponent of the 'Theory of Long Cycles'[5]. He observed that there are twenty to fifty year long cycles where capitalism plays a significant role. I don't know how he calculated this exact period of years. Later, however, another Marxist economist, Ernest Mandel, studied the long waves and short waves of capitalism. I really wish to know which stage of capitalism we inhabit presently. Perhaps, a prognosis for the future could be possible then. In his counterargument to tackle this periodic crisis of capitalism, an extremely right-wing American economist remarked that after all Marx was right. These dimensions that emerge out of such confessions would perhaps play a major role in the coming future. The so-called Marxist rule that we have had for thirty-four long years in West Bengal carried out not a single substantive experiment. On the other hand, the Yugoslavian model, vehemently criticised in Marxist circles, did carry out major experiments in worker's self-management. That the workforce would follow self-directed work processes, and regulate their production capacity themselves from within—I think it was a revolutionary step. Today European communists are changing their denomination, but they still function within the established tradition of European Social Democracy. This experience of functioning within a democratic framework will come to their immense aid in future. Today the communists in Italy, France or Spain are extremely active. None of them are staying silent in these times of global recession. These countries are consistently being paralysed and immobilised due to strikes, and this is gaining currency due to the active involvement of the communists. As far as my knowledge goes, there are communists involved even in the Occupy Wall Street movement. Some of them

5 Kondratiev Waves.

are socialists and some Trotskyites, but they are in it together. They are active in every country in the world, even in England. Therefore, it will be a fallacy to claim that experiments with Marxism have ended. Had the Indian communists attempted to carry out something worthwhile within the democratic framework of the nation, it would have benefitted them in the long run. All they are left with is renouncing the past in the name of introspection. Although I should mention that whatever little they have achieved should indeed be renounced without a shadow of a doubt. It is pretty late in the day to make a hue and cry around the Communist Party's (CPI[M]'s) monolithic and Victorian structure, or its totalitarian politics because these would yield no results. There comes a time in history when you are bound to pay your debt; there comes a time for confrontation and revenge. I don't think that this party is ready for any of it. I do not see any real, active engagement with Marxist thought in them. It is now high time to reformulate and reevaluate the Latin American Marxists' stance on internal colonialism, or about Gunder Frank's Dependency Theory. The world that seems all too familiar today may suddenly shift into someplace very different where everything is going to transform in a deep-seated manner. This change may not be restricted to a mere technological shift; it may bring about some fundamental transformations. Precisely because of this very reason, I think that there is an immense potential in Marxism. Its promises are lofty; its possibilities are nascent. Actually, I am not at all a person who belongs to the defeatist sort. As I have mentioned earlier, applied Marxism has not been in vogue for long and, therefore, its crimes should not be tantamount to the hollowing out of the entire argument of communism. Following the same logic then, as Terry Eagleton says, one needs to discard Christ for Inquisition. Whatever Stalin did is already done and dusted, so what? People like Slavoj Žižek today claim themselves as Marxists. He says that he opposes the logic of destroying the opposition in favour of an undemocratic single party rule. In fact, no communist today is in favour of such a rule because that sort of an administrative structure is extinct in our times. If Marxism has to advance under present conditions, it needs to acknowledge pluralism. In the near future, Russia too would see a major change as the communists there are getting stronger by the minute. I am optimistic that they will not repeat their mistakes this time.

Rajib: Nabarun-da, in your writings, alongside the human world, there are blind cats or Lubdhaks.

Goutam: In Nabarun-da's writings, the cat is a vital factor.

Rajib: Correct. How do you envision such an animated world devoid of human beings?

Nabarun: I have been brought up with several domesticated animals since childhood. Even to this day, dogs have their fair share of biscuits in our monthly groceries. I won't be living for long after they are gone. I know each one of them most intimately. I have had miraculous experiences in these relationships. I have heard about other astounding experiences too. For example, a pet dog went missing from his master's house during the First World War. His master was fighting a war from the trenches at that time. His wife wrote to him from England that, unfortunately, Prince had gone missing. The husband replied that she was not supposed to find Prince because he was with him. This means that the dog boarded a ship from England, got off in France and found his master. This is a real incident. Nowadays, I see no sympathy for these birds and animals. I am deeply startled by this unsympathetic attitude. Auden once wrote in one of his poems, 'We must love one another, or die.' This does not mean that humans should love humans alone; it means that man should also love beings that are non-human.

(…)

—Translated by Partha Pratim Roy Chowdhury

(The interviewers are Goutam and Rajib, representatives of the Bengali little magazine *Darkroom* [Kolkata 2012]. The interview was published in the little magazine and was later anthologised in 2016 in

Nabarun Bhattacharya's interview collection, *Aro Kathabarta*, 9–26, Kolkata: Bhashabandhan. Little magazine-based interviews often do not follow an academic style of interviewing with context, setting and full names of interviewers, etc. The text has been shortened and edited.)

Part II

Critical Essays on Nabarun Bhattacharya

Kolkata and the Poetics of Waste in Nabarun Bhattacharya's Spectral City

Anuparna Mukherjee

'One of the city's archives is its detritus'
—(Sheringham 2010: 1)

In his final unfinished work, *Mobologe Novel* (2017), Nabarun uses a striking image of graves lined up like spectral heaps in the still 'chloroform light of the moon' in a necropolis of Calcutta. These funerary architectures in the darkness form strange silhouettes that assume 'historical image of oversized mounds of dinosaur *excreta*' (Bhattacharya 2017: 64; emphasis and translation mine), as history laughs at the empire's infirm glory amidst the enormous waste (of lives), which ensued from the unmitigated ambition of the imperial overlords.

In another instance, delineating a comic banter between the venerable spectral crow, Dandobayosh, and the curator of the Victoria Memorial Museum in *Kangal Malshat* (2003), the former excoriates the curator with a curse—'in your next life you'll be born as an insect on the faeces. That too, not in this place. Somewhere else. Let's say either in Bardhhaman or Mankundu. Faeces-insect in a can of faeces. You will eat faeces, roll in the faeces and then one day die by sinking in that faeces' (Bhattacharya 2010: 294; translation mine).

In Nabarun Bhattacharya's creative oeuvre, there is an obsessive preoccupation with detritus, waste and scatological references which become a significant representational window for archiving the city-space. Even one may interpret the neologism in the title of his last novel as an instance of literary spoonerism, where word-switch can turn *Mobologe* into *Mol-bege* or an effluence of faeces (*mol* means faeces; *bege* means to flow rapidly). Thus, while the Fyatarus observe the metropolitan milieu from a certain elevation through their aerial maneuverers, the urban subalterns (both human and animals) also scale the city from the pits and gutters around which they envisage their everyday. This essay symptomatically dwells on Nabarun's excremental imagination against the cultural milieu of post-imperial Calcutta in his literary corpus through an engagement with the peripheral and the spectral.

The contemporary Kolkata, deeply riven with protean class/caste anxieties, is a dystopic city in Nabarun. There is an overwhelming presence of feculence, filth and litter in the urban ethos. This disenfranchised 'underclass' (Bhattacharya 2019: 37), or the 'nameless procession of human faces', 'labourers or farmers' (Bhattacharya 2019: 131), represented by his fantastical Fyatarus or the 'flying humans' may be viewed as an embodiment of this refuse which the modern metropolis attempts to conceal from the public gaze by shoving them off to dark, dank quarters in the urban peripheries. Their presence is incompatible with certain notions of order and aesthetics. However, the restive subalterns in the urban margins turn this treatment into a potentially subversive strategy through their choice of excremental words, expletives and the use of domestic and human wastes to threaten the spatio-cultural fabric of the bourgeois, neoliberal city. Filth becomes endemic to urban and literary forms, especially in the use of coarse, vulgar language in Nabarun. Hence, the essay concerns itself with the treatment of the various orders of refuse and garbage, coextensive with the manifold forms of urban violence and exclusion. This piece would simultaneously interrogate the fixation with filth in depicting fraught relationships between the spectral and the spatial in Nabarun's Kolkata—a city that was arguably raised on waste and sludge to a millennial wasteland in the 21st century. One may recall the Great Raven or Dandobayosh's scathing views on Kolkata's British foundation in *Kangal Malshat*: 'That buffoon (Charnock) founded Kolkata by defecating on the banks of Ganges' (Bhattacharya 2010: 295; translation mine). However, before moving specifically into Nabarun, it might be cogent to signpost the conceptual outlines around the ways in which 'waste' is broadly used in this essay. In *The Waste of the Nation*, Assa Doran and Robin Jeffery suggest what waste might mean in various sociocultural contexts:

> [W]hat makes something waste is a trickier exercise than it may first appear. Of course, anything that we don't want anymore, especially if it smells or disintegrates, is waste, junk, or garbage. In English, waste can be a noun, an adjective, or a verb. We may see a pile of wastepaper in an office or waste wood on a building site. Children are admonished not to waste food or money. And a person is sometimes said to be wasting away. A Marxist view of waste sees the bodies of laborers 'used up or wasted at accelerated rates in order to secure the most profit' and emphasizes an expandable, unorganized labor force whose lives are locked into dealing with waste materials. (2018: 5)

The authors purport that while waste might be a 'thing', it is engendered by 'physical and psychological process' (2018: 5). Unless society finds a way to confine or contain 'waste' in some fashion, 'it confuses and contaminates the surroundings of the people who created it. And people who regularly deal with waste, if the work is especially dangerous, loathsome, or stigmatized, may find their lives shortened and made miserable—laid waste, wasted away' (2018: 5). Depending on its form, nature, origin, size or recyclability, waste is classified into subcategories with varying nomenclature, indicating specific or generic qualities: dry or wet, household (garbage), human, industrial, treated/untreated, filth, dust or dirt. There again, each of these categories is imbricated in a complex nexus of socio-religious relations, specially 'filth' in popular imaginary with its manifold associations of pollution and purity. There is a robust scholarship on caste, taboo and cleanliness vis-à-vis purity in India that is not covered here, partly because it merits a separate research onto itself around the extensive debates it has generated in social sciences and literature; and partly because in the body of work under consideration, Nabarun in a classic Marxist way speaks of a wider spectrum of disenfranchised people as city underclass in the margins, without necessarily attending to the caste particulars. Nonetheless, one must acknowledge at the outset that the notion of 'garbage' or 'pollutant' in the Indian context cannot be removed from caste and the nested ideas of 'untouchability'[1]. In Nabarun's corpus of work under consideration,

---

1 For a conceptual distinction between 'touch' and 'contact', see Sundar Sarukkai (2012), 'Phenomenology of Untouchability'. In *Cracked Mirror*, 163–165. New Delhi: Oxford University Press.

caste, thus, becomes a spectral coordinate that is conspicuous in its visible invisibilisation.

This essay, again, does not concern itself with the granularities or the finer classifications between various forms of urban waste, but deals with it as a conceptual register whose manifold evocations occur throughout Nabarun's body of work. However, what is of use here is how the proliferating anxieties around hygiene, sanitation, aesthetics and religion in the social sphere of modernity created models of urban segregation which Nabarun seeks to subvert through his literature. Dipesh Chakraborty, in his essay 'Of Garbage, Modernity, and the Citizen's Gaze', significantly alludes to the distinction between 'inside' and 'outside', and how structurally 'dirt' elicits 'the problem of the outside' in sociocultural imagination (2002: 69). The demarcation between the auspicious inner sanctorum of the home or the 'habitat' and the outside, which is precariously exposed to impurities, is premised on the fear of contagion that might enter a bounded system through foreigners who import disruptive substances that 'threaten one's well being' (2002: 70) or dislocate the fundamental experiences of everyday altogether. A series of practises are, therefore, undertaken in almost every culture on a regular basis both as acts of protection and purification through which the 'inside is both produced and enclosed. The everyday practise of classifying certain things as household rubbish marks the boundary of this enclosure' (2002: 70); and because they are inimical to one's health and well-being, they are duly disposed beyond the threshold of the home.

In fact, this fear of pollution and the inside/outside question had plagued the residents of Calcutta from the early days of its inception and shaped the configuration of the city space into stratified zones based on race, ethnicity, class and caste. In colonial Calcutta, the faulty model of urban dualism that aspired a separation between the 'White Town' and its native counterpart was located in the fear of contamination through contact, thereby, creating a deeply hierarchal urban space that led to various forms of segregation and ghettoisation. Rudyard Kipling, for instance, spoke of the 'Big Calcutta Stink' in *The City of Dreadful Nights*, which he describes as a 'ferocious stench' (1899: 11) with a 'diffused, soul-sickening expansiveness' (1899: 8) referring to the city's origin from muck and mud, which its majestic colonial edifices were simultaneously trying to conceal and reveal. Kipling also alludes to the plague epidemic in Calcutta. He blames it on the indulgence of the British administration in allowing the infiltration of the 'Natives' in Calcutta Municipal Corporation, as a typical case of outsiders (as pollutants) ruining a well-wrought system:

> And in spite of that stink, they allow, they even encourage, natives to look after the place! The damp, drainage-soaked soil is sick with the teeming life of a hundred years, and the Municipal Board list is choked with the names of natives—men of the breed, born in and raised off this surfeited muck-up. (1899: 10)

His rhetoric shows a curious admixture of a certain civic consciousness and concern about public health with his usual imperious arrogance that was heightened by his disdain for the local populace who, for him, were inhospitable and unwholesome like the land on which the 'chance' capital of the British Empire was built.

The repeated emphasis on the 'Black Town's' pathetic sanitary system and its poor management of garbage in public spaces in European accounts legitimised the colonial state to eke out a hegemonic discourse of efficient governance that could potentially disregard any opposition to their modernising plans in the civic sphere. Simultaneously, such accounts also reflected a strong desire for a gated community by projecting an 'outside' through a ritual of enclosure. This solidified in the actual erection of 'elaborate artifices of delimitation—wrought-iron railings, masonry walls, and gates—often designed after European pattern books' (Chattopadhyay 2005: 92) around British residences. Yet, architectural historian, Swati Chattopadhyay, points out the paradox embedded in such a practise where marking the boundaries of the 'White Town' inadvertently acknowledged the existence of its spectral 'other' that haunted the fringes of colonial consciousness.

However, the 'Black Town' and the 'White Town' were not the only distinctions that separated the motley inhabitants of the city. The 'Native' locality itself was divided into several quarters (*paras*), broadly based on religious affiliations, class, caste and profession (in traditional Hindu set-up, caste and profession are often associative identities) which sedimented the social hierarchies and the corollary insider/outsider question to determine who should be included within the fold of the community, locality or the households by maintaining the 'purity' of these spaces (Guru 2012: 219). Such segregations, particularly based on caste, in the Hindu society dates to several centuries before the European colonisers made inroads into the Indian subcontinent. The practises predicated on 'purity' and 'pollution' were carried over to the colonial city, as the rural population from feudal villages started relocating in modern urban centres.

However, on the ground, these classifications, which largely reflected the perverse aspiration of the urban upper classes to avoid infection from the low-lying and the poor by drawing spatial boundaries, could not remain as discreet as they were conceived theoretically. 'Due to the compulsion of the modern conditions, untouchability', as Gopal Guru posits in the 'Archaeology of Untouchability', 'both as practice and as consciousness' found it 'difficult to remain on the surface of social interaction' in urban spaces. Hence, it was 'forced to hide itself behind certain modern meanings and identities'. (2012: 203)

Without generalising the Dalit experiences which might tantamount to trivialising the pathological and cultural stigma of 'untouchability' in a caste-ridden society, one can nonetheless locate various exclusionary practises with marginalised groups in the modern city, based on 'touch' and 'contact'. With the independence from the colonial rule, for instance, came the Partition in 1947 that reinforced new boundaries. Those who crossed the borders shared a common religion and language with the hosts, but were dissimilar in their everyday practises, parlance and habits. The two populations met each other as strangers who were identical in many respects, yet remained opaque and unfamiliar. The refugees aroused a sense of unhomely, stirring mixed emotions of suspicion, panic and guilt. Their settlements or the 'colonies', as they were called, were fundamentally deemed as sites of violent disorder. Their presence 'like a deluge' (Bandyopadhyay 2003: 25) often induced a similar sense of repulsion or fear of contagion associated with filth and dirt that the British previously felt about the natives of the 'Black Town'. They were, thus, treated as potential pollutants or miscreants who were kept at bay in the edge of the city.

The marginalisation of the urban poor, refugees and labourers that one witnessed over these years took a new shape in the last decade of the 20th century when the city opened its doors to globalisation. Under the neoliberal structure, the increased privatisation of public spaces led to coerced displacement of the underclass by the emergence of new gated communities. Alison Brown in her essay 'Urban Planning and Violence' situates the weight of such public spaces in cities of the global South:

> In cities of the global South, public space plays a central role as spaces of everyday practice for meeting and celebration, and are of crucial economic importance for street vendors, transport workers, and many other urban workers who depend on access to public space[2]. (Brown 2017: 86)

She further states:

> Some iconic spaces have symbolic significance due to their history or social claim; these are also where the geographies of protest are played out ... Both everyday practice and the markers of social symbolism are often repressed in urban planning interventions. (2017: 86)

To relate these concerns with the exploration of waste in Nabarun's creative oeuvre, one may read the contextualisation in the previous paragraphs for a framework to understand the Fyatarus (or the flying subalterns) as representatives of these marginalised social groups—the dalits, the pariahs and the refugees—encompassing all the 'hopeless cases, half-dead, abused, humiliated' (Bhattacharya 2015: 142). They are cast off like scarps as potent bearers of disease, pollution and impurity in the postcolonial city, and routinely denied access to spaces and services. The Fyatarus, however, possess the unique gift of flying and a predisposition for causing 'damage' to the properties of the rich. For example, in the short story, 'Fyataru', a veteran of this gang makes a catalogue of the swarm, who fly from different directions of the city to attack an upscale entertainment hub of the rich on River Hooghly

2 Here, the author alludes to one of her pervious publications in 2006 as a reference: *Contested Space: Street trading, Public Space and Livelihoods in Developing Cities*, Rugby: ITDG Publishing.

with trash, urine and faeces. They come from the red-light areas of Sonagachi, and other shady underbellies of the metropolis:

> From that dark side of Howrah, a sound of 'ole! ole!' could be heard.
>
> There they are.
>
> Who?
>
> All the Fyatarus of Howrah. They live in dirty alleys and slums like land snails in a colony. You give them free space and they are like the king—oh that sound, that roar.
>
> Like a wind-cutter at night, a few more war-cries were heard, 'Laila o Laila.'
>
> Khidirpore, Ekbalpore, Kantapukur—everyone is coming. Just hear them, and you'll know that they are the most fiery, chaotic lot.
>
> In a whisker, the sky became thick with the *fnyat fnyat snai snai* sound.
>
> Can you see that gang of people there, wearing rings on their fingers, with shirt and dhoti, they are the lot of *cheatingbaj*, the tricksters. All from North Calcutta. Though there are a few shop-owners too. (2015: 145–146; translation Sourit Bhattacharya)

These 'spectralised' denizens in the dark and obscure zones between the conspicuously visible flats and the footpaths in literature[3] are like ghosts or leftovers of another time. They are excess or '*udbritto manush*' ('surplus' people), in Nabarun's own words,[4] in the wasted margins of the contemporary metropolis who haunt the neoliberal city-space through incessant troublemaking. They object to the structural violence against the urban underclass for fostering an environment that makes them exiles in their own city by storming into the gated communities and spotless interiors—the malls, hotels, housing complexes, entertainment hubs—meant for a certain section of the society by guarding them against the intruders, to make a pandemonium. However, the Fyatarus, like the comic ghosts of Parashuram or Trailokyanath Mukhopadhyay in Bengali literature,

3 See Sanghita Sen's 'The Language of Nabarun's Novels', 218.

4 In the interview, 'Nabarun Bhattacharya Talks about Ritwik Ghatak', Nabarun speaks of '*udbritto manush*' (YouTube 3.40) which he uses synonymously with 'lumpen' or 'superfluous' (as in surplus, see YouTube 9.49) humans.

are largely mischief-makers. The aerial attacks on the upper classes are never meant to wound or kill anyone: 'Just frightening. Making the place dirty. Rampaging stuff. The fun's there' (Bhattacharya 2015: 142). Their inventory of weapons includes chilli powder, Molotov cocktail, socket bombs, firecrackers, none of which cause death. The Fyatarus spoil the entertainments of the rich by pouring from the sky congeries of 'broken stoves, sweepers' brooms, rotten potato curry with the weird goat-head soup, discarded toothbrush, exam scripts, the leftover hair collected from the salon, bed pan, etc.' (Bhattacharya 2015: 146). The choice of litters and excrements to threaten the urban bourgeoisie is a significant subversive strategy laid out by these subalterns who are viewed as refuse or 'excess' (*udbritto*) by the elites. This rhetoric of the upper class again speaks to the legacy of colonial modernity where the disciplinarisation of public space and their reforms relate to a category of 'aesthetics from which the ideals of public health and hygiene cannot be separated. It is the language of modern governments, both colonial and postcolonial.' (Chakraborty 2002: 66).

The existence of the poor in fetid slums and shanty towns dotting the contours of the modern metropolis is irksome to the aesthetics of the urban bourgeoisie. Their glaring poverty and 'uncouth' habits are an embarrassment to the polite society which attempts to conceal them from visibility. The impoverished underclasses are treated like excremental population, due to the pathologisation and the concomitant stigma of dirt and disease associated with their labouring bodies: 'The lower classes are literally lower—closer to the ground with its dirt they wallow in' (Morrison 2015: 47). The connection is further solidified by their relative proximity to those social classes dealing in filth and faeces—the scavengers, sweepers, those cremating the dead and cleaning the toilets—and, in turn, are forced to become 'repository of the impurities' (Guru 2012: 213) of the others. The cultural enfolding of the dirt into their bodies, makes them the embodiment of the filth that the polite society keeps outside its boundaries to prevent 'pollution crossing over' (Guru 2012: 210) from the garbage hordes.

A way to resist being the 'dumping ground' (Guru 2012: 214) of the garbage of the upper classes/castes might, for instance, lie in the refusal to partake in certain professions such as scavenging. It will impact the workers economically. Nonetheless, this prospect is equally threatening to the urban elites as Sandipan Chattopadhyay suggests in the concluding lines of *Kolkata Tumi, Kar?* (*Whom Do You Belong to, Kolkata?*):

> Even if you lock down each of the four gates of Kolkata Corporation, the city will live on as long as the [sweepers and scavengers] continue to work. Once they stop working, the manholes will choke with fifth. And, this will be akin to the stoppage of blood passing through the veins. Is one monsoon not sufficient to submerge Calcutta, if these men do not open the manholes and wait, wait for the entire night [for the water to pass]? These safai workers—these conservancy labourers on contract—mainly hailing from a certain district in Orissa, if they make a homeward journey, then the affected conversations in Calcutta Club to the toilets in Taj Bengal, all will close. The film-festival in Nandan will stop. The knit-picking of the poets in the coffee-house will stop. The squabble of the councilors will no longer be visible in *Doordarshan*. The convoys of the who's who with obscene hooters on their escort vans will stop.... (2006: 365; translation mine)

The other 'tactic', adopted by the Fyatarus, is to avenge the injustice meted out to the underclasses by attacking the 'beautiful' homes and gated entertainment hubs of the rich with garbage, which they hide at a safe distance to avoid contamination. The gratification that Fyatarus feel creating a raucous, or disrupting the skewed initiatives of beautification in gated urban spaces, also generate a vicarious 'wish-fulfilment' for the author.[5] He is appalled by the predicament of a large floating 'underclass', goaded by the bourgeoisie, in collusion with statist forces and their corporate allies, to live amidst muck. Expressing his anger at these spatial inequalities engendered by the new paradigms of urban development that bars the economically underprivileged from accessing these social spaces, Nabarun avers in conversation with *Kabitirtha* that:

> It is not good to watch the rampant roguery of the rich. But there is nothing much that I can do myself. For instance, I cannot wink at

5 Also see page 150 of his interview, 'Banano reality-r Biruddhe Lorai Korai Syot Lekhoker Kaj' ('The Job of an Honest Writer Is to Fight Against a Concocted Reality'), where he explicitly talks about the author's own wish-fulfilment through the anarchism of the Fyatarus. The conversation is anthologised in *Sob Kathabartha* (*All Conversations*) (2019).

> someone in a five-star hotel. So, I introduce four *Fyatarus* there. Let them do what they can. Foil the amusements [of the rich] and wreck a havoc. There is joy in spoiling their fun. I think, this is about seeking revenge by those who are slighted every day. Many of us are grounded with humiliations in our daily lives. Because the city insults us. Because it makes roads and shopping malls, which tell us that you are not welcome here. You are a *Fyataru*. If I wear my kind of clothes and visit these places, nobody would even acknowledge my presence. Now I cannot do anything about it, but at least, when it comes to Madan DS, they can do their bit and Purandar Bhat can write poems on them. (2019: 50; translation mine)

The spectral wings which facilitate the flight of the Fyatarus is largely unseen human counterparts. They symbolically speak of the hidden strength of the underclasses that are disregarded and deemed invisible, till the poor break out in angry/spectacular protest to shake the elites out of their comfort. Here, the wings which give the Fyatarus a spectral agency to make various aerial maneuvers, facilitate them to defy the urban segregation and fly to the elite quarters that are otherwise kept out of their reach. They are no longer 'despicable' beings sniveling in the dirt; they return the garbage of the elites to their own homes which the rich dump onto the poor. It is their fitting reply to the bourgeois for treating the marginalised groups like a trash in the city.

Elsewhere, countering the lopsided development projects led by the capitalist cronies, and the consequent beautification drives that exclude the working class from the benefits of urban infrastructure, Nabarun conjures a certain 'inaesthetics' of waste and filth as an alternative, that pervades his literary imagination. Consider the opening gambit of *Herbert* where he conjures the shoddy lifeworld of Harbart Sarkar, sullied with excreta, urine and vomit:

> The frothy-foaming light-dust of the streetlights. Everything slippery with heat. And from the pits of their bellies, curdled chops and chana and whisky and rum and ice-water roaring up into their throats. Swarms of cockroaches seething out of the gutter grilles and flying up into the streetlights' glow. Koka vomiting against the Dutta-house gates—hot, sour, and slithering vomit—Borka could still smell its acid

> reek. Daktar and Koton playing piss-cross games. Like a dirty sack, an oily cloud suddenly covers the moon. (Bhattacharya 2019: 1)

His fixation with filth becomes particularly manifested in the unabashed deployment of slang or the language of the gutters as an implicit critique of middle-class respectability. The Calcutta cockney that his urban underclass speaks is purposely offensive, inflicted with coarse and libidinal humour. One must navigate through the putrescent pools of shit and piss in the poems and parodies of the Fyataru poet, Purandar Bhat, as he angularly mocks the upper classes' cultivated civility in *Kangal Malshat*:

> The wasps flying, the hornets flying, the bees are in the sky
> The moment the bums are uncovered, they sting hard and fly
> From the space the turd-eating vulture throws down his shit
> Bengalis are not only bastards, they're helpless to the last bit. (2010: 303; translation mine)

In another poem, Purandar relates with a dramatic vigour (despite claiming to be opposite), what might be called a trajectory of his insignificant life with a generous dose of dark humour:

> There is no drama in my life at all
> In the cotton-field will I go and crawl
> My life is without a dream I say
> Lizard am I, eat insects and eggs I lay
> My death will not make a headline at all
> I'll break the law by pissing on the palace wall (2010: 263; translation mine)

Nabarun explains in an interview that this impulse behind de-aestheticising speech through 'conscious use of slangs' (Bhattacharya 2019: 19–20) is a normal function of language in his writing. He underscores how against the stilted vocabulary of the polite, the 'ejaculation' of the low-brow street argot, infuses verve and spontaneity. In an interview given to Qaushiq Mukherjee for his documentary, *Nabarun* in 2015, he asserts:

> Any human in a sound state of health should normally use expletives in a speech, and they do so—here the expletives are not specifically used to mean anything, it's a mode of expression. It bespeaks a

> language's vitality and strength (Sen 2016: 216–217; translation mine).

Nabarun makes a strident claim in his 'Poem on Vietnam', collected in *This Valley of Death Is Not My Country* (*Ei Mrityu Upattaka Amar Desh Na*), that words are not 'passports or cosmetics' to 'please the illiterate editor of a monopoly Daily' (Bhattacharya 2004: 17). They are 'grenades' targeted at deconstructing the rhetoric of imperialism. A way of achieving this in his corpus is the incessant production of verbal/textual waste that trashes the language of the bhadraloks (genteel) in urban drawing rooms. His literary inaesthetics is championed by those who are treated like vestigial population in the urban map, despite the services they render. His characters, thus, generate a poetics of detritus, waste and excrement within the text-scape, or what Susan Morrison pithily calls 'fecopoetics' (Morrison 2015: 2)[6], by challenging the dominant political and cultural institutions to break through the oppressive nexus of order. They confront their conditions of precarity by owning up their affective or embodied experience of living amidst grime and filth, to deploy litters, both literally and linguistically, for attacking the elite's disdain towards dirt. Mary Douglas proclaims in her seminal work, *Purity and Danger*: 'dirt is essentially disorder' (2001: 2). Through an effective use of garbage as a political tool, characters in Nabarun's literary repertoire, such as Fyatarus, foil the efforts of the upper class 'to organize the environment' (Douglas 2001: 2) by forging a 'manufactured reality' (Bhattacharya 2019: 150) in the neoliberal city-space.

In Nabarun's writings, there is a strange nostalgia for a decaying city, the wasted remains of a bristling metropolis that once was. He finds an enduring quality in the shadowy mansions in old *paras* (localities) that one believes would remain 'untouched by time from time immemorial' (2019: 44) until one sees the old houses being 'riven apart by shouting and screaming, and then shackled back together by walls and doors built up in the unlikeliest of places' (2019: 44). However, even in these neighbourhoods, changes have crept in surreptitiously when developers 'tore down some of those ancient homes and replaced them

6 'The ecological and poetic dimensions of feces' (Morrison 2015: 2)

with the new-fangled multi-storeyed' (2019: 44). Nabarun had once complained that in the rat race of development, Calcutta has become a city of the deads, of mummified people, which can 'no longer inspire poetry' (2019: 155) in this 'acquisitive society' (2019: 49). In *Herbert*, the narrator indicates the waning of this old order:

> The main road had once been lined with tall trees whose soft shadows would fall upon the double-decker buses like a cool caress. Now the trees were gone. Now, only the frantic frenzy of traffic. The pushcart men had a favorite resting spot in the neighborhood—that was gone. (2019: 44)

Against this changing ethos in the grip of globalisation's intractable forces, Nabarun's fiction invokes the spectres from the colonial times—Begum Johnson, the Great Raven (*Dandobayosh*) or the Wild Cat—who watch over the urban-space with a special sense of entitlement. As spectral citizens inhabiting the city through centuries, they simultaneously impart a notion of permanence or 'fixedness' in space as opposed to the constant churning of the metropolitan landscape; and equally evoke a specific sense of 'waste' in being 'surplus' (*udbritto*), or 'carry-overs' from another age. Every historical break with the past, posits Susan Morrison, (in this case, the changes referring to the shift from colonial to the postcolonial regime through India's freedom and Partition, or Calcutta's more recent transition from the modern to a millennial city under the aegis of neoliberalism) 'creates garbage; results in leftovers ... The trashing of the past is an integral strategy of progress; yet the 'debris of a life [somehow] continues as the ghost of the present' (Morrison 2015: 61). These ghosts, like rubbles of another era, survive the present as figures of 'anachrony' who do not quite belong to the new configuration of the city. Quite rightly then, the spectres of old Calcutta join the urban proletariats—the Fyatarus, the *choktars*, the failed writer, the browbeaten, etc.—who are equally made redundant in reclaiming the city-space with those insalubrious objects in which they fester.

'Waste' as a conceptual register, thus, braids together the spectral and the proletarian to restore agency to the peripheral. It also provides a powerful lens to interpret the emaciated urban brickscape, struggling to embrace the framework of globalisation which in the global South works as a new 'avatar' of imperialist domination, widening the material inequalities between the urban population. Nabarun's work draws a direct correlation between capitalist overconsumption and defecation when he envisages Calcutta: 'broken, maimed, burnt, melted, and battered into a toxic synthetic city whose skylines are perpetually covered with a poisonous mist'. (Bhattacharya 2010: 253; translation mine) It is an end product or the trash engendered by the new circuit of development.

The conventional narrative of Calcutta's British origin tells us that the city had germinated from marshes and malarial wastelands. However, its fecund soil and waterbodies fostered cultivation and trade and held the city through its growth. But the barren waste to which it is reduced after successive periods of abuse, betrays a frightening aftermath of capitalist exploitation. In his narrative arc, as we move from *Herbert* to *Kangal Malshat,* and then to the unidentified city in *Khelna Nagar* (*Toy City*), a more terrible image of this urban necropolis consumes the readers' imagination. The unnamed industrial conurbation around a burnt-down toy factory in *Khelna Nagar* (1998) becomes the very embodiment of urban dystopia. Following the closing of the factory in a fire-wreckage, the place has been reduced to a dumping ground of nuclear waste. Everything one touches here is poison. As one degenerates from one stage to the next, in this all-engulfing wasteland, the world becomes devoid of animals. Even the most resilient pariah dogs in *Lubdhak* (2000) are nowhere to be seen. Conversely, a robust, disruptive nostalgia for the old-world scrapes, and the discarded, dehumanised urban population who do not fit into contemporary city-space that permeates through Nabarun's literary universe has a definitive political purpose. Nostalgia generates affective excesses when it overwhelms us with the past. His narrative channelises the affective charge in these nostalgic residues into a subversive critique to tap the deeper and graver disorders in the present. It is a call to humanity to take responsibility for its own action.

References

Bandyopadhyay, Manik (2003), 'The Final Solution'. In *Mapmaking: Partition Stories from Two Bengals*, translated by Rani Ray. Kolkata: Srishti.

Bhattacharya, Nabarun (1994 [2019]), *Herbert*, translated by Sunandini Banerjee. New York: New Directions.

——(2004), 'Viternamer Upor Kobita' ('A Poem on Vietnam'). In *Ei Mrityu Upattaka Amar Desh Na* (*This Valley of Death Is Not My Country*), 16–18. Kolkata: Saptarshi.

—— (2010), 'Kangal *Malshat*' ('The War Cries of the Vagabonds'). In *Upanyash Samagra* (*Collected Novels*), 229–280. Kolkata: Dey's.

—— (2014), 'Nabarun Bhattacharya Talks about Ritwik Ghatak'. Available at https://www.youtube.com/watch?v=VIuC9Gv-R2o (accessed on 30 May 2019).

—— (2015), 'Fyataru'. In *Sanglap 2:1*, translated by Sourit Bhattacharya. Available at http://sanglap-journal.in/index.php/sanglap/article/view/98/87 (accessed on 29 January 2017).

——(2017), *Mobologe Novel*, Kolkata: Bhasabandhan Prakashani.

—— (2019), *Sob Kathabarta: Nabarun Bhattacharjer Bibhinno Sakkhatkarar Atmokathan* (*Conversations: A Collection of Interviews and Personal Narratives*), Kolkata: Bhasabandhan.

Brown, Alison (2017), 'Urban Planning and Violence Cause or Catalyst for Change?', *Economic and Political Weekly*, 52(7): 83–90.

Chakrabarty, Dipesh (2002), *Habitations of Modernity: Essays in the Wake of Subaltern Studies*. Chicago: University of Chicago Press.

Chattopadhyay, Sandipan (2006), *'Kolkata, Tumi Kar?'* ('Whom Do You Belong to, Kolkata?'). In *Upanyash Samagra-3* (*Collected Novels*), 313–365. Kolkata: Ajkal.

Chattopadhyay, Swati (2005), *Representing Calcutta: Modernity, Nationalism, and the Colonial Uncanny*. London: Routledge.

Doran, Assa and Robin Jeffrey, eds (2018), *Waste of a Nation: Garbage and Growth in India*. Cambridge. Massachusetts: Harvard University Press.

Douglas, Mary (2001), *Purity and Danger: An Analysis of the Concept of Pollution and Taboo*. London: Routledge.

Guru, Gopal (2012), 'Archeology of Untouchability'. In *Cracked Mirror: An Indian Debate on Experience and Theory*, edited by Gopal Guru and Sundar Sarukkai, 200–222. New Delhi: Oxford University Press.

Kipling, Rudyard (1899), *The City of Dreadful Nights and Other Sketches*. New York: Alex Grosset.

Morrison, Susan S. (2015), *The Literature of Waste: Material Ecopoetics and Ethical Matter*. New York: Palgrave Macmillan.

Roberts, Emma (1836), *Scenes and Characteristics of Hindostan, with Sketches of Anglo-Indian Society*. Philadelphia: Carey, Lea & Blanchard.

Sen, Sanghita (2016), 'Nabaruner Upanyasher Bhasha' ('The Language of Nabarun's Novels'). In *Nabarun Bhattacharja: Manan o Darshan* (*Nabarun Bhattacharya: Thoughts and Philosophy*), edited by Adway Chowdhuri and Arka Chattopadhyay, 211–222. Kolkata: Aihik.

Sheringham, Michael (2010), 'Archiving'. In *Restless Cities*, edited by Matthew Beaumont and Gregory Dart, 1–17. London: Verso.

Fyataru As Political Society: Nabarun Bhattacharya and the Postcolonial Politics of the Governed

Anindya Sekhar Purakayastha

Civil Society

By Purandar Bhat

Wearing an expression of embarrassed unease on his face
Panchu was defecating in public
His discomfiture was visible from the passing train
Lo! beneath the trees, menfolk gather to sip country liquor
In the past, we had the Sahibs
Now only the CPIM
Any idea what is in store for us next?
Civil Society has answers to all the questions
they know who rules or who are the ruled
wherever you go
everywhere you encounter the real nation
the temple and the mosque
Panchu and Ramjan
coalesce and script their inherent ethos of co-living
and yet, Civil Society takes all the credit

—(Bhattacharya 2009: 56)

I believe it is no longer productive to reassert the utopian politics of classical nationalism. Or rather, I do not believe it is an option that is available for a theorist from the postcolonial world. Such theorist must chart a course that steers away from global cosmopolitanism on the one hand and ethnic chauvinism on the other. It means necessarily to dirty one's hands in the complicated business of the politics of

> governmentality. The asymmetries produced and legitimized by the universalisms of modern nationalism have not left room for any ethical neat choice here. For the postcolonial theorist, like the postcolonial novelist, is born only when the mythical time-space of epic modernity has been lost forever. (Chatterjee 2004: 23)

This chapter situates Nabarun Bhattacharya and his fictional universe within the matrix of deep socio-political asymmetries produced by colonial modernity as enunciated by Partha Chatterjee in his *Politics of the Governed* (2004), and it tries to investigate the contingencies of postcolonial politics through Nabarun's rendition of existing power equations and social anomies. His textual world is sustained by his fictive characters, the Fyatarus—the postcolonial anarcho-subalterns—who defy the normative logic of civilised status quo, and register the agonies of the 'small voices of history' produced by the modernist logic of growing accumulation by dispossession. Nabarun, therefore, epicalises the dirt, the discarded margin or the non-civic commoner. His fictional protagonists, Fyatarus, dwelling in the filth, swear by the political philosophy to dirtify, to threaten the establishment and to destabilise the status quo—'*Fyatarus* are committed to sabotage, subversion and urination at the establishment' (Bhattacharya 2004: 14). He erects the stature and solemnity of the non-pomp and coronates the precariat through a celebration of people's democracy and subaltern angst. This chapter identifies him as one of those writers who vigorously fumes against class elitism of the civic space. He consciously vandalises what Partha Chatterjee calls 'the mythical time space of epic modernity'—modernity that posits, according to Benedict Anderson, the homogeneous empty time of global capital that elbows out myriad heterogenous temporalities of the non-Euro-modern, the non-civic and the norm-deviant. Nabarun, like a true postcolonial writer, as described by Chatterjee, dirties his hand in the muckheap of real life—a terrain deglamourised and yet fantasised to actualise real decolonial liberation for the people (Chatterjee 2004: 23). The vitriolic *lebenswelt* of his creative gestalt conscripts a phenomenology of the non-voiced and the unseen. His Fyatarus can fly; his imaginative discs of revolution (*chakti ka khel*) are visible and yet elude the grasp of authorities; his vehicle of subversive plotting; the revolutionary submarine of beggars; *Kangal Malshat* makes a clandestine and stealthy move—all these point to his penchant for addressing the submerged and simmering dynamics of subaltern upheavals that foreground the non-voiced and empower the 'reject[s]' (Goh 2014) of our society. Through all his works, he articulates the growing undercurrents of existential agonies, unifying silently to launch a blistering attack on the ostentatious normalcy of civilised life. This chapter, while focusing on Nabarun's literary *oeuvre*, demands an alter-aesthetics or 'inaesthetics' (Badiou 2005) of literary perception. Borrowing Nabarun, this chapter, too dares the readers, rather dares to grab the readers by their necks, to defamiliarise their norm-centric fascination for seductive syntaxes and tailor-made semantic orders, or the assured fructified horizon of interpretive *jouissance*. I will show how discarding the modular and the normative, Nabarun rallies for 'Fyatarufication' or 'Fyataru-fiction'—a whiplash of narrative upsurge popularised by Nabarun's rebellious self or his Fyatarus or the *choktars*, his fictive protagonists who can dare to say that '[t]he civic serendipity and nonchalance of metropolitan literary somnolence must be dislodged by the political rhymes of ruralised, and grounded verse/poetry is to be weaponized, needs to be independent and daring/… the stereotyped tools of versification is to be embellished with a position of militancy' (Bhattacharya 2016: 10–11). This is a clear rallying cry to wage war against civic elitism that advocates the ideology of docile citizenship and dishonest complicity. Deflating this culture of civic equanimity and our established literary equipoise, Nabarun could speak of a different genre of incendiary verse:

> When the wind is heavy with the smell of revolutionary blood
> Allow the explosive soil of poetry to erupt
> … the burning torch of poetry
> the fierce Molotov cocktail of poetry
> the flame of poetry
> Let all these aspects of poetry sustain these incendiary desires for revolution (Bhattacharya 2016: 12)

His is, therefore, a committed terrain of arsenal rhymes: '*petrol r aguner kobita*' (poems sculpted in the smithy of fire and petrol). His entire literary universe explodes with the ethos of a barricade

Muse—a rebellious principle of educating, agitating and organising public consciousness on the fault lines of the existing social structure. His investment of complete faith on the deterritorialising *potenza* of literature equips his slender and non-descript books with a seismic capacity. I would argue that for Nabarun, the matrix of literature is forged in militancy; it cannot allow even the poet to wallow in civic niceties and mellifluous scintillations, rather, at times, even the poem grabs the poet by his neck as Nabarun's *oeuvre* rebukes our collective indifference and civilised anomies. 'Sometimes, the poem grabs the poet by his neck' (Bhattacharya 2009: 10) because we have bartered away our real creative self 'in the bourgeoise market, we, the poets are sustained by the daily dose of ennui and frustration/subsequently we commercialize the flesh of rotten poetry/[...] let beggarly children come and kick me out, they should unmask my unscrupulous being' (Bhattacharya 2009: 10). Having made his objectives clear, Nabarun also declared his war of position in unequivocal terms—a position that testifies his siding with the fringe, with the underdog and not with the civic upper echelons of society—'one who is completely dispossessed/knows that his ensuing end is about to take him to the crematorium/hence he does not bother to care for this empty glamorous world/ Adopting a rebellious posture/he imagines the flyover and the roads as his weapon to vandalize this rotten world/ he cares a hang for the cacophony of the city/Whether I am alive or dead/my writings and I side with this poor rebel' (Bhattacharya 2009: 23). Nabarun has perhaps no parallel in Indian literature, his is not mere literary Bolshevism, or literary sloganeering, because that would have been easier, his is a heightened imaginative courage that challenges or provokes the very edifice of practising literary paradigms—his Fyataru-texts constitute the lexicon of rebellion, they generate semantic tremors whose seismic after-effects disrobe and deconstruct all existing conventional claims of aesthetic supremacy and literary authenticity. If Edward Said called for worlding the text, Nabarun, I would say, not only worlded, walked an extra mile, peeled off the surface of the world to foreground materiality, allowed all the suppressed outcries of the dispossessed to magmatise. If Hopkins invented the sprung rhythm, it would not be an exaggeration to say that Nabarun is the progenitor of a new type of significatory kineticism—an eruptive guerrilla rhythm of social vision that enacts an evental effect in the Badiouian sense:

> *The Land of Scoundrels*
>
> I live in the land of scoundrels, here merchants produce and motivate poets
> and poets allow them to be motivated
> I live in the land of scoundrels
> where the government supported by the intelligentsia
>
> evicts the poor by demolishing their makeshift shanties in the dead night of winter
> I live in the land of scoundrels
> where munching on inane phraseologies
> poets metamorphose into cows or vice versa
>
> I have chosen my own ways
> Therefore, I reside in the company of the discarded steam rollers
> I sit by them and listen to the stories of how new paths are made
> (Bhattacharya 2009: 41)

This quoted poem clearly testifies the points made so far, Nabarun's angst with the systemic anomies and his deliberate siding with the discarded section of our society. Having introduced Nabarun and his literary proclivities, this chapter approaches him in the context of postcolonial 'politics of the governed', reading in that process his entire *oeuvre* as weaponisation of dissent—an explosive literary corpus that exposes the aporias of postcolonial Indian democracy. Borrowing existing critical optics available in works, such as *Literary Radicalism in India* (Gopal 2009) and *Literary Activism: Perspectives* (Chaudhuri 2018), I would inquire how Nabarun has powerfully conjoined literature and radical politics to unpack the ideological field of the Indian nation state, adopting in that way, the position of the radical exile, as enunciated by Edward Said, to critically intervene in the arena of postcolonial governance, citizenship rights and class struggles. I would argue that for Nabarun the postcolonial nation explodes as the conflictual site of dissensus and his prototypical postcolonial protagonist, the Fyataru, emerges as, what Partha Chatterjee called, the 'political society'—the disenfranchised group, distinct from the elite category of civil society—that acts as the incorrigible saboteur to demolish our systemic discriminations and inequalities. I consciously situate Nabarun among the global constellation of decolonial thinkers such as Frantz Fanon and Aime Cesaire. Like them, he too constituted a narrative of resistance that would characterise any form of postcolonial *politics of the governed.* Nabarun's *oeuvre* is marked by a conscious defiance of the brutal real through a recourse to an unreal (Dasgupta 2015), an unreal which in his radical envisioning becomes more real as he populates this unreal real with the architects of social change—his fictional protagonists, the Fyatarus and the Choktars—the new urban precariats, the 'new dangerous class' (Standing 2011). In Nabarun's vision, they are the constituents of postcolonial popular sovereignty, the people-power who can reinscribe a new social order. In what follows I would initially elaborate Partha Chatterjee's idea of political society or postcolonial popular politics and inquire how closely Nabarun exemplifies these concepts through his fictional narrative of revolutionary praxis as actualized by the Fyatarus and the Choktars. To do that, I shall revisit his primary texts—*Kangal Malshat* and *Fyatarur Bombachak O Onnanno* and *Fyatarur Kumbhipak*—where his entire focus is on the commoner, a domain on which even postcolonial historiography did not pay much attention till the Subaltern Studies school of historiography rectified such flawed modes of postcolonial representation.

In his essay, 'Subaltern Studies as Postcolonial Criticism' (2010), Gyan Prakash analysed how Marxist historians failed to do real justice to the margin as their 'mode-of-production narratives merged imperceptibly with the nation state's ideology of modernity and progress … [S]ubaltern studies plunged into these historical contests over the representation of the culture and politics of the people' (Prakash 2010: 216). Nabarun as a postcolonial writer adopted this people-centric view of literature, dichotomised the elite and the subaltern domains within postcolonial conditions that get manifested in the gap between civil and political society:

> […] the emergence of mass democracies in the advanced industrial countries of the West in the twentieth century produced an entirely

> new distinction—one between citizens and populations. Citizens inhabit the domain of theory, populations the domain of policy. Unlike the concept of citizen, the concept of population is wholly descriptive and empirical; it does not carry a normative burden. (Chatterjee 2004: 34)

From the above observation, two lines of political systems emerge in postcolonial politics—one is the thread connecting civil society with nation-state founded on popular sovereignty and granting equal rights to citizens, and the other emerges through the networks aligning population with governmental agencies implementing numerous policies of social security and welfare. While the first way ties with normative political theory of the last two centuries, the second line of thinking belongs to a different aspect of politics. Partha Chatterjee distinguishes it from the 'classic associational forms of civil society' and calls it 'political society'. Chatterjee clubs the first line of civil society paradigm as *bourgeois society* in the sense used by Hegel and Marx and in the Indian context that sphere is inhabited by a relatively 'small section of the people whose social locations can be identified with a fair degree of clarity' (Chatterjee 2004: 38). Constitutionally speaking, all citizens are supposed to be granted equal rights and, therefore, they are to be considered equal members of the civil society but in reality it does not happen that way. Most inhabitants in India are not proper members of the civil society and are not regarded in that way by the different arms of the state. They are viewed as members of population groups who are to be both looked after and controlled by the state. I would argue that Nabarun situates his Fyatarus and his Choktars among these population groups who are not accommodated within the boundaries of civil society. They inhabit the unorganised subaltern domain and rage their battle with the postcolonial state from within that position.

Fyataru As Political Society

As the domain of political society or Fyataru-society (if I may use this term) gets emboldened and empowered through their negotiation and conflictual relation with the nation-state, members of the civil society and the constitutional state are bound to protest and complain saying that 'modernity is facing an unexpected rival in the form of democracy [political society].' (Chatterjee 2004: 41) Modernity with its baggage of norms and civic rules belongs to the elite horizon of civil society, and real democracy is actualised through the persistence of Fyatarus and Choktars who continue their battle to eke out a living in this unequal world of capitalist division. Nabarun has exactly demarcated this split between modern civic rules and social norms with the non-modern political domain of unending negotiation—a process in which the members of the population groups (the Fyatarus) have to resort to vandalism, illegality, paralegal strategies, rebellious plots, etc. so that they can deepen their rights within the structures of postcolonial governmentality.

In his *The Politics of the Governed* (2004), Partha Chatterjee clarifies that his focus of analysis is 'certain relations between governments and populations' (Chatterjee 2004: 3), something that determines popular politics of 'well over three-fourths of contemporary humanity' and civil society according to Chatterjee will appear

> as the closed association of modern elite groups, sequestered from the wider popular life of the communities, walled up within enclaves of civic freedom and rational law. Citizenship will take on two different shapes—the formal and the real. And unlike the old way, known to us from the Greeks to Machiavelli to Marx, of talking about the rulers and the ruled, I will invite you to think of those who govern and those who are governed ... democracy today, I will insist, is not government of, by and for the people. Rather it should be seen as the politics of the governed. (Chatterjee 2004: 4)

Chatterjee in this context also critiqued Benedict Anderson's idea of nation living in 'homogeneous empty time' or 'the time of capital'—a temporal simultaneity within whose domain, 'capital allows for no resistance to its free movement. When it encounters an impediment, it thinks it has encountered another time—something out of pre-capital, something that belongs to the pre-modern.' (Chatterjee 2004: 5) In that way, capital characterises such opposition as 'archaic or backward'. Chatterjee also discarded Anderson's idea of 'unbound seriality of everyday universals of modern social thought' (Chatterjee 2004: 5), such as nations, citizens, revolutionaries, bureaucrats, workers, etc., which is opposed to the 'bound seriality of governmentality' that relies on finite totals of enumerable classes of population produced by modern census and the modern electoral systems. Bound serialities for Anderson are 'inherently conflictual' and they produce 'tools of ethnic politics'. Politics in the Andersonian modernist sense 'inhabits the empty homogeneous time-space of modernity' (Chatterjee 2004: 6). Chatterjee disagrees with this proposition, saying that 'people can only imagine themselves in empty homogeneous time; they do not live in it. Empty homogeneous time is the utopian time of capital' (Chatterjee 2004: 6). So, the real space of modern politics according to Chatterjee is constituted of 'heterotopia' and to ignore this reality is to skip the real for the utopian. The postcolonial world, according to Chatterjee, suggests the 'presence of dense and heterogenous time'—Chatterjee prefers to call it the 'heterogenous time of modernity' (Chatterjee 2004: 8). I situate Nabarun's creative universe within this theoretic logic of Partha Chatterjee to argue that Nabarun successfully reflects through his textual world the conflictual relation between the utopian dimension of the homogeneous time of capital and the harsh realistic plain of the heterogenous time of governmentality. Fyatarus and the Choktars embody the heterogenous terrain of the non-capital, and their consistent subversion of the universal rulebook of law and civic norms typify their hostility to the narrative of the homogenous line of a unified nation, something the postcolonial nation-state projects itself to be.

Fyataru, Distributive Justice and the Prose of Counter-Insurgency

The postcolonial Indian state, according to Sudipta Kaviraj, emerged primarily as a bourgeoise state safeguarding the property-related interests of the moneyed class, and post-1947, the postcolonial Indian state did not go for an all-out structural change of social relations of existing forms of political economy; rather it resorted to a system of 'passive revolution', which was slow growth of molecular changes in socio-economic relations in a society (Kaviraj 2010). The bourgeois nationalist elite, therefore, was given power to hegemonise the social terrain in independent India, and popular sovereignty was not actualised. Kaviraj in his *Imaginary Institution of India* (2010) analysed the functioning ideology of the postcolonial Indian state and showed how post 1947 the Indian state adopted both the logic of bureaucracy and logic of democracy (Kaviraj 2010: 223) to bolster the rhetorical narrative of the developmental state and bureaucratic state control, something which had an antecedent in colonial India. The 1970s saw the first democratic upsurge in India with political mobilisation against Emergency and the Naxalite uprising which was brutally repressed by state power, betraying its anti-people nature. Nabarun in many of his poetic works have captured this phase. Works like *Transforming India* (Frankel et al. 2000) substantiate how democratic institutions and practises unleashed in India a slow and gradual process of transformation in the social, cultural and politico-economic terrain. So, if the postcolonial state colluded with the comprador class and allowed only a slow process of passive revolution that does not facilitate structural reform, the populace is left with one option only—to rebel, to agitate, to organise. This is exactly what the political society does. In *Kangal Malshat* and *Fyatarur Kumbhipak or Fyatarur Bombachak O Onnnanno*, Nabarun scripts such a narrative of subaltern insurgency.

The textual world of *Kangal Malshat* (*War Cries of the Vagabonds*) begins by reporting macabre and bizarre happenings, human heads chopped off with sharp instruments found on the banks of River Ganga, human skulls dancing beneath the Calcutta sky on 28 October 1999, etc. The police witnessed all these and the media sensationalised them in its reportage. As the reader gets bewildered by this absurd beginning, Nabarun chastises us by saying—'At the fag end of this murderous century what did you expect, melodious bird songs? Hymnal chords in the neighbourhood?' (Bhattacharya 2003: 7) Nabarun hits out at the civic reaction to such manifestation of the macabre, arguing that our collective degradation is bound to emanate in such forms of the unreal or the surreal. Departing from the usual custom or literary decorum, Nabarun rebukes the reader, calling the reader a bastard, for whom no writer should waste any time (Bhattacharya 2003: 10). The primary target of Nabarun's ire in this book is Bengali civil society who according to him have forgotten their hoary past of radical dissent, colluding now with the ruling structure of power in a state of utter compromise and complicity. Opposed to this civic space stands the incongruously discordant voice of Vodi and Nolen, the Choktars, the incorrigible saboteurs of Bengali political society who dabble in strategic illegalities, sabotage and subversion to dismantle the existing power structure. The Choktars along with the Fyatarus fulminate against the unscrupulous ways of the civil society stakeholders—they speak through the use of vulgar expressions, using slangs as weapons. *Kangal Malshat* is written in episodes and each episode is equivalent with the move of the revolutionary subaltern submarine named as *Kangal Malshat*. This is indeed unique in structure and thematic innovation, each chapter attempting to mobilise public consciousness to rage against social injustice and democratic deficit. The backdrop of this book is the burning ghat of Kyaoratola in Kolkata characterised by filth, squalor and the macabre, with corpses arriving for the crematorium to consume it, we encounter a beeline of corpses, the body carriage, the sardonic ambience and against this eerie backdrop, Nabarun introduces us with Madan, DS and Purandar, the three leading Fyatarus, sitting in this cremation site. The discerning reader can immediately understand the symbolic overtone of society at large being compared with the crematorium, a corpse land or a wasteland where death reigns supreme and the Fyatarus position themselves as observers and fence-sitters in this death land of millennial degradation. In a single stroke of artistic marvel, Nabarun deglamourises the façade of polish and the pseudo-glitter of modern metropolitan civic life is taken off to foreground the dark shingles of life—the crematorium, dirt, unending slangs, wine bottles, empty religious rituals after death, etc. are all devised here to project the basic non-elegance of the modern life-world. Vodi, the prime Choktar, directs Nolen, his lieutenant-in-arms, to open the '*chaktir ghor*' (the war room of revolution) as the '*chaktir khel*' (the subterfuge of revolutionary arms struggle) is on the offing and when that happens, the perfect alliance between Choktars and Fyatarus is solemnised ('When the revolution begins, Fyatarus align with the Choktars' (Bhattacharya 2003: 22). Now who are the Choktars? One is familiar with terms like doctors or moktars (lower level lawyers), but Choktars? In reply to this, Nabarun defines the Fyatarus and the Choktars in the following way:

> You cannot find the Fyatarus or the Choktars among doctors or lawyers or law clerks. Fyatarus and Choktars are not among the elites or familiar ones. Nobody therefore knows about them … Hence questions like who are the Fyatarus or who are the Choktars make no sense and they are pointless questions. Fyatarus are Fyatarus and Choktars are Choktars, that's all. But, yes this much can be said that Choktars are known for creating nuisance, in launching agitations or a pandemonium. (Bhattacharya 2003: 22–23)

Suffice it to say that these fictional creatures are members of the urban underbelly; they are the fence-sitters, members of the urban precariat, the new dangerous class who flaunt their hostility to civic norms and in Nabarun's works they deliberately forge a new vocabulary and a new way of living which destabilises formal civilities, a cover which we use to stabilise existing power equations in a society. Vodi, the lead Choktar, rents his dilapidated house for *ashuvo anushthan* (non-pious enterprises), something strange and gives an immediate jolt to our civic mentality, even though we know that all these corrupt machinations are constantly going on all around us with our silent collective support. Our unscrupulous pretentions prevent us to acknowledge the existence of these nefarious aspects of reality and as members of civil society we shy away from this reality, assuming it to be a part of the impure—a filth stock to be avoided and denied even though we are perennially sustaining this sordid dimension of our social malaise. Choktars defy this civilised façade; they own up this rotten filth, encounter it only to dislodge the root of this rottenness. Hence, they rent their house for impious activities—an act of engagement with the muckheap of life. They rationalise this too:

> See, everyday countless impious activities are going on! […] illegal Law suits, corrupt business, destroying marital ties, vicious electoral deals, amassing purchase orders through nefarious means, brooding enmity, cheating […] women trafficking, political horse trading, etc.—all these are constantly being conjured and pursued by all and that is why I rent only those who are involved in all these dark activities. (Bhattacharya 2003: 24)

Vodi's father, Dandobayosh, is an incorrigible saboteur, appearing in this novel as an aged crow who can break temporal barriers, can fly invisibly, can acquire omnipresence and can radically intervene anywhere—he has handed down that revolutionary lineage to Vodi, the lead Choktar. Speaking in his choicest slangs even with his own son, he supervises the build-up of the revolutionary plot being hatched by Vodi, his associates and the Fyatarus. I would argue that Nabarun uses Dandobayosh as history itself. Choktars play the vanguardist role and the Fyatarus are the revolutionary followers—*Choktar leader, amra cadre* (Bhattacharya 2003: 29). Like his radical outcasts who dabble in continuous political tussle with the existing power set-up, Nabarun too believes in the prose of counter insurgency, his textual practises are steeped in the principle of sickle script, acting as political whiplash, something the Fyatarus and the Choktars do:

> We are political poets, we do not wallow in stereotyped inanities. Our writings are always robust and politically aggressive. It's aglow with the fire of life. Few can survive its glaring whiplash. (Bhattacharya 2003: 30)

Armed with their rage potential against social anomies and civil dishonesty, Fyatarus swear by the carnivalesque and a commitment to subversion. *Kangal Malshat* is motored by this agitational energy of the postcolonial precariats—its arsenals aim at the citadel of civil society and its intellectual claims:

> what is visible in the periscope of *Kangal Malshat*, the revolutionary submarine of the subalterns is the pervasive dominance of the civil society intellectual elites [...] these charlatans flaunt their empty intellectuality and hegemonize the social scene with their exclusive views. They have been doing this for ages. Fyatarus are targeting these festering minds, they look for opportunities to devastate these elite intellectual class who are lifeless and submissive in all spheres. (Bhattacharya 2003: 38)

Fyatarus betray a true form of literary bolshevism that erupts with veritable semantic vitriol and exasperated articulation. Purandar Bhat, the Fyataru poet, writes his suicide note in the following way that speaks volumes about his position on civic life and living in this decaying world:

> The Fucking World
> Purandar Bhat (1948–1999)
>
> My life is devoid of any meaningful event
> hence I shall squander away my life in cotton fields
> … my death shall not figure in the headlines
> I shall urinate on the palace walls to violate the laws … (Bhattacharya 2003: 47)

In a similar vein, Fyatarus call this civic world '*haramir hat*' (civic space, a land of traitors) (Bhattacharya 2009: 9), and the section on 'Basonto Utsobe Fyataru' ('Fyatarus in the Spring Carnival') consistently draws our attention to various civil society extravaganzas, their vulgar show of money and social indifference and, by doing this, Fyatarus generate public outrage and collective angst. Nabarun's brilliant rendition of Fyatarus exposing the corrupt sham and follies of civil society stake-holders in the section 'Sushil Samaje Fyataru' ('Fyataru in Civil Society') (Bhattacharya 2009: 46–56) provides a post-civil society optic to deflate the routinised razzmatazz and designed clamour (candle light marches, group email-dissents, etc.) of civil society. Fyatarus reiterate that million candlelight marches on various issues are powerless to actualise a new political economy of redistributive logic. The civic space is accommodationist and colludes with the existing norms. It is only in the hurly-burly of popular politics of subversion, enunciated by Fyatarus that emerge out of their real existential needs, that one can forge a politics from the below. Nabarun, the chronicler of subaltern war cries (Purakayastha, 2015), materialises the real Naxalisation of semantic force and shrapnel rhymes through a vigorous rebuttal of civic docility and unscrupulous norms.

Nabarun through his fictional outpourings has captured the bizarre canvas of the contemporary *wasteland* where human beings cannibalise other fellow beings in the name of *laissez faire* and where the state has failed to provide the necessary succour for the needy and suffering multitude. While many others before him have also engaged with such issues of state coercion, social anomies and economic Darwinianism, Nabarun's uniqueness lies in the radical brilliance and efficacy with which he captured the state of collective angst, existential cynicism and economic disparities of a society that valorises the doctrine of the simulacrum and hedonistic self-enclosure to conscript the ideology of status quo and conformism (Purakayastha 2015). I would conclude by saying that for Nabarun, nothing could be more vulgar and anarchic than the continued endurance of poverty and other forms of social coercions and the one and only way out of the pervasive cult of subservience, the tradition of enduring collusion with the existing system is through revolution—*fyant fyant snai snai*—the sound created by the flight of the Fyatarus, the presaging of revolution. Fyatarus, the subaltern forces of immanence, are everywhere, in every nook and corner of our elitosphere—they are lurking around the civic space, the book fair, in the glossy glitzy lavish marriage parties, in poetry festivals, social ceremonies, fashion parades, etc.—waiting to pounce on, just looking for the best moment to subvert, to devastate. It is because of this resuscitation of the radical rage potential in an age when compromise and conformity have become the only norm, the legacy of Nabarun Bhattacharya would remain with us. In a society which is blinded with the seduction of hierarchy, over-consumption, privilege and interpellation, Nabarun's *prose of counter-insurgency* would continue to provide the necessary grammar of resistance, so lacking in this pervasive ambience of mindless subservience as practised by the members of our so-called civil society.

(All transcreations from Nabarun's texts are by the author)

References

Badiou, Alian (2005), *Handbook of Inaesthetics*. California: Stanford University Press.

Bhattacharya, Nabarun (2003), *Kaangal Malshat*. Hooghly: Saptarshi.

——— (2004), *Fyatarur Bombachuk O Onnanno*. Hooghly: Saptarshi.

——— (2009), *Fyatarur Kumbhipak*. Kolkata: Bhasabandhan.

——— (2016), *Eei Mrityu Upotyaka Amar Ddesh Na*. Kolkata: Bhashabandhan.

——— (2009), *Rater Circus*. Kolkata: Bhasabandhan.

Chatterjee, Partha (2004), *The Politics of the Governed: Reflections on Popular Politics in Most of the World*. New Delhi: Permanent Black.

Chaudhuri, Amit (2017), *Literary Activism: Perspectives*. Kolkata: Oxford University Press.

Dasgupta, Subhendu (2015), 'Nabaruner Obastob Kimba Asol Bastob', Nabarun Bhattacharya Special Issue, *Bhasabandhon Patrika*, Kolkata: Bhasabandhan.

Frankel, Francine R., Zoya Hasan, Rajeev Bhargava, and Balveer Arora, eds (2000), *Transforming India: Social and Political Dynamics of Democracy*. New Delhi: Oxford University Press.

Goh, Irving (2014), *The Reject: Community, Politics, and Religion after the Subject*. New York: Fordham University Press.

Gudavarthy, Ajay (2013), *Politics of Post-Civil Society: Contemporary History of Political Movements in India*. New Delhi: Sage.

Kaviraj, Sudipta (2010), *The Imaginary Institution of India*. New Delhi: Permanent Black.

Purakayastha, Anindya Sekhar (2015), 'Narrator of Subaltern War Cries: Nabarun Bhattacharya and the Literature of Dissidence', *Economic and Political Weekly*. 50: 42.

Prakash, Gyan (2010), 'Subaltern Studies as Postcolonial Criticism'. In *Indian Political Thought: A Reader*, edited by Akash Singh and Silika Mahapatra. New York: Routledge.

Standing, Guy (2011), *Precariat: The New Dangerous Class*. London: Bloomsbury.

Counter-History, Counter-Memory and the *Harami*: The Fictional World of *Kangal Malshat*

Anustup Basu

Nabarun Bhattacharya's *Kangal Malshat* (*The War Cry of the Vagabonds*) is a novel about bureaucratisation and Bengali in-worldliness, both of illicit and rogue modern origin. It is one that joyously casts itself against the instrumentalisation of politics, language, imagination and memory in the era of late capital. As aficionados of Bhattacharya's fiction well know, *Kangal Malshat* is an interim moment in a longer tale about periodic run-ins between a soft-Stalinist Left-Front-ruled West Bengal State Government (1977–2011) and a motley crew of rabble-rousers comprising of Fyatarus (flying men) and Choktars (black magicians). The ruling order is marked by a provincial Bengali left-wing paternalism, afflicted by a growing irrelevance, both in relation to a changing Indian federalism as well as a wider globalisation. The anarchists on the other hand are aided by a trinity of spirits in the legendary Calcutta dowager Begum Johnson (1725–1812), Dandobayosh, a giant, venerable crow and, in later novels, by Bonberal, an Asiatic jungle cat who is a literary descendent of felines in Bulgakov's *Master and Margarita* and Saki's *Tobermory*. This trinity is a burlesque approximation of epic pantheons, guiding the retailed anarchy of the Fyataru–Choktar combine with their encyclopedic knowledge of the occult, modern politics, science, warfare and history. They display wondrous powers of speech, telepathy, omnipresence and anticipation in scuttling intrigues hatched against the Fyatarus–Choktars by incompetent state functionaries, the facile media or powerful sections of the civil society.

This universe was inaugurated in 1995 by a series of short stories featuring the Fyatarus, later anthologised as *Fyatarur Bombachak* (first published 2001) and *Fyatarur Kumbhipak* (2009). These short tales feature a trio of flying men—Madan the hustler, DS the low-end share market tout and Purander Bhat the failed poet—engaging in a series of anarchic adventures to inflict 'damage' on the pieties and hygiene of a Calcutta elite caught between old feudal entitlements and incomplete embourgeoisment, between an older Anglophone colonial culture and current winds of American-style, consumer-driven globalisation.[1] The cosmology is extended in *Kangal Malshat* (2003) when the Fyatarus meet the Choktars, who are sorcerers, probably of Aghori Tantrik inspiration. The Fyataru–Choktar combine is formed at a predestined hour for the unleashing of a swarm of magical airborne automatons called *chaktis* (discs). The Choktars mastermind such chaotic events once every 150 years to rattle the world. The self-animated *chaktis*—sized between bottle-caps and manhole covers—decapitate the Police Commissioner of Calcutta (without killing him), lobotomise a group of eminent city industrialists, and generally bring about a series of inexplicable events which culminate in Marshall Bhodi, the commander of the Choktars, declaring a frontal war against the state government. The state functionaries are subsequently bewildered and panicked by aerial bombardments of garbage, muck and shit by flying Fyatarus, *chaktis* dominating the skies like UFOs, a quixotic military operation spearheaded by a three centuries old rusty 'small dick' canon made by the Portuguese and horrifying spectacles like old slime-covered tin cans climbing out of sewers and marching the streets like European knights in bloody armour. The government sues for peace and the novel ends with a provisional compromise between the warring parties.

The fictional world is extended in *Mausoleum* (2006), in which Bhodi organises a media circus and a pay-per-view public spectacle around his own faux death and mummification through an ancient technique based on hibernating pythons. The Choktars and Fyatarus make a lot of money from this con-venture, and, in the process, precipitate a crippling existentialist crisis on the leaders of the ruling Communist Party in relation to rationalism, superstition, deification

1 See Samrat Sengupta's (2015) astute reading of the emergence of the Fyatarus in an era of left obsolescence and post-Fordism.

of humans and the historic mummification of V. I. Lenin. In *Mobologe Novel* (apparently incomplete, posthumously published in 2014), the rebels plan and execute fresh intrigues. Bhodi's chief military officer, retired Major Ballav Bakshi, sequentially launches V1, V2 and V3 rockets across the Calcutta skyline. The events once again lead to widespread panic and considerable administrative headache in the final days of the Left Front government.

The rebels, such as Purander Bhat, the failed poet, or Madan, the hustler, generally come from urban lower-middle to working-class backgrounds. Under Bhodi's leadership, they gradually embark on a series of vernacular emulations of global corporatism: a cottage petroleum company, a publishing house, aphrodisiacs and sundry consumables like devotional CDs and Bhodi Cola centred upon the godman cult. The rebels are marked by a naturalised, vernacular sexism bordering on misogyny, rustic insularity and class *ressentiment* of the deprived that refuses to take the form of an organised politics. It is a vapid, insecure Bengali masculinity, perpetually under the existentialist shadow of personal cuckoldry (Madan, DS) as well as a historical obsolescence in the techno-financial metropole. Bhattacharya identifies this as part of a collective Bengali neurosis on the lines of the Koro Syndrome—that delusional state when a culture-bound individual is afflicted with the overpowering belief that his genitals are shrinking and disappearing (2016: 82–83).

The members have different political leanings. Bhat is a declared 'half-Maoist'. DC is a plebian opportunist. Dandobayosh, the giant crow, is an astute but frazzled interlocutor of late 20th-century Leninism. Bhodi's almost entirely provincial anarchism, on the other hand, is never weighed down by cultured bourgeois erudition or radical introspection. He simply wants to be important enough to own a private helicopter. Between the eclectic, gross naturalism of the rebels and the bureaucratic inertia of their enemies; between Bhat's vulgar eloquence and Dandobayosh's encyclopedic erudition or Begum Johnson's deep historical witnessing across centuries, the world of the Choktars and Fyatarus present an armada of typologies, figurations and movements. These come together, unravel and reassemble by way of dynamic alignments and polarities. The play of these figurations, along with the ghosts, the beasts and the clutter of the city, dramatise the tensions and missed encounters in the Bengali modernity project. Such movements feature competing temporal imaginations, voids of oblivion, as well as vectors of untimely remembrance. Literary fiction, in this case, rehearses an ongoing crisis of language and memory. It does so by dismantling bureaucratic machines of representation.

I will argue that the extended Fyataru–Choktar saga is not a romance of subaltern insurrection. It is also not a monstrous parable or allegory awaiting *interpretation* in that direction. Rather, it is an enacted implosion of the political, juridical, scientific or aesthetic language games of a Bengali modernity project. This fictional universe is a baroque disarticulation of liberalism's discourses of constitution (freedom, equality or the secular) as well as 'postmodern' nostalgias for the same. It is baroque in the Benjaminian sense, as a massive 'ongoing' expression of unremitted desires. The texts may not be *interpreted* precisely because they fracture all hermeneutics of interpretation. They unfold a cosmology in which one does not abandon the quest for meaning but has to proceed without the assurance of a providential narrative of means and ends. That is, one can only *go along* with the text by abjuring theological eschatologies of life, mission and death, as well as secularised forms of the same, like the powerful Hegelian teleology of historical redemption and self-consciousness. The works do not 'represent' the world in a nihilistic manner, but joyously call it to judgement, exposing its dominant conceptions as a medley of bureaucratic realisms.[2] It is, therefore, not very productive to *read* into these texts or read between the lines. There is nothing inside or between them. Instead, it is far more useful to follow its tracings, extend its excesses, add three jokes to its one and augment its dismantling of the regimes it inevitably inhabits—of politics, aesthetics, revolution, art or the novel—while writing itself out. Attempting a 'professional essay' on Bhattacharya's work—marked by a proper beginning, interpretive middle and conclusive end—is, therefore, a fatal mistake, for it would be an unthinking capitulation to one of the very bureaucratic

2 For an enlightening discussion on Bhattacharya's work in relation to Michael Löwy's notion of 'Critical Irrealism', see Sourit Bhattacharya (2016).

machines, that of industrial literary criticism, that the encyclopedic anarchy questions at every step. I, therefore, offer a series of scattered speculations—with the native informant's irony and mischief as well as cosmopolitan deliberations—and promise to stop when the word count runs out.

Then, what exactly is a bureaucratic machine? It is one that tries to systematise disciplines and pieties of Enlightenment, norms of justice, equity and production in accordance with the requirements of a capitalist governmentality. The classical diagram here is a Weberian one, based on a sociology of the *ultima ratio*, by which legal intelligence could be subject to regular calculation and a stable schema of juridical cognition. Human knowledge production, communicability and forms of anticipation had to be submitted to capital as singular ontology and destination. Historicity had to be visualised from the vantage point of eternal bourgeois peace rather than perennial subsurface war between the races, the castes, the genders or the classes. Representation had to be formalised within the auspices of liberal parliamentarism, civil society and the rational state. The state itself had to be tied to economism, and politics had to gravitate towards an impersonal scientism of 'development', private property and trade devoid of risk. This template of modernity was a bourgeois tempering of European republican revolutions, by which the former royalist or aristocratic transcendence of the state was to be neutralised and absorbed into an immanent 'great administration' of things. In an ideal sense, bureaucratisation had to wed the positivistic applications of the modern physical sciences with an overall technological production of social life itself. In that vein, the impulse extends to language, poesis, gnosis and imagination; it involves consigning all memories and forms of remembrance to what Foucault would call the Jupiterean history of victors. Bureaucratisation of culture, amongst other things, means submitting all forms of storytelling to a dominant mythography of power. A true act of novelisation that shudders the bureaucratic imaginary—in all its disciplinary and therapeutic dimensions—thus, has to contend with the already-there bureaucratisation and market of the novel form itself.

Disarticulating bureaucratic idealism means exposing the machine for what it is: a formation of means without ends. It is a bourgeois engine that perpetually defers that thing called modernity in favour of perpetual *modernisation*. The specific idea of modernisation here is something we get from Rajni Kothari.

> A 'modernizing' society is neither modern nor traditional. It simply moves from one threshold of integration and performance to another, in the process transforming both the indigenous structures and attitudes and the newly introduced institutions and ideas. (Kothari 1997: 58)

The crank and other noises of the machine is a constant reminder that there is no achieving modernity, but only assemblages of modernisation that go by other names like 'development', 'growth', 'law and order' or 'progress,' now determined in neoliberal terms. Bureaucratism demands a statist monopoly of realism and cognition. It does not actually foreclose miracle or magic but announces that the magic of the state and the theologism of the market (with its hidden hand) as the only valid forms of transformation and destining.

This is a western diagram of power, an inheritance of colonialism and the 1950 passive revolution of the constitutional republic in the postcolonial milieu of *Kangal Malshat*. The bureaucratic assemblage draws from the Anglophone Civil Service of the Raj, indigenous feudal and comprador traditions of the bhadralok and, indeed, state capitalism in the erstwhile USSR. It is, therefore, a historical mishmash of contrary pieties and paternalisms, inspired at once by Warren Hastings, the purported 19th-century Bengal Renaissance, the CIA and Joseph Stalin. Let us call it a *harami* bureaucracy, a 'bastard' one, in the spirit of the novels. The word in itself should not be a pejorative (indeed, the texts warmly democratise it), but in this case, it may be strategically marshalled to dispel certain monogamous pieties of the state: that the aim of bureaucratisation is actually to wed the past to the present, tradition with modernity, development with welfare or science with dogma.

Establishment bureaucratisation appears in many forms in Bhattacharya's work: security, surveillance, law and order, weather reports, sexology, entrepreneurship, cricket, media, history or literary criticism. This imagination is enfigured in Comrade Acharya, the leader of the Communist Party, the lecherous curator of the Victoria Memorial Museum, P.D. Paul, the postmodernist, terrorism expert Syambhajan Batabyal or Mr Sikdar, the Director of the Calcutta Positional Astronomy Centre. The assault on the bureaucratic imagination is woven into the patterns of textualisation. That is, in the manner the texts tie and untie themselves in the act of fabrication, featuring small and large forms of surprise, shock or the burlesque. The police officer in '*Boimelay Fyataru*' shouts the Anglophone legalese, 'Pilferer! Pilferer!', instead of the colloquial '*Chor*! *Chor*!' when he spots DS and Madan picking up charred books from the precincts of the 1997 Calcutta Book Fair which, after an illuminating address by Chief Guest Jacques Derrida, was deconstructed by a fire within a couple of days (N. Bhattacharya 2015: 38). In *Kangal Malshat*, the beheaded and bewildered Police Commissioner Joardar wonders how such a thing could happen without advance warning from official channels. With stoic determination, he learns how to balance his severed head and have soup with gentlemanly poise. He dutifully reports to a meeting with the chief minister after securing his head under a 'STUD' monogrammed motorcycle helmet confiscated from an underling. Joardar's head, however, rolls out when he takes his headgear off as a show of respect to visiting beauty contestants who swoon immediately. Embarrassed, he insists that he is no ghost, and the whole thing was just a matter of 'minor adjustment'. The CM rebukes him for working with a detached head but lauds his sense of responsibility. He demands an investigative report on the decapitation from the Director General of Police, who too appears with a helmet on his head (N. Bhattacharya 2017: 131–163).

In contrast, the rebels of this fictional world are special not because they successfully rival the panoptic and military resources of the state. It is because they confound the state and civil society's hermeneutics of suspicion, their cataloguing powers and modes of instrumentalising language. The state struggles and fails to define Fyataru–Choktar antagonism as phenomena that can be included in a calendar of expected hostilities: terrorism, crime, larceny or sedition. The problem with the rebels is not that they challenge the state's military-industrial command of the skies, but that they fly without capital or technological investment. They exercise their 'Black Magic' to create untimely *events* rather than *phenomena*. The event, as perhaps Bergson would say, comes with unique memories of its own, denying the state its habitual serendipity. The phenomenon, on the other hand, is readily accountable within the state's stable frameworks of cognition and classification.[3] The real crises of the Bengal bureaucracies, therefore, lie in *representing* matters like the carnival of ghosts in *Kangal Malshat* or the mysterious mummification in *Mausoleum* within the grid of statist realism. This is a problem because the thing that cannot be represented cannot be governed. The occult is that which is unprecedented in the archive of statist anthropology. The untimely is the one that is not contained in the state's chronometric temporality and its machines of anticipation.

The 'bureaucratic machine' is, thus, a diagram of *modernising* power. We are using it to gain access to a fictional universe with many entry points and labyrinths. It is in this vein that we may propose a kinship of souls between Nabarun Bhattacharya and Franz Kafka. We can do so in the spirit of playfulness that the works themselves demand, and not in terms of inevitable identity or positive inspiration. Bhattacharya could be placed in the company of many other affiliate minds in Bengal (Hutom Pyacha, Sukumar Roy, Parashuram, Troilokyonath Mukhopadhyay or Jagadish Gupta) and across the continents (Mikhail Bulgakov, Isaac Babel, Italo Calvino or Pater Bichsel). The invocation of Kafka is, therefore, just one way of critically grasping a multiplicity. Bhattacharya himself invokes the Bohemian Jew at one point in *Mobologe Novel.* He does so tellingly to indict Bhodi himself for bureaucratising the rebellion. 'The outcome of the chickenshit insurrection of the Choktars partly mirrors that Kafka written good news that all revolutions vaporize like camphor and what remains is a world-wide bureaucracy.' (2016: 76). Accordingly, a smug Bhodi bureaucracy entrenches itself, especially after the launch of the V1 rocket: pointless conversations, siesta followed by siesta, lazy delegation of responsibilities to pass the buck, periodic huffing and puffing like Leonid Brezhnev, consuming tankers of country and foreign liquor

3 See Basu (2003).

and indulging in that serious pastime cultured Anglophone gentlemen call 'ball scratching'.

Kafka and Bhattacharya were fellow travellers in a broad path of negative theology through the void of the modern. The negation is marked by an absence of providence and redemption, a transcendent law, pieties of the subject or valorisation of guilt. The legal apparatus here becomes a maze because it is shown to be without god and father. The people are 'missing' in a political sense, because the city is filled with orphans and somnambulists, while officious officers chasing them are marked by a crippling lack of imagination. A radical questioning of Cartesian humanism by way of gallows humour and grim irony is supplemented by the delegation of appetites, shock, violence and intelligence to animals. The creatures and insects in Bhattacharya—from the venerable crow Dandobayosh to the cockroaches smoked out of sewers—are, thus, kindred to the beasts in Kafka: Josephine the mouse, the giant insect in 'Metamorphosis', rats and other animals in 'The Burrow', 'Memories of the Kalda Railroad' or 'The Investigation of a Hound'.

Such topoi apart, there are two general features of this kinship worth highlighting. The first of these pertains to the question of realism already broached. In her classic study of Totalitarianism, Hannah Arendt observes in passing that writing at the twilight of the Austro–Hungarian Empire, Franz Kafka had turned into a humourist of the macabre. He had given expression to a minoritarian life of perpetual accidents that always seemed to take place between blind destiny and Weberian social constructivism. Kafka, therefore, a writer of plebian lore and parables, was essentially a realist. This is a thought one can extrapolate onto the fabulous, the grotesque and the beastliness in Bhattacharya's fiction. His art is aimed 'to complete what reality had somehow neglected to bring into full focus' (Arendt 1973: 246). Accordingly, the magic of this realism unravels the arrangement by which the modern bourgeois state kills God only to secretly monopolise magic as exception, theodicy and divination, replacing a *theologia revelata* with its own psychobiography. In contrast, Bhattacharya's plebian realism mobilises radical, minoritarian energies of counter-memory against providential narratives of empires past and present.

The second feature pertains to the widely recognised cult affect Bhattacharya has had on the norms and practises of Bengali prose. However, it would be a mistake to limit its importance merely to a colourful babble of the unwashed—the dialects of dirt-lanes, bordellos or sleazy watering holes—intruding into domains of respectable culture and expression. That is, it would be an error to view this novelisation merely in decorative terms, as within an already-there grid of anthropological understanding by which bhadralok-culture has always judged, admitted or sequestered the eloquence of the vulgar. Rather, the unleashing of such expressive energies would be similar to what Deleuze and Guattari, via Kafka, call becoming a nomad, an immigrant and a gypsy in relation to one's own language. That is what makes Bhattacharya a writer of 'minor' literature in Bengali, not a writer of Bengali literature. 'A minor literature doesn't come from a minor language; it is rather that which a minority constructs within a major language' (Deleuze and Guattari 1986: 16). The visibilities and statements in Bhattacharya's work de-territorialise dominant institutions of the major language. His words and images acquire novelising powers by refusing to submit, in the last instance, to any of the presiding ontologies of Bengali Being—be it in terms of an agonistic *Bengaliana* drawn from the 19th-century Bengal Renaissance, the 20th-century nationalism and left-wing politics or even the contemporary lightness of being *Bong* in the era of American globalisation.

Becoming a linguistic nomad means exiling oneself from the framework of bureaucratic realism, missioned by the state as arch lexicographer, cryptologist and controller of language with demiurgic power. Rebellion, in Bhattacharya's works, therefore, often takes the form of riddles, cryptic messages or psychological conundrums presented to the state, be it Choktar Sarkhel's enigmatic track on dinosaurs that mysteriously disappears from police files, or Purander Bhat's 'suicide note' entitled 'The Ass-fucked World' that flouts all norms of idiomatic propriety, logical progression and bourgeois poetic license. The schizoid text locates the floundering but lustful Purander between bestial appetites and the polis of human play, between cotton fields and palaces, and between urine and a confectionary named after Countess Charlotte Canning (1817–1861), the first Vicereine of the Raj.

> There is no drama in my life at all
> I dive, therefore, on cottonfields I crawl
> No dreams have I either, only the dregs
> A lizard am I, to eat bugs, lay eggs
> No headlines will happen when I die
> On palaces I pee; the law, I defy
> On my death no cats will be a-mourning.
> Sweet Ledikeni, to salute Lady Canning.
> One foot on hell, the other on heaven falls
> `A cannon erect, and two cannon balls (2017: 58–59).

Bhattacharya locates the problem of discovering a language of novelisation in a data-driven universe of awry information flows and an industrial evisceration of memory. That is, in a dispensation of power that produces an electronic book of the world that only the state can read in real time. He counters this ordered reality by unleashing energies of laughter, neurosis and utopian thinking that clog efficient circuits of information.[4] The planetary state of the geostrategic satellite and micropunctual electronic surveillance, at different moments, mistakes a garden umbrella to be a missile, and a brand of saris to be RDX explosives.[5] The fiction is, however, self-conscious about the impossibility of fiction itself interrupting the data stream. The fiction writes itself into the world and then folds the world and the act of writing itself into the next act of fabrication. The novel, in its serialisation, is alert to reports and information about the novel's serialisation. The narrator of *Kangal Malshat* pauses midway to respond, in fictional time, to reader comments in real time. In the middle of *Mobologe Novel*, he visits the fictional author, Bajra Ghosh, to discuss further developments in *Mobologe Novel* (2016: 75–76).

---

4 In this context, see also Adheesha Sarkar's (2015) insightful reading of Bhattacharya's fiction in relation to Peter Marshall's work on the modern anarchic-utopian tradition that stretches from Sorel and Bakunin to Gandhi.

5 '*Global Terror O Fyataru*', in *Fyatarur Bombachak*, 119–125, and '*Fyatarur RDX*', in *Fyatarur Kumbhipak*, 177–199.

When totality cannot be book-ended, the novel never ends; it merely moves from one caesura to the next, folding the world onto and extending itself. It lives and flourishes beyond the death of the writer. The stories brim with a plethora of non-obligatory tropes: a Hollywood B-movie with flying, man-eating fish, the Lady Diana funeral or Johann Strauss Junior's *Blue Danube*. They are rife with jocular asides, snide interruptions and profound citations from many intellectuals, from John Stuart Mill to Michel Foucault, or the obscure Bengali poet Anita Roy. These operate in a double layer of irony. At one level, they point to the twilight of true remembrance in the sea of information. At another level, they function in a manner similar to an ongoing mischief Ramanujan recalls to begin one of his magnificent essays: 'Walter Benjamin once dreamed of hiding behind a phalanx of quotations which, like highwaymen, would ambush the passing reader and rob him of his convictions' (Ramanujan 1999: 140).

The mock-heroic quest for Totality automatically becomes a matter of low-tech, voluptuous cannibalisation of a kinetic sea of information. The prolific and tireless researcher Sarkhel authors a series of studies pertaining to dinosaurs and their tantra practises, sex lives, poetic works and military strategies. These works philosophise on the diminishment of epic entities in time with proper amplification of contemporary visions: magnify a fight between lizards to understand how dinosaurs fought (Bhattacharya 2017: 144). In *Mobologe Novel*, Sarkhel reveals that he has been on a perennial hunt for the mystic 'sky records' of everything, from literary works to shopping lists, cat fights or speeches. These, as per the antinomian Theosophist Helena Blavatsky's writings, could be in the possessions of secretive ancient Lamas in Tibet. Dandobayosh is a master of the ancient astrological craft of *Nakhadarpana*, which allows one to use his nails like a mirror to see the past, present and future, as bright as images on an LCD television screen (2016: 239).

Bhattacharya's style marshals energies from below to stretch the Overton Window—the permissible range of ideas and voiced feelings in a given climate of propriety, opinion and taste—of the Bengali literary. Figures, animals, ghosts or elemental forces, therefore, become immediately political, imbued with collective value precisely because they become drifters and fugitives in relation to the *polis*.

It is, therefore, to the city we turn in the closing movement of this essay. There is a moment in the short story '*IPL-e Fyataru*' when Purander Bhat and Madan proceed toward DS's ancient, dilapidated house. The alleyways leading up to the building present a palimpsest of an originary world of gross naturalism and a determined milieu of town-planning. The originary world creeps and oozes out of the surface of the latter in the form of poisoned mice with swollen bellies lying flat like knocked out wrestlers, vegetable skins, moss, crows and diseased cats fighting over fish bones amidst dead cockroaches, a three-legged dog and an elemental soundscape comprising television noise, rickshaw horns, radio, cries of babies, women and caged parrots (2015: 140–141). Tree roots and unlawful vegetation creep with infinite patience and strangle buildings of the old city to reclaim them. There are also beastly energies lurking beneath the surface, as Madan reminds DS on another occasion, when the latter insults a rat near Curzon Park by offering it the peel instead of the banana. Madan warns that the disgruntled rodent might seek DS out using a great underground network of tunnels that connects and subliminally controls everything, from the State Secretariat to the General Post Office or the Police Headquarters. There have been twenty-six cases since the British era, when rats have traced enemies out and castrated them at night.[6]

Such moments are part of an archaeological figuration of the changing city, perpetually caught between a historical field of problems and an abstract metropolitan diagram of value and bureaucratic planning. The abstract diagram seeks to overwrite and rationalise the beastliness and dirt (which anthropologist Mary Douglas once described as 'matter out of place') of the former. That is, it seeks to reinvent all spaces as prime real estate and submit all temporal imaginations to a Calvinistic futurism of capital. The contrary image of originary worlds oozing out of determined milieus and exhausting them comes from Deleuze: 'The originary world only exists and operates in the depths of a real milieu and is only valid through its immanence in this milieu, whose violence and cruelty it

6 '*Kobi shommelone Fyataru*', in *Fyatarur Bombachak*, 62.

reveals' (Deleuze 1986: 125). This is a sentiment shared enthusiastically by Bhattacharya in a declarative moment in *Kangal Malshat*:

> The Calcutta that is being broken, twisted, roasted, dissolved, crushed, and plucked into an unknown metal and synthetic assemblage—that Calcutta has its true friends in the lunatics and the pipistrelles. Along with some decked-up women, dogs, bats, cats, owls, rats, mice, cockroaches, beggars, and ants. Mosquitos, flies, the last few asphyxiating butterflies, moths, and sparrows, mynas, crows and kites too join the group. If someone has been left out, for them this space remains open without a period mark'. (Bhattacharya 2017: 40)

In that spirit, we could add dry skeletons of cats, eggshells or minor actors like Bolai, the driver, or Kali, the whore.

These are Bhattacharya's schizophrenic inventories and itineraries. They violate what Ranciere would call a distribution of the bureaucratic/Brahminical sensible: '[that] system of self-evident facts of sense perception that simultaneously discloses the existence of something in common and the delimitations that define the respective parts and positions within it' (Ranciere 2004: 12). Objects, figures, beasts, insects and animations are unmoored from their assigned places in the order of things. They are rendered afloat and inevitably acquire an aspect of terror. This is perhaps best illustrated in the weaponry mobilised by the Choktars and Fyatarus in their wars against the state machinery: human excreta and urine, bassine brooms, stale potato curry, used toothbrushes, water bombs made of muck-filled water, rotten snails, frogs, a 300-year-old Portuguese made 'small-dick' cannon, Mungeri muskets, Mughal cutlasses, a pair of opera glasses or Molotov cocktails. These are fired, bombarded from the skies or magically animated. The arsenal reaches its peak in *Mobologe Novel* when Bhodi redirects his childhood pyrotechnics towards his own nuclear missile fueled by charcoal and Sulphur, with deadly atoms of sugar or flour inside a homeopathic bottle as warhead. The state, on the other hand, sticks to conventional instruments like .303 rifles, tear gas, grenades and a few torture manuals procured from Israel's Mossad and South Africa's OCI.

The fictional city is a phenomenal space as well as a space constructed through oneiric journeys into spectral history. Ghosts from Calcutta's past—Job Charnock (1630–1693) or Robert Clive (1725–1774), apart from Begun Johnson—populate it. The city echoes with the hum of dead and forgotten poets: Kumudranjan Mullick, Akshay Kumar Baral or Kalidas Roy.[7] It bears the imprints of popular saints like Kangal Harinath and Lochan Goswami; it houses statues of forgotten patriots covered with birdshit; it holds onto the disappearing footprints of Bengali entrepreneurs or aviators. Joseph Stalin and Mikhail Kalashnikov make ghostly and teleported appearances in *Kangal Malshat*, speaking impeccable 19th-century Bengali. Towards the end of the novel, a group of intellectuals write an open letter to the state government urging peace. The signatories include Bengal's literary giants like Tagore, Bhodi's own ancestor Atmaram Sarkar, obscure spiritualists like Bishudhananda Paramhansa, as well as Werner Heisenberg or Karl Gustav Jung.

The fictional space becomes a clamour of resonances and a kaleidoscope of visions without bureaucratic guarantees. It unfolds a perverse network of memories, interests and forces. The convolution of temporalities and the war cry of the beggars present a primal nightmare for the modern: that of a renewed ruralisation of the city. This is a reversal of fortunes that pertains to a striking observation made by Marx in the *Grundrisse*: 'the modern [age] is the urbanization of the countryside, not ruralization of the city as in antiquity' (Marx 1973: 479). It is by besieging and confining the rustic outside that the modern city conquers terror and assures itself. In relation to that purported urban normal, the Fyatarus and Choktars are noxious tissues in the city imagined as organic mass. They splinter bureaucratic compositions when they should not and refuse to extinct themselves when they should. One could end by illustrating this city as pharmacopic entity and the rebels as indefatigable allergen with a beautiful figuration in Thomas Pynchon's *Gravity's Rainbow*, whose V1 rockets probably resonate in *Mobologe Novel:* 'what if the Ci-ty were a growing neoplasm, across the centuries, always chang-ing, to meet exactly the chang-ing shape of its very worst, se-cret fears?' (Pynchon 1973: 202)

---

7 See Chakravarty (2005) for a critical elaboration of the vast, untimely archive that Bhattacharya brings to bear against the contemporary screen-city.

References

Arendt, Hannah (1973). *Origins of Totalitarianism*. New York: Harcourt.

Basu, Anustup (2003). 'State of Security and Warfare of Demons'. *Critical Quarterly,* 45 (1–2): 11–32.

Bhattacharya, Nabarun (2010). '*Mausoleum*'. In *Uponyash Shomogro.* 417–504. Kolkata: Dey's Publishing.

———(2015). '*Fyatarur Bombachak*' and '*Fyatarur Kumbhipak*'. In *Fyatarur Bingshoti*. Kolkata: 7–125; 126–213. Bhashabandhan.

———(2016). *Mobologe Novel.* Kolkata: Bhashabandhan.

———(2017). *Kangal Malshat*. Kolkata: Bhashabandhan.

Bhattacharya, Sourit (2016). 'The Margins of Postcolonial Urbanity: Reading Critical Irrealism in Nabarun Bhattacharya's Fiction'. In *Postcolonial Urban Outcasts: City Margins in South Asian Literature*, edited by Madhurima Chakraborty and Umme Al-wazedi. New York: Routledge, 39–54.

Chakravarty, Aritra (2005). 'Reading and Resistance in the Works of Nabarun Bhattacharya'. *Sanglap 2:1.* Available at http://www.sanglap-journal.in/index.php/sanglap/article/view/88/137.

Deleuze, Gilles (1986). *Cinema 1: The Movement Image*, translated by Hugh Tomlinson and Barbara Habberjam. Minneapolis: University of Minnesota Press.

Deleuze, Gilles and Felix Guattari (1986). *Kafka: Toward a Minor Literature*, translated by Dana Polan. Minneapolis: University of Minnesota Press.

Kothari, Rajni (1997). 'Caste and Modern Politics'. In *Politics in India*, edited by Sudipta Kaviraj. New Delhi: Oxford, 57–70.

Marx, Karl (1973). *Grundrisse*, translated by Martin Nicholaus. London: Penguin Books.

Pynchon, Thomas (1973). *Gravity's Rainbow*. New York: Viking, 202.

Ranciere, Jacques (2004). *The Politics of Aesthetics: The Distribution of the Sensible*. London: Continuum.

Ramanujan, A.K. (1999). 'Is There an Indian Way of Thinking: An Informal Essay'. In *The Collected Essays of A. K. Ramanujan,* edited by Vinay Dharwadkar. Oxford: Oxford University Press.

Sarkar, Adheesha (2015). 'The Impossible Demands of Nabarun Bhattacharya'. In *Sanglap 2:1*. Available at http://www.sanglap-journal.in/index.php/sanglap/article/view/89/139>.

Sengupta, Samrat (2015). 'Strategic Outsiderism of the Fyatarus: Performances of Resistance by "Multitudes" after "Empire"'. In *Sanglap 2:1*. Available at <http://www.sanglap-journal.in/index.php/sanglap/article/view/93/145>.

A Cyborg Goddess? Baby K and the Symbolisms of Gendered Violence

Priyanka Basu

This chapter focusses on the character of Baby K from Nabarun Bhattacharya's collection of stories entitled *Baby K Parijaat* (2013). As a less-explored character in comparison to his much-celebrated 'Fyatarus', Baby K upholds what can be described as 'the non-recognition of the "other" which inevitably leads to an explosive finale' (Ray 2015). Baby K amounts to what can be highlighted as 'the modern consumerist hybrid cyborg woman' (Sengupta 2014). Bhattacharya places her within the stark realities of US Imperialism and in the dystopic landscape of Calcutta as a modern-day colony of America. Following from Donna Haraway's formulations in *A Cyborg Manifesto* (1991), this chapter will analyse Baby K not just as an 'other' but as a cyborgian entity who, on the one hand, internalises the systematic societal, political and sexual violence, and, on the other, employs this internalisation to conduct the final violence in the explosion—a veritable striking back by the subaltern which Bhattacharya repeatedly stressed in his writings. Does Baby K signify a larger collective in her marginality and resistance? Or, does she stand out as a singular actor in the consumerist, neo-capitalist, postmodern world of technological advancement and epistemic violence? In the current world threatened by climate crisis, forced migrant mobilities and social media opening up as an alternative space of global collective activism, Baby K offers and remains an enigmatic example of subversive action within the larger performativities of gender roles, ideations and idealisations.

Introduction

In inflammable and consumption-led times like these, and in an unabated growth of distortion it would be fitting to consider *these short*

> *stories* [sic] as a document of my political perception(s). Have I been able to make my point? I am saying these words with the Buddha's 'Fire Sermon' in mind. Everything is burning; although the fire is not visible. However, it will be visible at some point. And I, too, am racing towards an incineration. Bravo![1] (Bhattacharya 2013: 7)

In his 'Prelude' to the collection of short stories entitled *Baby K Parijat* (2013), the author Nabarun Bhattacharya points towards the editorial choice of arranging the stories that seem to be standing like 'the bar-dancers of Bombay'. This reference (or allusion) is not coincidental to the narrative logic of the seven short stories strewn together in the volume—'Aaguner Mukh' (The Face of Fire), 'Parijat O Baby K' (Parijat and Baby K), 'Baby K', 'American Petromax', 'Fire Fight', 'Baby K and Spiderman Parijat' and 'Baby K, Parijat, Pangapal, o Markin Samrajyabad' (Baby K, Parijat, Locusts and US Imperialism). Evidently, the protagonist is Baby K, the rather inscrutable brevity of whose name shrouds her identity as a sex worker, thus, almost immediately referring back to the visualisation that Nabarun creates in describing his stories as a row of Bombay's poised bar-dancers. If flesh and desire are recurring motifs in these stories, the overarching theme, as Nabarun himself spells out, is that of fire. Borrowing directly from the 'Fire Sermon Discourse' of the Buddha, Nabarun lays bare the crux of the matter—*sabbambhikkaveāditttam* ('Bhikkus, everything is burning').[2] The fires of lust, hate and delusion that the Bodhisattva emphasises, and, thus, links them to the sensory qualities of sound, odour, flavour and tangibles remain the guiding principles of an amorous relationship between the central characters—Baby K and Parijat.

It might seem incongruous at a glance as to why the first of the seven short stories in the volume—'Aaguner Mukh'[3]—is included despite its seeming non-relation with the rest of the stories and regardless of the absence of the central characters (mentioned above). However, as the

1 Translation mine. All translations, unless otherwise mentioned, are mine.

2 For a discussion on the 'Fire Sermon', see Bhikkhu 1981.

3 'Aguner Mukh' was first published in 2001 for the magazine, *Ebong Shayok*. For a discussion on the short story with regard to the concepts of ritual and re-performance, see Basu 2015: 70–89.

sequential logic of the stories unfolds, the first story seems to follow directly from Nabarun's pronouncement of the predominant objective correlative, that is fire. Rather than an Aristotelian Physics of beginning-middle-end, Nabarun follows a Heideggerian defiance of the linearity of time, thus, moving back and forth into historical time[4]; the consequent repetition of scenes and events stems from the authorial intention of documenting his own political perceptions. Perhaps then, none of the other characters in Nabarun's universe appear more politically volatile, more subversive and more annihilating than Baby K.

The name 'Baby K' is a hypocorism for 'Baby Khanki' (Baby Whore) who upholds what can be described as 'the non-recognition of the "other" which inevitably leads to an explosive finale' (Ray 2015).[5] Following from the way Sengupta (2014) phrases Baby K—'the modern consumerist hybrid cyborg woman'—this chapter will discuss the extents to which this central character can be understood as a cyborg goddess through the symbolisms of fire and violence. As a petrol-consuming, economically self-sustaining sex worker, Baby K defies the collective non-identity that is (albeit, sarcastically) accorded to the bar-dancers standing together. She defies the inflexible binaries of human and machine to become what Donna Haraway underlines as 'chimeras, theorized and fabricated hybrids of machine and organism' (1991: 150). Perhaps, the significance of this puzzlingly subversive/explosive entity of Baby K has never been more relatable, given the current global events that we are faced with every day, growing climate crisis, forced immigrant mobilities, deepening religio-political polarities and social media activisms being some of the vital ones.

Does Baby K signify a larger collective in her marginality and resistance? Or, does she stand out as a singular actor in the consumerist, neo-capitalist, postmodern world of technological advancement and epistemic violence? Extending the cyborgian paradigm in looking at her character, could we possibly offer an alternative reading of Baby K

4 I have argued elsewhere how historical alignment and literary practise of amplification recurs in Nabarun's stories. See, Basu 2015: 70–89. Additionally, this phenomenon could also be understood as 'telasthesia', or a perception of distant events of the past through extra-sensory means.

5 For a discussion on the wordplay on 'K' see Ray, 'The War Cry of the Vagabonds', p. 68.

as an entity transcending natural hierarchies and more contextualised in a post-humanist, post-cyborgian world order? Baby K and Parijat are invariably the products of a deconomy (Mann 2003) that Nabarun historicises or carefully aligns through past, present and future events in history. I am borrowing the idea of deconomy from Steve Mann's definition of decon. 'Decon', he writes, 'is about people, places, things, or shall we say, displaced without their things'. However, the enigma of Baby K lies in her volatile presence, negating any scope decontamination and bringing in an explosive finale that is captivatingly eventful even though seemingly deferred. In the following section, I will flesh out the character of Baby K through the two introductory short stories in order to show how her transgressive ability to burn down existing structures is a possible indication of a post-feminist world order.

Cyborg, Miniaturisation and Historical Allusions: Who Is Baby K?

In his ongoing work on the visual platform, digital collage artist Uğur Gallenkuş juxtaposes images from the Western world with those of the war-torn Middle East: 'The corresponding pictures demonstrate the political climate and lifestyles between the two areas. The apparent opulence, overindulgence, and consumerism of the West is a popular topic for Gallenkuş'(Barnes 2018). Gallenkuş' activist portrayals are one among many of the visual images, reportages and op-eds that circulate on the social media every day beckoning the polarities and escalating crises of geopolitical entities. More importantly, it also brings us face to face with the crises of affect/being affected in a post-truth world of attack, denial and 'ideological impasse'.[6] There is repetition in the way images/opinions/information are assimilated, presented and re-used and this is how 'annoyance-based-repetition' makes us ignorant (simultaneously leading to deafness in a new deconomy) (Mann 2003).

If Fyatarus are characterised by their 'strategic outsiderism' and as 'a community of the ungovernable' in Nabarun's magic

6 See Gopalakrishnan 2016, 'Life in Post-Truth times'.

realist world (Sengupta 2015), Parijat and Baby K are products and inhabitants of a deafness-based new deconomy. The near refrain-like imageries of (Calcutta) city buildings caught in fire and the warnings of the Fireman (to Parijat) about explosive fiascos that Baby K is capable of, underline how both acts are home-bred and rooted in the stifling socio-political realities. Nabarun has time and again referred to the idea of explosion in his writings—the bullet in *Auto* and 'Amar Kono Bhoy Nei To?' (I Hope I Have Nothing to Fear?), the dynamite in *Herbert* and the ammunitions in *Juddho Poristhiti*—highlighting constantly how the possibility of devastation-as-action is embedded in an immediate, socio-political condition and not orchestrated from beyond. Baby K belongs to this world of Nabarun where he repeats imageries of broiler species and Molotov cocktails. Yet, she stands out not by the virtue of a unique explosive event as the finale, but in carrying in herself the risk of explosion at any moment; that we inhabit a current world connected by possible explosion and extinction of species is a reminder that Baby K embodies and parodies.

We are introduced to Baby K on a rather unexciting winter night in Calcutta when Parijat, a fat medical representative, roams around on his moped to find a petrol pump and, more importantly, a sex worker. It is in this uneventfulness that he spots Baby K, a short woman dressed in sky blue, drinking petrol at a filling station. It eventually becomes clearer from a conversation between Parijat and the employee at the filling station that she is quite 'popular' and that her tongue flashes blue light when she speaks (Bhattacharya 2013: 30). The image that immediately comes to mind from this description of Baby K is that of a cyborg.[7] Baby K symbolises what Donna Haraway underscores as the appearance of cyborgs in a myth: 'The cyborg appears in myth precisely where the boundary between human and animal is transgressed' (1991: 152). They 'signal disturbingly and pleasurably tight coupling' (1991: 152) and 'are ether, quintessence' (1991: 153). Miniaturisation remains a guiding feature of cyborgs. The qualifying suffix in Baby K's name is

7 'A cyborg is a cybernetic organism, a hybrid of machine and organism, a creature of social reality as well as a creature of fiction' (Haraway 1991: 149).

suggestive of this miniaturisation, something that Susan Stewart writes is 'effected by magic, not by labour' (1993: 60).

It is possibly by indicating this miniaturisation in introducing Baby K, and affirming later again in the subsequent stories, Nabarun attempts not only to place her in his magic realist literary world but to transpose her (and Parijat) in a cause-and-effect manner to the setting of the Iraq War (2003–2011):

> There is an infallible logic behind this magic. Bush has gone to Baghdad because he wants petrol. Baby K could also go to Baghdad because she drinks petrol. Parijat's role in Baby K's journey to Baghdad is thus similar to the role of American soldiers in Bush's journey to Baghdad. (Bhattacharya 2013: 43)

Baby K, however, stands in contrast to a '*Videodrome*, a man who has merged so completely with his medium that he has a cavity in his torso into which videocassettes can be inserted' (Conrad 2016: 188). The idea of consumption, on the other hand, is conjoint in Baby K and a *Videodrome*. A *Videodrome* has the capacity 'to equate thinking with browsing, surfing, or flicking through data' (Conrad 2016: 188). Baby K is both an object and a symbol of consumption, the latter becoming more evident when Nabarun builds her as a metonymy for USA's insatiate thirst for oil in the Middle East.[8]

In fact, through her explosive annihilating possibilities that are achieved ultimately, Baby K is perhaps in line with Nabarun's array of characters who belong to the socially and economically marginalised quarters of the society. Women characters in Nabarun's literary universe are sparse, yet Baby K retains and upholds a critique that is pertinent even today in the face of global consumption, the ongoing war on nature and natural species and ideological polarisations across the world. In this sense, Nabarun does not segregate Baby K from his marginal yet forceful characters who are capable of upturning the establishment. Perhaps by investing petrol-drinking and explosive

8 For example, see Prof. Sanjay Mukhopadhyay's lecture on Nabarun Bhattacharya and Baby K at Jadavpur University on 16 December 2018, available at https://www.youtube.com/watch?v=R8yzW6czKM4 (accessed on 28 May 2019).

qualities in her, Nabarun has chosen to indicate the collective uprising of disenfranchised groups of whom women as sex workers remain particularly evident; from US imperialism to local power structures Baby K symbolises the possibilities of that collective uprising from her sexual–social position.

The two stories in the beginning—'Baby K Parijat' and 'Baby K'—work together in establishing her character through chance encounters, intertextual references and historical alignments. In 'Baby K Parijat' the section following Parijat's chance encounter with Baby K describes in narrative brevity Parijat's quest for his love interest (Baby K). He roams aimlessly (perhaps in a non-achieving circular motion) on his moped looking hard for her. Nabarun alerts the readers that this is the only information we have and that nobody knows more than this, hence, there is no use in rambling any further (2013: 31). In this tenacious resolve of Parijat and in the monotony of repetition, Parijat is historically aligned to an event in the preceding story, 'Aguner Mukh'—a story set in the autumn festival of Calcutta in October 1972—where a mechanical female voice from Calcutta Telephones kept offering best wishes to the protagonist on the other side of the telephone receiver (Bhattacharya 2013: 14). As I have argued elsewhere, the 'predictability of a cultural ritual in its annual re-performance' works as a recurrent theme and image in Nabarun's writings (Basu 2015: 73). The banality of re-performance and ritual under social arrest that is pronounced in 'Aguner Mukh' is carried further in 'Baby K Parijat' and 'Baby K'. Yet, in this apparent non-eventfulness lies the possibility of subversive violence, a possibility embodied by Baby K as a cyborg, as a living Molotov cocktail.

The reference to Molotov cocktail repeats itself in Nabarun's stories. In one instance Nabarun reminds his readers of the use of Molotov cocktail and flame throwers by the American military in Vietnam to burn down the huts of poor civilians. In another, it assumes a human form capable of conducting a 'spectacular' explosion among the US military in occupied Baghdad. In the section entitled 'Every game has its end' in the story 'Baby K', Nabarun transposes Parijat and Baby K to occupied Baghdad, offering two possibilities: first, the one in which a Humvee vehicle of the American military is blown up by Iraqi guerrillas leaving the former panic-stricken and aimlessly firing bullets, one of which hits Parijat, leaving him dead; second, one in which the soldiers lust for Baby K and, in their attempt to make her smoke a cigarette (a Lucky Strike or Camel), instigate her explosive capacities. Nabarun writes: 'This is not a secret that there are no parallels to Americans in conducting irreparable mistakes (2013: 44). A Molotov cocktail like Baby K could explode as the smoke from the cigarette reached her LPG breath, but this remains one of the many probabilities that act refrain-like in Nabarun's narratives. Instead, it is Parijat whose blood is induced heavily with petrol as he ends up having sex with Baby K that night. Unaware of what the consequences of this contamination could be, Parijat is warned once again by the Fireman: 'What else will happen? You'll burn!' (Bhattacharya 2013: 45).

Perhaps, this is Nabarun's way of reminding what Haraway underlines as the potential of cyborgs: 'Cyborg gender is a local possibility taking a global vengeance' (1991: 181). This possibility, as a manifesto on cyborgs clarifies, can be achieved through affinity/affinities. The act of inducing petrol into her lover's body is nothing short of a political act, an act that binds characters like Parijat and Baby K in their non-entities within consumerist, dystopic city-space marked by uneventfulness. Such aggravating consumerism is captured aptly in the thoughts of Fireman who equates Baby K as a new kind of sex worker as mobile-phone cameras, DVDs and home theatres infiltrate the market. Baby K as a fictive, magic realist presence is a cyborgian political tool critiquing the 'phallogocentric' (or the 'blasphemous' in Haraway's argument), something that Sourit Bhattacharya and Arka Chattopadhyay sum up thus: 'Literature doesn't become political by imparting knowledge; instead it becomes political by questioning a "phallogocentric" (phallic as well as logocentric or reason-centric) construction of Statist knowledge by installing non-knowledge' (2015: 7). Baby K generates 'an effect as well as an affect of the bizarre' (Bhattacharya and Chattopadhyay 2015: 10).[9] While bizarre is

9 For example, note the Fireman's awe in hearing about a petrol-drinking sex worker, which he immediately aligns with another unbelievable incident—that of the police stealing the erstwhile Chief Minister Jyoti Basu's ATM card. See, https://www.thehindu.com/2004/11/06/stories/2004110602761100.htm (accessed on 28 May 2019).

strongly connected to how myths are generated and circulated, Baby K passes on from being a myth to a political language: 'There is a myth system waiting to become a political language to ground one way of looking at science and technology and challenging the informatics of domination—in order to act potently' (Haraway 1991: 181). In the following section I will discuss the symbolisms of fire and destruction that align Baby K as a marginal entity to a neo-capital global wasteland.

The Face(s) of Fire: The Mundane, the Unpredictable and the Hopeful in Baby K

In an 'Introduction' to his collection of short stories (1996), Nabarun writes about a daily life of the oppressed—'a strange kaleidoscope'—through which he sees himself and his times. It is a life governed by everyday coercion, neo-colonialist strategies and cultural imperialism; for Nabarun the lack of hope that was once a promise of the new century has ensued from the lack of the organised Left to critique itself, to bridge the ever-growing gap between ideology and practise (or more importantly, people). The theme of the mundane uneventful, as argued earlier, has been repeated through new symbols in Nabarun's works. In *Khelna Nagar (Toy City)*, for example, we find the accumulation of toxic explosive chemical waste as a result of a colony affected by civil war. It is a toxic waste that awaits uneventful days to succumb to death by a 'capitalist bomb'. In 'Fire Fight', the uneventful accumulation is replaced by the images of Calcutta buildings catching fire and burning relentlessly. Nabarun describes these burning buildings as uneventful enough not to make it to the front pages of newspapers in the same way that the fire brigade doesn't care to extinguish them, and news of murders, explosions and mass killings go unnoticed after a certain point.

There is a recurrence of the possible or the probable in the stories around Baby K. In Parijat's intrusion into occupied Baghdad on his moped (discussed earlier) or the sudden shift of scene in present-day Calcutta to a setting during the Second World War. In 'American Petromax', an inebriated Fireman reminisces about a reference to the powerful American Petromax brought into Calcutta during the

War. Nabarun writes: 'Parijat and Baby K's story however, remained documented as a nearly unknown historical event in the Calcutta of the Second World War' (2013: 52). In the narrative that follows, Baby K is abducted by American War soldiers who, like the previously visualised event in occupied Baghdad, propel her towards a violent explosion in a dance bar by allowing her to smoke a king-sized Marlboro cigarette. 'Later on the Military Forensic Bureau of the US army—after detecting the forty-one roasted corpses in that bar burnt to ashes, comprising thirty-seven water soldiers, three waiters and a burnt compressed pygmy female body—came to the conclusion that the explosion was just similar to the usual Molotov cocktails' (Bhattacharya 2013: 55). If Baby K explodes and kills a bunch of American soldiers with her in this instance, in the following story she leaves Parijat by choice for another man who is better capable of satiating her daily and ascending need for consuming petrol. While none of these events might seem plausible enough, they might be connected by what Nabarun introduces in 'Fire Fight' as the theory of the Black Swan; something that explains and links Baby K's explosion or her conscious departure to the inexplicable incidents of Calcutta buildings on fire.

Nassim Taleb (2007) explains black-swan events as those with high impact but less possibility of taking place. For example, the terror attacks of 9/11 recount as a black-swan event impacting immediate and ensuing global communities, perceptions and reactions. In Nabarun's world, and more potently in the world of Baby K, fire/explosion carries the promise of becoming a black swan event, of becoming the performable spectacular.[10] It is a world in which marginal creatures like Baby K (and Fyatarus) assert their subversive potentials through acts of desecration, blasphemy and explosion. In its truest cyborgian sense and self, Baby K defies the paternal/male control and upholds what Haraway sums up thus:

> Unlike the hopes of Frankenstein's monster, the cyborg does not expect its father to save it through a restoration of the garden—that is, through the fabrication of a heterosexual mate, through its completion

10 For a discussion on theatricality and performability in Nabarun Bhattacharya's short stories, see Basu, 'Texts of Power', *Sanglap* 2015.

> in a finished whole, a city and cosmos. The cyborg does not dream of community on the model of the organic family, this time without the oedipal project. The cyborg would not recognize the Garden of Eden; it is not made of mud and cannot dream of returning to dust. (1991: 151)

Cyborgs 'are the illegitimate offspring of militarism and patriarchal capitalism' (Haraway 1991: 151), and as illegitimate offspring they are often unfaithful to their origins and consider their fathers 'inessential'. The defiance of the cyborg is an outcome of centuries of domination by man over automatons. Victoria Pihl Sorensen in her analysis of sex workers, cyborgs and the image of the woman, terms this as the 'domestication of natural forces':

> In the history of automatons, a pattern emerges: The domestication, or power over, 'natural forces' corresponds with the simulation of animals, women, people of color, and children. 'Domestication of natural forces' is a metaphor for dominating those made to be other. (2018: 21)

Baby K belongs to a group of those who have been made to be the 'other'; as a sex worker her physical labour in male sexual appeasement is historically considered as non-work and, thus, disreputable. This double marginalisation—first as a woman, and then as a sex worker in a neo-liberal, consumerist capitalism—is asserted continually by the Fireman as he advises Parijat to 'leave the whore and return to the family'. Parijat remains a 'chaste hero', a veritable Spiderman who as Theresia Heimerl (2017: 55) puts it, spends his 'cinematic life languishing and pining' for his lady (in this case, in his love for Baby K).[11] Quite fittingly then, Nabarun devotes an entire story—'Parijat and Spider Man'—to situate this romance-driven helplessness in developing Parijat as a foil to the Fireman, the latter being representative of a profession marked by violent risks; the accompanying images of the a giant-like Fireman 'whose jumbo shadowy presence reminds one of the colossal yet idiotic statues of the Soviet era' (Bhattacharya 2013: 71). Baby K denies this

11 Heimerl in her discussion on sex and violence in comic book screen adaptations also shows how 'the entire field of sex and violence assumes quite a different colouring with regard to both heroes and villains if we examine traditions other than the Western, Christianity-based tradition'.

embodied structural binary of the male world that Parijat-Fireman stand for in their intoxicated philosophising and collective camaraderie. She denies this face of patriarchal capitalism writing[12] in the Cixous-esque sense of claiming her own body/individuality. She discards Parijat and moves onto choosing her clientele. Eventually, she proceeds even further to explode and demolish a consumerist-capitalist hierarchy inhabited equally by Parijat-Fireman or the American GI soldiers.'

The explosive finale in the last story, 'Baby K, Locusts, Parijat and US Imperialism', is perhaps more of a violent reminder than a closure for the narrative, containing within itself the immense possibilities of sustained violence, regeneration or extinction in what Lyotard (1984) terms as 'petite narratives'. In fact, the stories in the Baby K series do not follow a sequential logic/action pattern, leaving them rife with the promises of becoming such 'petite narratives' in themselves. The final story begins with locusts invading the Calcutta sky and city scape with a premonition of a 'black swan' event. Nabarun himself warns the readers of a remarkable twist in his own story but urges them to read two books—*No Easy Day* (2012), a military memoir by Mark Owen on the mission of killing Osama Bin Laden in Abbotabad, and *Counterstrike: The Untold Story of America's Secret Campaign Against Al Qaeda* (2011) by journalists Eric Schmitt and Thom Shanker. There is a dismissal in Nabarun's authorial voice here about half-baked knowledge/intellectualism that remains occluded in truths mediated by mainstream news/imagery/State machinery and does not see beyond it. It is an occlusion that ensues with surveillance and keeps global powers ongoing, the perforation of which is reified by Baby K at the end of the story. Animal imageries (especially of cats), as we have seen in Nabarun's other writings, are common and not in the least incidental to the plot(s). In this case, Nabarun stretches the images further, to include locust-like cyborg-insects in the shape of drones—'ultra-small flying robots capable of performing surveillance

12 Haraway (1991: 176), too, stresses on writing which 'is pre-eminently the technology of cyborgs' and discusses how '[c]yborg politics is the struggle for language and the struggle against perfect communication'. 'Cyborg writing is about the power to survive, not on the basis of seizing the tools that mark the world that marked them as other' (175).

in dangerous territory'.[13] In the final turn of events, as miniature drones (a part of CIA's secret operation) infest Baby K and Parijat's tiny cohabitation—a space that is dangerously volatile with cans of petrol and inflammable air—and a near volcanic blast kills real and cyborg-insects alike. 'A huge fire of this kind is possible only when a lot of Molotov cocktails explode together' (Bhattacharya 2013: 106) and the subsequent smell is like the 'scent' of funeral fires.

Conclusion

Bodies are maps of power and identity where cyborgs are not exceptions (Haraway 1991: 180). Through her cyborgian existence and more so in the final ghastly spectacle, Baby K pre-empts the possibilities of feminist collectives built through affinities and not by identity politics alone. Nabarun's forte as a rebel writer has always been to bring out the promises of violent revolutionary outcomes from within the people living at the margins, at the lower echelons of global centres and powers. Baby K is one such peripheral entity who, unlike the grandeur and restorative prescriptions of sci-fi superheroes, is simply able to assert her subversive presence. The scopes of reading and analysing Baby K beyond the cyborgian paradigm are multiple/multi-dimensional, and this chapter has attempted to situate the character within the ambit of ongoing global developments in feminist theories and practises.

References

Anthes, Emily (2013), *Frankenstein's Cat: Cuddling up to Biotech's Brave New Beasts*. Great Britain: Oneworld.

Anthes, Emily (2013), 'The Race to Create "Insect Cyborgs"'. *The Guardian*, 17 February. Available at https://www.theguardian.com/science/2013/feb/17/race-to-create-insect-cyborgs (accessed on 31 May 2019).

13 See, Anthes, 'The Race to Create 'Insect Cyborgs', 2013. It is interesting to note that '*Baby K Parijat* was published in the same year as that of Emily Anthes' book *Frankenstein's Cat*, the latter discussing the initiative of the US military in designing cyborg-insects functioning as surveillance machines (or drones).

Barnes, Sara (2018), 'Side-by-side photos show heart-breaking contrast of Western World and War-torn Middle East', *My Modern Met*, 30 November. Available at https://mymodernmet.com/digital-collage-artist-ugur-gallenkus/ (accessed 26 May 2019).

Basu, Priyanka (2015), 'Texts of Power, Acts of Dissent: Performability and Theatricality in Nabarun Bhattacharya's Short Stories', *Sanglap: Journal of Literary and Cultural Inquiry*, 2 (1) [Supplement]: 70–89.

Bhattacharya, Nabarun (2013), *Baby K Parijat*, Kolkata: Saptarshi.

——. (2004), *Khelnanagar*, Kolkata: Saptarshi.

——. (1996), *Nabarun Bhattacharyer Chhotogalpo*, Kolkata: Pratikshan.

Bhattacharya, Sourit and Chattopadhyay, Arka (2015), 'Nabarun Bhattacharya: An Introduction', *Sanglap: Journal of Literary and Cultural Inquiry*, 2:1 [Supplement]: 1–15.

Bhikkhu, Ñāṇamoli (1981), *Three Cardinal Discourses of the Buddha: The First Sermon, the Sermon on Not-Self, the Fire Sermon*, Kandy: Buddhist Publication Society.

Cixous, Helene (Summer, 1976), 'The Laugh of the Medusa', *Signs*, 1 (4): 875–893.

Conrad, Peter (2016), *Mythomania: Tales of Our Times, from Apple to ISIS*, London: Thames & Hudson.

Gopalakrishnan, Amulya (2016), 'Life in Post-Truth Times: What We Share with the Brexit Campaign and Trump', *The Times of India*, 30 June. Available at https://timesofindia.indiatimes.com/blogs/to-name-and-address/everything-but-the-truth-what-we-share-with-the-brexit-campaign-and-trump/ (accessed 26 May 2019).

Haraway, Donna (1991), 'A Cyborg Manifesto: Science, Technology, and Socialist-Feminism in the Late Twentieth Century', in *Simians, Cyborgs and Women: The Reinvention of Nature*, New York: Routledge, 149–191.

Heidegger, Martin (1962), *Being and Time*, trans. J. Macquarrie and E. Robinson, Oxford: Blackwell.

Heimerl, Theresia (2017), 'Rampant Lechers, Chaste Heroes: (De-)sexualised Violence in Comicbook Screen Adaptations', *Journal for Religion, Film and Media*, 3 (1) [Drawn Stories, Moving Images: Comic Books and their Screen Adaptations]: 45–57.

Lyotard, Jean Francois (1984), *The Postmodern Condition: A Report on Knowledge*, trans. G. Bennington and B Massumi, Minneapolis: University of Minnesota Press.

Mann, Steve (2003), 'The Post-Cyborg Path to Deconism', *CTheory*, 18 February. Available at https://journals.uvic.ca/index.php/ctheory/article/view/14705/5576 (accessed 26 May 2019).

Pihl Sorensen, Victoria E. (2018), 'Dolls Who Speak: Sex Robots, Cyborgs and the Image of Woman', MA diss., The City University of New York (CUNY), New York.

Ray, Dibyakusum (2015), 'The Vagabond's War Cry: the "Other" in Nabarun's Narrative', *Sanglap: Journal of Literary and Cultural Inquiry*, 2:1 [Supplement]: 52–69.

Sengupta, Samrat (2014), 'Ideology of the Lips: Feminine Desire, Politics of Images and Metaphorization of Body in Global Consumerism', in D. Banerjee (ed.), *Boundaries of the Self: Gender, Culture, Spaces*, 168–179, Newcastle upon Tyne: Cambridge Scholars.

——. (2015), 'Strategic Outsiderism of Fyatarus: Performances of 'Resistance' by Multitudes after 'Empire', *Sanglap: Journal of Literary and Cultural Inquiry*, 2:1 [Supplement]: 90–112.

Stewart, Susan (1993), *On Longing: Narratives of the Miniature, the Gigantic, the Souvenir, the Collection*, Durham: Duke University Press.

Taleb, Nassim Nicholas (2010), *The Black Swan: The Impact of the Highly Improbable*, London: Random House.

Dancing Skulls and Red Hibiscus Flowers: Nabarun's Tantric Imaginaries and the Radical Aesthetics of Subversion

Carola Erika Lorea

Nabarun Bhattacharya's capacity to criticise contemporary politics and denounce inequality with the weapons of the bizarre, the spectral and the trivial has led several scholars to discuss his oeuvre as magic realism. Rarely, however, the author's use of the magic and the occult has been specifically analysed in its vernacular contextualisation. Are Tantric-like characters a peculiar feature of Nabarun's novels? How are blood-thirsty and belligerent mother goddesses accommodated in his narratives and why? What is the influence and the contemporary relevance of esoteric and Tantric traditions in Bengali literature, and how do these relate to the work of Nabarun Bhattacharya? This chapter seeks to explore similar questions by discussing the popular imaginaries and the politics of cultural representation of Tantrism in Bengal, and the ways in which these have been employed in Nabarun's radical aesthetics. I will primarily focus on the novels, *Harbart*, *Bhogi* and *Kangal Malshat*. Before that, I will historicise and problematise both scholarly and popular representations of Tantra and the occult in modern Bengal to provide a backdrop for understanding Nabarun's fascination with, and use of, Tantric imaginaries.

At the sole mention of the term Tantra in modern Indian languages, most interlocutors react with shock and bewilderment, because of complex historical and sociocultural reasons that tinge the term with scandalous, illicit, transgressive and dark tones. While Tantra in the West has come to be associated with erotic New Age-ish thrills and sexual massage techniques, Tantra in South Asia is typically associated with black magic, powerful but frightening occult powers and immoral behaviours (Urban 2003; McDaniel 2012). The controversial status of

Tantra in the perception of Bengali intellectuals can be traced back to the 19th century, resulting from complex and composite ideas drawn from local orthodoxies, colonial views and Christian missionaries' concerns. British Orientalists and Indologists often depicted Tantrism as Hinduism's 'last and worst stage of medieval development' (Monier-Williams 1894: 112), or as the most 'degenerate phase' of Buddhism (Waddell 1895: 129). Colonial ideas were selectively internalised by bhadralok intellectuals, Bengali nationalists and religious reformers. Rational, universalistic and scientific concerns started to shape ideas on how a modern Indian religiosity ought to be. Tantric practises and traditions were found to be incompatible with this vision, as demonstrated by the scathing attacks on Tantra pronounced by reformers, such as Swami Dayananda Saraswati, or by Ram Mohan Roy, according to whom the Tantric cult of Kali involves unspeakable and offensive instances of debauchery (1817: 26–27). Unmerciful critiques abound also in the writings of Bhaktivinoda Thakur, the doyen of reformed Vaishnavism (Lorea 2018b). The Bengali Sanskritist Benoytosh Bhattacharyya described Tantric practises as 'diseases' to be treated and eradicated from modern India (1932: vii). In this light, Nabarun Bhattacharya's incorporation of Tantric imaginaries can be seen as part of the author's commitment to rehabilitate and recover elements otherwise forcefully left behind in the process of social change that constructed our perception of 'modernity'. Elements perceived as obsolete, marginal, superstitious or incompatible with a modern Indian nation are promptly brought to the fore in Nabarun's subversive creations. These, I would argue, include indigenous traditions and personalities that belong to religious and esoteric realms.

Not all representations of esoteric Indian traditions during British colonialism were scabrous and malicious. Bengali scholar Gopinath Kaviraj (1887–1976), for example, systematised the study of Tantric texts, creating an overarching ontological system, ennobling the philosophical and religious relevance of Tantra as a precious heritage. Strongly sympathising and intellectually glorifying the rich Tantric tradition, Arthur Avalon's books found a very enthusiastic reception among the Indian public (Taylor 2001: 144). The perception of Tantra as a valuable key to access higher knowledge and secret wisdom is what we find in the popular *Tantrabhilashir Sadhusanga* by Pramod Kumar Chattopadhyay (1941). This unusual travelogue recounts the spiritual wanderings of the author, who travelled extensively between 1911 and 1918 to meet and learn from living Tantric masters. Still widely read in West Bengal, the book's amateur-ethnographic accounts of ordinary and extraordinary events, mixed with personal notes and drawings, provided material for imagining, consuming and reproducing Tantra in modern Bengali literature.

In the same period, Western traditions of occultism, spiritualism and theosophy—rooted in fascination for, and reinterpretation of, 'Oriental' philosophy—powerfully entered the discourse of Indian politics and spirituality, cross-fertilised with local ideas and practises. The ubiquitous influence of occultism in the shaping of modernist aesthetics has only recently been taken into rightful consideration (Bauduin and Johnsson 2018). The impact of 'occulture' (the dissemination of occult discourses and topoi into mainstream culture, according to Christopher Partridge, 2004) on literary and artistic creations was not immune from transnational networks and global connections. The use of planchettes to mediate with the spirits of the dead had gained some popularity in late 19th and early 20th-century Calcutta. Spiritualist séances became an object of fascination and gained currency among Bengali writers. Rabindranath mentions his planchette experience in *Jibansmrti* (*My Reminiscences*, 1944). Bibhutibhushan Bandyopadhyay, one of the leading figures of literary realism, used to communicate with his deceased mother and first wife via the planchette (Bandyopadhyay n.d.). The same author employed a fictional Taranath Tantrik in two of his short stories in 1940 (see Bandyopadhyay 2016). Whereas, modernity has often been assumed to be stripped of magic and supernatural beliefs, as the culmination of the Enlightenment's faith in rationality and the teleological development towards complete secularisation, occult and paranormal phenomena permeate the very core of modern literature.

Nabarun Bhattacharya is certainly fascinated with the esoteric world of Tantric practitioners and their transgressive practises, which legitimise the infringement of middle classes' taboos. Tantric ritual consumption and offerings of alcohol, for example, are recurrent images in his novels (Lorea 2018). I suggest that the reason lies not only in the Tantric use of alcohol per se, but particularly in the Tantric subversion of notions of purity and impurity, a subversion that rehabilitates classes of people, objects and ideas otherwise oppressed by orthodox notions of cleanliness versus ritual pollution. The sacralisation of socially forbidden substances and behaviours, both in Tantric practises and in Nabarun Bhattacharya's novels, permits a transgression that is liberating on a ritual, cosmological and political plane. The Tantric concern for ritual subversion in order to encompass dualities is adopted in Nabarun's politically committed narratives, where the rich and the poor, the rational and the magic, the low and the high, the centre and the margins are intermingled and blurred, in the underlying commitment to equality. This operation is embedded in a longer literary history dealing with the cultural representation of indigenous knowledges and Tantric tenets. For example, the famous Bengali scholar of Shaktism, Narendranath Bhattacharya, found in Tantra an ancient projection of widespread Marxist ideals. He traced Tantra back to an archaic, matriarchal and class-free society based on the power of labouring classes, and juxtaposed it with patriarchal, caste-based Brahmanical Hinduism (Bhattacharya 1974). Narendranath Bhattacharya's Tantra is 'a religion of the oppressed masses' rooted in a kind of 'primitive socialism' (Urban 2003: 167). In a similar fashion, after Independence, a number of scholars of Bengali literature and folklore (that is Sudhir Chakrabarti, Shakti Nath Jha, Tushar Chattopadhyay) have brought under the limelight the literary corpora and spiritual practises of low-caste Tantric lineages (Baul-Fakir, Kartabhaja, Balahari, Sahebdhani, Matua, etc.) tracing them back to the Carvaka and Lokayata traditions of this-worldly, atheistic, anthropocentric and egalitarian thinkers. The complex relationship between Marxist ideals and traditional systems of spiritual knowledge are constantly interrogated in Nabarun's oeuvre, at times clashing and, at other times, supporting each other.

In *Harbart* (first edition 1993; see Bhattacharya 2011), the homonymous protagonist starts a small private business as a spirit medium. This proves to be a decently remunerative activity and a source of status for the otherwise mediocre and disempowered life of Harbart. The novel features some important themes in connection with the occult which will recur throughout Nabarun's oeuvre: Spiritism, death and the afterworld, the power of mantra, the meaning of sacrifice, the fascination for Tantric mother goddesses, the underlying questioning of rationality and its relation to communist ideas.

Harbart developed an irresistible attraction for the concept of death, at least since he found a skull and a few bones in an old trunk. This passion might be an inheritance from his grandfather Beharilal Sarkar, whose books Harbart enthusiastically adopted and employed for his spiritualist business, particularly *Poroloker Katha* (*All About the Afterworld*) by Mrinalkanti Ghosh, and *Poroloker Rahasya* (*The Mysteries of the Afterworld*) by Kalibar Bedantabagish. Nabarun uses excerpts from these two works as a narrative device with contrapuntal regularity. But he could have as well used any other cheap *Porolok*-themed booklet that abounded in popular Bengali literature at the time: *Moroner Pore* (*After Life*), *Porolok o Pretatattva* (*The Afterlife and the Science of Ghosts*), *Planchete Poroloker Kotha* (*On the Afterlife and the Planchette*), among others (Bandyopadhyay n.d.). On the other hand, Harbart's Naxalite nephew Binu, perhaps the only person to show empathetic and friendly sentiments towards him, would dismiss Harbart's fascination for the vernacular literature on the paranormal: 'all this rubbish [...] it's all fraud' (48).

And yet it is after hearing Binu's voice in a dream populated by crows—messengers of the dead and mediators of the ancestors—that Harbart remembers Binu's diary, hidden behind Kali Ma's poster in the puja room, initiating and substantiating his idea to start a business of communication with the dead. The dark goddess of the cremation ground appears generously in the pages of Nabarun's novels; for example, in Harbart's delirious vision: 'Pray to Shyama or Dakshini Kalika, Crinccring hum humhringhring ... Cringcring the secret Kali kringdring the funeral Kali om Kali frightful submerged bloodshot-eyed eager to eat flesh and skin' (110).

Nabarun indulges with sophisticated details in describing occultist methods and techniques that Harbart did or did not use, showing us his profound knowledge of 19th-century European spiritualism. Qualified as a 'sort of medium' and basically 'a freak' (68–69), Harbart did not use the American Fox sisters' 'rapping' strategy, nor did he employ invisible writing, like William Eglinton is believed to have demonstrated in Calcutta in 1881.

Occasional automatic writing and some attempts at psychometry could not suffice to place Harbart in the 'great tradition' (69) of Charles Richet (the French physiologist, born in 1850, interested in ectoplasm and psychic materialisations), Frederic Myers (born in 1843, pioneer of psychical research in automatic writing and the subliminal self) or with the contributors of William Stead's *Borderland* magazine (a publication that focused on spiritualism and psychical research, from 1893 to 1897). Harbart could not heal nor mesmerise anyone; nor could he compare with the fascinating Casanova, who used to pass himself as an occultist to impress women, or with the legendary Count de Saint Germain (125), presumably a Rosicrucian and an alchemist. Harbart is rather a disturbed social misfit depicted with sympathy and depth, who makes free use of indigenous as well as exotic ideas of death and beyond.

Nabarun's fascination for the anti-discursive and non-narrative power of language accompanies all the characters who walk on the uncomfortable edge between the obscure and the rational. In this sense, Harbart's obsessive and delirious mantra (cat bat water dog fish … cat bat water dog fish…) connects to the Fyataruṣ' absurd mantra for taking flight (*fyant fyant snai snai*), and also to Bhogi's incessant murmuring of secret and unintelligible syllables on his journey towards his decapitation. These characters are incarnations of Nabarun's critical stance against the hegemony of Western rationality. The latter is represented, in *Harbart*, by the annoying and arrogant characters forming the delegation of the Rationalist Association, who visit Harbart's room to take pleasure in humiliating and delegitimising him. Shouting and weeping, Harbart clumsily attempted to defend himself ('I am not lying. Ghosts exist. Ghosts will always exist'; 123) while the Rationalists threatened to prosecute and expose him publicly, incapable of any humane sympathy. 'What these creatures need to cure them is Stalin … If only this had been Stalin's era!' (ibid.), proclaims one of them, incidentally, remarking the unwritten pact of solidarity between certain rationalist and communist forces in their mission to delegitimise and suppress spirit mediums, folk healers and Tantric renouncers. This is corroborated in field-work-based scholarly literature. For example, according to June McDaniel's ethnography of Shakta Tantrics, during the Left Front government in rural West Bengal *sadhus* and practitioners have suffered tremendous persecution (McDaniel 2012: 148, 159). In Da Costa's work, leftist theatre in rural Bengal misrecognised a long history of indigenous health practises and goddesses of health in people's lives, posing the access to modern Western medicine in a mutually exclusive relation to the lived religion and healing practises (Da Costa 2013: VII).

Harbart ultimately explodes with an uproarious detonation inside the crematory oven, turning his pathetic death into the sounded, disrupting protest of a 'dead human bomb' (139). Harbart's final gesture is divested of weakness and mental insanity, and serves instead as an anticipation of the parable of Bhogi's self-immolation. This final sacrificial action, as absurd and bizarre as it may be, is better than no action at all. The quote that Nabarun borrows from Dwarkanath Ganguly—'Unless you offer great sacrifice/This India will never rise, never rise' (64)—can function as the rhetorical bridge between Harbart's bizarre and inadvertent resistance and Bhogi's lucid and premeditated self-sacrifice.

The novelette *Bhogi* (*The Expiator*; see Bhattacharya 2007) first appeared on *Baromas* magazine in 1993, the same year as *Harbart* was published as a novel. This meta-story recounts the short encounter of the city-dwelling Mithil with one of a particular class of creatures called Bhogi. In the evocative flash-forwarding incipit, a decapitated head rolls on the shore, rocked back and forth by the foaming waves in a dark and stormy night. The head has thick, long hair and a long beard. The cut running through the neck looks like the executioner had too many a glass of cheap country liquor. Nabarun will replicate and multiply the picture for the starting scenario of *Kangal Malshat* (*The War Cry of the Vagabonds*), where a multitude of rolling heads are brought by the high tide on the banks of the river Ganges, performing a grotesque 'skull dance' (2003: 8).

Despite his fairly high education in English medium, Mithil is an unemployed and unmarried youth maintained by an affluent aunt, and has just recently quit taking drugs. He has just returned from a religious folk festival observed in the Bengali ritual calendar as part of the *Gajon* celebrations, which the author describes elaborately. Self-mortifying pilgrims dance with sticks at the rhythm of frenzied percussions. The initiated devotees perform a *danse macabre* and the ritual jump from a high bamboo platform (2007: 68–70). It is significant to note that the antecedent of the main events takes place during *Gajon*, a ritual festival comprising practises of piercing, penances and self-mortification. Among these, *carak* (hook swinging) was banned in British India, while the ritual parade with dancing skeletons and skulls (*marakhela*, *mukhakhela* or *naramunda nritya*) was banned by the endeavours of Christian missionaries, and is still widely criticised by the Rationalist Association (Ferrari 2010: 187–189).

Parade of the Sannyasis Displaying Human Remains, As the Concluding Part of the Festival of *Gajon*, April 2010.
Photograph courtesy: AP/Press Association Image Associated Press

Mithil is brought there by his sort-of-guru, who speaks in a rural dialect and represents Mithil's 'guide' in this 'ethnic phase' of his life, introducing him to fairs, rituals and folk religious narratives (i.e. *bonbibirpala*, 70) which remain otherwise extraneous to the urban educated youth. Like much of *Harbart*'s astrological and spiritualistic intertexts, in *Bhogi*, indigenous and grassroots religiosity appears from the very beginning as an alternative knowledge to give sense to a capitalist and individualist reality permeated by ethical emptiness. Mithil's 'guide' conducts him to his first meeting with Bhogi, a mysterious character that never finds a clear-cut definition in existing social boxes; he is a *sadhu*, but not the 'classic type'. He comes to stay for a few days only, and then, after the ritual offerings (*bhog*) and the sacrificial beheading (*boli*), he dies (70). His mission is redemptive: he comes to drive away injustices, tyrannies and corruption (70, 113).

Like a reflection of the social imaginary of a Tantric *sadhaka*, Bhogi has thick hair, wild beard and worn out clothes. He reads people's minds and is able to predict the future. He generously hands out herbal remedies and protective amulets, in the fashion of a village *gunin*. He incarnates village wisdom, juxtaposed with urban intellectual knowledge. His rustic non-standard Bengali betrays his lack of formal education, while his only mention of his childhood reveals a context of abject poverty and displacement. In his words, 'bhogi' is not a personal name but rather a collective noun, like 'tiger', or 'crocodile' (86). From time to time, the world needs 'a' Bhogi, to expiate its ugliness.

Nabarun adorns the main story with scattered references to 13th-century-Christian flagellants, washing the planet's sins away by shedding their blood (73); the Babylonian ritual of treating a thief like a king for three days and then executing him; the self-immolation of Vietnamese monks (82); the self-afflicting practises during *Gajon*; the worldly renunciation of the intellectual protagonist of Tarkovsky's 1986 movie *The Sacrifice* (120), providing us with terms of comparison to locate Bhogi's agency. Bhogi (Pongal) is also the name of a South Indian festival. On that day, people discard or burn old, ugly and derelict things to regenerate the annual cycle of normal order, marking transformation and purification in the passage from the old to the new. The imagery of *Bhogi* freely flirts with Christian notions of atonement and self-sacrifice, scapegoat narratives and Tantric ritual catharsis. It simultaneously plays with the Indic mythological framework of the cyclical descent of avatars, who restore the degeneration of moral and cosmological order (*a-dharma*, a recurrent term in the novel).

Bhogi does not emerge as a passive sacrificial victim, but as a fully active political subject, a 'common man' dying in a 'poetic protest' (120).

In the concluding part, he walks to the seashore where his executioner awaits him while sharping the machete and polishing the stone where Bhogi will accomplish his destiny. At the end, the filmic meta-narrative is revealed: Bhogi walks off the set while holding his own decapitated head, an excellent artifact of the Madras Sundaram Studios, 'like a trophy' (119). Bhogi's sacrifice can only exist in the dreamlike world of cinematic representation; not in reality, where only speculators exist ('This is the year of the scam! *Ham sab chor hai*!' is the motto reiterated by one of the characters; 78). However, the director confesses that inspiration for the plot was freely drawn from real events that are said to happen in Assam (119): a state notoriously rich in Tantric lineages, black magic and Shakta pilgrimage sites—Kamakhya above all.

It is in Kamakhya, in fact, that Atmaram Sarkar has learned his esoteric knowledge (Bhattacharya 2003: 64). He is the revered ancestor of the lineage of the Choktars, the Tantric-ish beings that populate *Kangal Malshat*. Together with the Fyatarus, they mobilise the ungrammatical manifesto of an impossible revolution. These are remarkably collective entities: just like the Bhogi type, Choktars and Fyatarus are not personal names but rather collective nouns. The narrative structure moves away from individualism and empowers instead the collective force of the characters. Hence, Nabarun's fascination for sects, cults, guru-disciple circles, which encompass the individual and share the force of collectivity while countering mainstream conventions. The leader of the Choktars, Bhodi and his wife, Bechamoni, are insistently portrayed like a Tantric guru and guru-*ma*, respectively. 'Could they be of the Kapalika sect … like those you still read about nowadays on the newspaper for their human sacrifices?' (21), asks Borilal at the beginning of the novel, after the initial 'dance of the skulls' on the shores of the Ganga. Bhodi confesses later on in one of his usual fits of anger that he has accomplished the *sadhana* of the Aghoris under the guru-mentorship of a certain Datta Babu (143). Responding to the popular representation of Tantric preachers, Bhodi is often surrounded by a circle of devotees who generously offer him bottles of booze, while Bechamoni wears a garland of red hibiscus flowers, gets often possessed, ball-dances with high-class ghosts and pronounces mantras for obscure enchantments during her sleep. Like the stereotypical Tantric magicians, the Choktars host in their decrepit mansion a plethora of 'inauspicious events' (19) ranging from breeding ghosts to various sorts of curses and spells.

The worship of Kali, the sacred space of Kalighat—themes already present in both *Harbart* and *Bhogi*—and the celebration of Kali Puja occupy a prominent place in *Kangal Malshat*, particularly in their spooky and left-handed conjugation. A horde of ghosts of defunct rowdies, gangsters and Naxalites celebrates Kali Puja with an aerial bombardment of fireworks and an endless stock of booze. The ghosts engage in the 'red hibiscus competition' (ibid. 52): a deadly mix of alcoholic drinks, called 'the ancestor of cocktails', is poured in a giant drum, where a red hibiscus, the flower offered to the goddess, floats on the surface.

Kali worship was infamously associated by colonial observers to criminal thuggees, dacoits and perpetrators of political violence (Urban 2003: 73–85). Colonial politics of cultural representation have often associated Shakta and Tantric cults to subversive and violent insurrectionist groups. Unsurprisingly, the revolutionary army of sannyasis depicted in Bankimchandra's *Anandamath* (1882) are devotees of the Mother Goddess, who became a representation of the occupied motherland. The radical, anticolonial society of rebels articulated in Aurobindo's *Bhawani Mandir* (1905) similarly revolves around a religio-nationalist cult of the goddess. This history connects Nabarun's character Bhodi, the camouflage-clad Tantric guru, with military boots who heads a clumsy supernatural guerrilla, to older representations of Kali worshipers as politically violent and rebellious.

Throughout the text, Nabarun introduces excerpts from and references to premodern religious literature, devotional poetry and manuals of spirituality. The narrator sharply criticises the readers who are not familiar with this kind of literature. Educated Bengalis only bother about quoting Foucault, Bakhtin and Gramsci, like parrots (67), but they remain embarrassingly ignorant about indigenous religious and philosophical heritage. He cites, for example, the sayings of Nigamananda Saraswati (ibid.), the yogi who used to meditate on a leopard skin; the poems of Haribor Sarkar (121), the Matua *kabiyal* and saint-composer; and the Shakta doctrine exposed by Mahanambroto

Brahmachari (109). The readers are reproached for their alienation from local forms of knowledge, while the Marxist influence on urban Bengali intellectuals is to be blamed for the diffusion of cultural atheism (121). Nabarun opposes this tendency by showcasing his mastery on a vast repertoire of indigenous sources. To justify the credibility of the flying Fyatarus, for example, passages from the oldest texts of Hatha Yoga are quoted, comprising the *Shiva Samhita* and the *Gheranda Samhita*, together with stories from the lives of Christian saints and the prison memoires of Aurobindo (98–99). As already noted, Anglo–European material is playfully integrated or juxtaposed with indigenous countercultural traditions. The operation rehabilitates and rediscovers the potency of local, informal, non-institutional traditions as prototypes for alternative knowledges, capable of challenging the rationale of modern Western science and the ontological foundations of neo-liberal capitalism. Tantric practises function, in this sense, as the countercultural par excellence (Kripal 2012: 435–456). In his creolisation of Western spiritualism, ethnic magic and Tantric imaginaries, Nabarun Bhattacharya closely reminds us Usha Iyer's masterly discussion of the portrait of the Tantric in Hindi horror films (Iyer 2013). Coming from a history of prejudice, the Tantric appears in a number of movies, constituting the frightening 'Other' since the 1970s. The characters of this 'filmic folklore' came to inform much of the popular perception of Tantrism. In their semiotic osmosis, interweaving Western folkloric figures, African voodoo, motifs of Tantra, possession and occultism, these filmic Tantrics share several traits with Nabarun's Choktars.

Spiritual and occult realms of esoteric knowledge provide Nabarun and his characters with instruments and methods to deal with social injustice. In front of the failure of legal justice, Nabarun searches for a larger universal justice in the karma–dharma complex ('a' Bhogi comes to fix the *a-dharma* condition) or in the inexorable laws of astrology. 'Today is a day of great astrological alignments' informs us Bhodi at the beginning of the novel/insurrection: 'it's the divine play of Atmaram Sarkar' and his army of flying saucers, which are 'destined to dance every 150 years' (164) to give a temporary lesson to those in power. Astrological conjunctions and the manifestation of a universal destiny provide sense where human societies perpetrate senseless and selfish exploitation. Indigenous systems of knowledge, excluded by the inexorable imposition of the rationalist and secularist dogmas of modernity, are unearthed and valued as they have answers to deal with injustice and death. This aspect clearly links Nabarun's guru-esque sorcerers to their predecessor Taranath Tantrik, the powerful astrologer and intriguing orator who first appeared in Bibhutibhushan Bandyopadhyay's short stories. Taranath Tantrik achieved his success through the six short stories of Bibhutibhushan's son, Taradas Bandyopadhyay (1985), and with his novel *Alaatchakra* (2003). The two babus, dressed in white dhoti who are the eager listeners of Taranath Tantrik's incredible stories of extreme *sadhana* with corpses and spiritual training at the cremation ground, are presented to the readers while listening to the radio and smoking cigarettes at the tea stall. The radio announces the 1939 invasion of Poland by Hitler's forces. On this side, there is famine; on that side, there is a world war: both sides are marked with death. Is there any chance to understand and control death? This is the preamble to the first visit to the anachronistic and yet potent knowledge shared by Taranath Tantrik. It is the Tantric possibility of ritual transgression, and the systematic Tantric methodology of dealing with the frightening, the repulsive and the forbidden, that allows personalities like Taranath, Bhogi and Bhodi to represent, for the modern reader, a countercultural alternative endowed with hope.

To summarise, this article has discussed how elements borrowed from Tantric traditions figure in Nabarun Bhattacharya's work, and how Nabarun's interest for the spiritual, the spectral and the occult is inseparably connected to his radical aesthetics of subversion. The normalisation of the *Bhadralok* opinion on Tantric cults is subverted and employed in Nabarun's characters and plot design with a coherent shift from the spiritual to the political. On one hand, the interest and inclusion of esoteric dimensions, deployed with sophisticated erudition, is part of the author's characteristic style: in both language and content, Nabarun invariably takes the margins, the rejected, the non-standard and brings them to the fore. On the other hand, his work enacts a continuation of historical and literary Bengali ways of understanding, producing and consuming Tantric imaginaries. This attitude is evident in the artistic and cultural production that closely follows Nabarun's footsteps. Contemporary usage of the Tantric in Bengali cinema, literature and graphic novels suggests a continuation of Nabarun's legacy. The filmmaker Qaushiq Mukherjee (known as Q), for example, has recently directed a TV series based on the figure of *Taranath Tantrik* (2019), but complemented it with his typically indulgent, eccentric and pulp aesthetics. The same Qaushiq Mukherjee has directed a documentary movie *Nabarun* (2018). His interest in depicting the urban margins with obsessive focus on transgressing middle-class mores has led to the consideration of his cinema as a flag-bearer of Nabarun's aesthetic tradition. The artistic collective Gandu Sampraday (composed of Q, Surajit Sen and Sambaran) has authored a graphic novel revolving around the delirious life of Gandu, embedded in the glorified squalor of Kolkata's margins (see Gandu Sampraday 2019). The illustrations profusely employ Tantric visual vocabularies. The goddess Kali appears with insistence, uprooted from devotional contexts and inserted instead in an urban anarchic scenario as a hyper-sexualised representation of Bengali male anxieties.

A Contemporary Representation of the Goddess Kali in the Graphic Novel *Gandur Mundu* by Gandu Sampradaya (2019).

Contextualised within the background of the controversial historical relationship between Tantra, Victorian mores and bhadralok culture in Bengal, Nabarun's oeuvre and his legacy can be traced in several genres and media, encompassing Bengali vernacular productions. This short contribution suggested that Nabarun's use of Tantric imaginaries adopted the notion of subversion from the ritual context and transposed it into a political scale, where the repulsive becomes sublime, and the outcast becomes a vehicle towards a multi-layered liberation (*mukti*), intended simultaneously as spiritual salvation, and as freedom from social oppression.

References

Bandyopadhyay, Bibhutibhushan. (2016), *Bhoutik o Aloukik Golpo (Taranath Tantriker Golpo),* Dhaka: Bornayan.

Bandyopadhyay, Nilanjan. (n.d.), 'Pret Baithak', Nilanjan Bandyopadhyay. Available online: https://nilanjanbandyopadhyay.wordpress.com/other-writings/essays/প্রেতবৈঠক/ (accessed 27 May 2019).

Bandyopadhyay, Taradas. (1985), *Taranath Tantrik,* Kolkata: Mitra and Ghosh.

——— (2003), *Alaatchakra*, Kolkata: Mitra and Ghosh.

Bauduin, Tessel M. and Henrik Johnsson, eds (2018), *The Occult in Modernist Art, Literature and Cinema*, Cham: Palgrave Macmillan.

Bhattacharya, Nabarun. (2003), *Kangal Malshat,* Kolkata: Saptarshi Prakashan.

——— (2007), *Auto O Bhogi,* Kolkata: Dey's.

——— (2011), *Harbart,* trans. A. Sinha, Chennai: Tranquebar Press.

Bhattacharya, Narendra Nath. (1974), *History of Śākta Religion,* Delhi: Munshiram Manoharlal.

Bhattacharyya, Benoytosh. (1932), *An Introduction to Buddhist Esoterism,* Oxford: Oxford University Press.

Chattopadhyay, Pramod Kumar. (1941), *Tantrabhilashir Sadhusanga,* Kolkata: Ajit Srimoni.

Gandu Sampraday (2019), *Gandur Mundu*, Kolkata: Oddjoint.

Iyer, Usha. (2013), 'Nevla as Dracula: Figurations of the Tantric as Monster in the Hindi Horror Film', In M. Sen and A. Basu (eds), *Figurations in Indian Film*, 101–115, London: Palgrave Macmillan.

Kripal, Jeffrey. (2012), 'Remembering Ourselves—on some countercultural echoes of contemporary Tantric studies', in I. Keul (ed), *Transformations and Transfer of Tantra in Asia and Beyond*, 435–456, Berlin: De Gruyter.

Lorea, Carola E. (2018), 'Ghosts, Drunkards and Bad Language: Translating the Margins of Nabarun Bhattacharya's Kāṅāl Mālsāṭ', *Sanglap: Journal of Literary and Cultural Inquiry,* 5 (1): 36–50.

—— (2018b), 'Sectarian Scissions, Vaishnava Deviancy, and Trajectories of Oral Literature: A Virtual Dialogue between the Bengali Songs of Bhaktivinod Thakur (1838–1914) and Duddu Shah (1841–1911)', *ZeitschriftfürIndologie und Südasienstudien*, 35: 83–114.

McDaniel, June. (2012), 'Modern Bengali Śākta Tāntrikas: Ethnography, Image, and Stereotype', in I. Keul (ed), *Transformations and Transfer of Tantra in Asia and Beyond,* 147–164, Berlin: De Gruyter.

Monier-Williams, Monier. (1894), *Hinduism,* London: Society for Promoting Christian Knowledge.

Nabarun (2018), [Documentary Film] Dir. Q, India: Oddjoint.

Partridge, Christopher. (2004), *The Re-enchantment of the West: Alternative Spiritualities, Sacralization, Popular Culture and Occulture*, London: T&T Clark International.

Roy, Ram Mohan. (1817), *A Defence of Hindoo Theism in Reply to the Attack of an Advocate for Idolatry,* Calcutta: Rammohan Ray.

Tagore, Rabindranath. (1944), *Jibansmriti, in Rabindra Racanaboli vol. 17,* Shantiniketan: Visva Bharati.

Taranath Tantrik (2019), [Web series] Dir. Q, India: Hoichoi.

Taylor, Kathleen. (2001), *Sir John Woodroffe, Tantra and Bengal: 'An Indian Soul in a European Body?'*, London and New York: Rutledge Curzon.

Urban, Hugh B. (2003), *Tantra: Sex, Secrecy, Politics, and Power in the Study of Religion,* Berkeley: University of California Press.

Waddell, Laurence Austin. (1895), *The Buddhism of Tibet or Lamaism,* London: W. H. Allen.

The Revolt of the *Bête Machine*: Animality, Language and Resistance in *Lubdhak*

Aritra Chakraborti

'God, in the dream, illumined the animal's brutishness and he understood the reasons, and accepted his destiny; but when he awoke there was only a dark resignation, a valiant ignorance, for the machinery of the world is far too complex for the simplicity of a wild beast.'

—Jorge Luis Borges, 'Inferno, I, 32', *Dreamtigers*
(Borges 1964: 50)

I

On 28 May 2013, a small child somehow managed to fall into the gorilla enclosure at the Cincinnati Zoo and Botanical Gardens. Eyewitnesses claimed that the child had shown prior intentions of entering the enclosure. He had proceeded to climb the fence, and then lost his grip of the railings and plummeted around fifteen feet, into the moat around the enclosure. As the onlookers started to scream in panic, a silverback Western Lowland Gorilla named Harambe approached the boy. Shocked and distressed by the screams of the people, Harambe seemed to drag the boy through the shallow water of the moat. The Dangerous Animal Response Team (DART) was summoned, who proceeded to shoot and kill the gorilla, and 'rescued' the boy.[1] This was, apparently, a standard procedure where the life of a human visitor is always prioritised (Kim 2017: 2).

1 For a detailed study of the impact that Harambe's 'murder' had on the discussion about the condition of animals held in captivity, see Doyle 2017.

In the aftermath of Harambe's death, which some went so far as to call murder, protests erupted all over the world. Numerous animal rights activists questioned the logic by which the values of the lives of two creatures were weighed against each other. Threatened from manmade climate change, poachers and mining companies encroaching upon their natural habitat, the population of the Western Lowland Gorillas has declined catastrophically in the last few years (Rainey et al.: 2010).[2] Sparing Harambe's life and mounting a more constructive effort to rescue the human boy would not have seemed illogical for several extremely obvious reasons. Yet, decision was quickly made by the authorities: the life of the human was always more valuable than that of an ape, no matter how endangered the latter was. Harambe was killed even before the true meanings of his actions could be understood. For the zoo authorities, he was always a threat to the humans around him.

In captivity or in their natural habitat, animals live in a world that is constantly shaped, perverted, occupied and destroyed by a species that has staked their claim over the entire planet. Do animals have any logical existence beyond their naming, describing, classifying and analysing by humans? Humanity has benefitted from the contributions of animals in every walk of life: they have laboured and donated their bodies for consumption, scientific experimentations and various modes of commodification.[3] Even in relative freedom, animals live in forests which are constantly threatened by human action. As wild creatures, pets, 'samples' or 'produce', humans continue to manipulate and mutilate them, unmindful of the impact on the very being of animals. Even the pets, that humans profess to love, are often abandoned when their usefulness ends or when they become too expensive to maintain (Sharkin and Ruff 2011: 275–289).

This chapter studies Nabarun Bhattacharya's novella *Lubdhak* (2000), a fable where animals, similarly mistreated, revolt against their

2 For more details about Western Lowland Gorillas, their population and living conditions, see the WWF website: http://wwf.panda.org/knowledge_hub/endangered_species/great_apes/gorillas/western_lowland_gorilla/.

3 Nineteenth-century radical reformer, author and labour activist Samuel Bamford recognised the rights of the domesticated animals who contribute to the betterment of the human society yet suffer in the hands of their cruel masters. See Bamford 1967: 50.

largely ungrateful human 'masters'. While *Lubdhak's* premise might be fantastical, and the final solution to the problem of human apathy towards animals that this text proposes might be too catastrophic, the essential questions that it presents in front of the reader, mostly through the voices of its non-human protagonists, is nonetheless devastating in their seriousness.

It is safe to say that despite years of coexistence, humans are yet to fully comprehend animals. There is always a fear of the unknown that lurks behind the veils of familiarity: the pet dog needs to be leashed, neutered, spayed and vaccinated; the bull in the farm needs to be constantly tied to his station, the faithful horse is trained to breed and pull the cart and race for the amusement of his human masters, but summarily put down when the humans are harmed. History, though, is not without the examples of the occasional animal resistance to human occupation of the planet (Hribal 2011). This chapter analyses how, in Nabarun's novel, animals use various methods, especially coded language that humans cannot comprehend, to counter a world of human dominance.

II

What is an animal, anyway? Animality is often defined as something that exists not only on its own, but also as an example of *everything a man is not*. One of the main differences that has come to define animality as fundamentally different from humanity is the apparent lack of rational imagination, or the inability to express complex rational ideas using structured language. Ancient Greeks were convinced that animals lacked the power of logos (*λόγος*) or reason (Sorabji 1993: 7). Once, after Plato had described 'man' as a 'hairless bipedal animal', Diogenes arrived at Plato's Academy the next day, holding a plucked cock as an example of what Plato's idea of a man was (Diogenes 2012: 32). This was Diogenes's way of reminding the great Greek philosopher that there was more to humanity than the mere physical description. While Plato's most famous student Aristotle had given animals and plants the 'scientifically proven' right to possess souls, he did not give them the ability to 'reason' or the capacity of 'rational thoughts' (Johansen 2012:

74). Descartes, on the other hand, thought that animals were soulless machines (*bête machine*) that functioned like clockwork engines (Baker and Morris 1996: 34–36). Also, one of the most important ways in which Descartes had differentiated between animals and humans was that humans had access to the use of a more complex form of language, something animals could not be a part of.

These theories, while largely contributing to the crippling anthropocentric bias of Western biological sciences, did not go unchallenged (Cottingham 1978; Harrison 1992). Jeremy Bentham in 1789 had questioned this obsession with the superiority of cohesive language, and advocated that the focus should be shifted to the very wellbeing of the animals (Bentham 1907: 342).[4] Nevertheless, the idea of the animal, or the 'brute', as something that was essentially beneath the human being, had been cemented in the Western mind by mid-17th century. Talking animals, a common metaphor in children's fiction, therefore, attracted more complex and darker interpretations. As a terrifying underbelly of adorable talking animals that populate children's fiction, the Western canon is littered with examples of loquacious animals that try to trick humans with their powers of speech. This usurpation of language often appears as a mark of evil. In European folktales, the Devil often appeared as a talking animal—at times functioning as the witch's familiar (Wilby 2011; Klaits 1985). For every innocent sheep, like the one found in the poetry of William Blake, there was a talking wolf trying to lure Little Red Riding Hood away from safety.

In recent times, philosophers have tried to adopt a more nuanced vision of animal existence. Martin Heidegger proposed a new interpretation of the animal–man difference through his exploration of the various facets of *Dasein* (existence), whereby, man, the rational

---

4 Bentham's main question was the boundary that separated humans from animals, and the logic behind the imposition of such a boundary:

> 'What else is it that should trace the insuperable line?… But suppose the case were otherwise, what would it avail? the question is not, Can they reason? nor Can they talk? but, Can they suffer?'

See Bentham 1888: 311

animal, is not merely something that exists, but attempts to *exist in connection with the world that it inhabits* (Heidegger 1962: 209). This is where the very nature of the existence of man is different from that of any other object or animal. Man is not merely the entity that exists; man is also the existing being that can locate itself within a discourse about its existence. Heidegger points out that the Greeks, the original proponents of the notion of man being the *animal rationale* or the thinking animal, had no word for 'language'. For the Greeks, the essence of language was 'discourse' (Heidegger 1962: 208–209). Since *λόγος* entered the Greek philosophical canon primarily as a form of assertion, *this* was the kind of discursive paradigm by which they understood their very rudimentary sense of *Dasein*. The connection between mere *expression* and *language*, therefore, is problematised to include not only the idea of *rational use of language*, but the effort to rationally express oneself beyond the scope of instinctual existence.

Heidegger went on to make further distinctions about the nature of *Dasein* of different entities. The stone, or any other inanimate object, for that matter is 'worldless'. It is unaware of its existence, and its existence is defined only by the perception that other living beings have about it. The man, on the other end of this spectrum, is the 'worldmaker', in the sense that humans are *attuned* with the world, making themselves accessible to the world and, at the same time, having access to the world. The animals, however, are 'poor in the world'; they have the capacity to exist, and be aware of their existence, but they are not attuned with the world (Heidegger 1995: 186–200). Non-human creatures do not perceive the world beyond the primary instinctual drivers of their actions such as self-preservation, sustenance and procreation. Beyond these basic needs, animals do not know how to interact with the world that surrounds them, like humans do (199–208).

Heidegger's reinterpretations put subtle chains of human superiority on animality. One can never ascertain if Heidegger was an inspiration behind Nabarun's vision of animal suffering and rebellion in a human world. His non-human protagonists, though, traverse an anthropocentric inferno that is enformed by Heideggerian notions of human superiority. Here they are, in every sense of the world, the poor and the dispossessed, constantly upstaged, hunted, hurt and persecuted up to a point where they do not see the possibility of restoring balance in the world. They cannot inform their human oppressors that the violence inflicted by them is driving the animals into a corner from which there may not be a way back.[5]

The main characters in *Lubdhak* are stray cats and dogs of Kolkata. Gypsy (a former pet, abandoned by his 'human masters') and Kangajano (literally, someone whose ears have grown anew) are the two dogs. Along with them, there is a cat who remains unnamed throughout the novel. Tortured and abused, all three bear witness to and, eventually, participate in a mass revolt, by leaving Kolkata in the form of a silent march, utterly rejecting the mastery that their human masters claim upon them.

III

Lubdhak begins with a city that has lost one major element from its soundscape—the sound of non-human animals (Nabarun 2010: 383).[6] The city lies on the brink of an apocalypse: the dog-star Lubdhak (Sirius), angered by the suffering of the animals in this city, has sent a planetoid hurtling towards Earth, headed straight for Kolkata. As the humans of the city stare at Armageddon, the animals, who know what is coming, have already left. For creatures with superior intelligence, linguistic capabilities and all the machinery around them to play with, humans are incredibly out of touch with their environment. They may be able to speak, write and read in all the languages that they have created, but they cannot read the languages of Earth as easily as animals can (Hough 2010: 58–85). Animals can sense disasters from quite some distance—temporal or spatial (Kirschvink 2000). What remains bafflingly difficult for humans, had become a matter of everyday life for animals (Tributsch 1982).

5 For a comparative analysis of the 'othering' of animals in fictions featuring 'intelligent animals', see Dibyakusum Ray's article, 'The Mute, the Stoic and the Rebel: Animals in the Works of Mikhail Bulgakov and Nabarun Bhattacharya' (2016).

6 'Lubdhak' was first published in the Puja edition of *Disha Sahitya* in 2000. In 2006, a single volume edition was published by Abhijan Publishers. For this chapter, the quotations have all been sourced from *The Complete Novels of Nabarun Bhattacharya* (2010). All the translation of Nabarun's novel are mine.

It all began with a drive to cleanse the city of stray cats and dogs. Cleansing of cities, however, is not an entirely novel concept. Cities are some of the grandest metanarratives of modern human society; each ruling political class tries to control the growth of the city. They modify its various parts to suit their idea of development as per their own political and social ideology. Encasing all the different voices, ethnicities, cultural, religious and political voices that animate a modern metropolis (Certeau 1984: 91–130; Lefebvre 2003: 103–114), though, a city is always the product of urban planning policies that shape its identity—policies that are controlled by people who have their own agenda. The city is, thus, a text that is continuously being written by whoever is in power. At times, forceful attempts to remodel a city into its most desirable shape have yielded tragic results. In 1996, reports emerged that in Mexico City, street children were being persecuted and killed as a part of the country's war on drugs and crime. Similar incidents have been reported from major cities in Brazil, Guatemala, El Salvador, Colombia and Argentina in South America (Sluka 2000: 5—6; Breuil and Rozema 2009). Vulnerable sections of the cities' population were systematically targeted and eventually removed from the cityscape one way or another. In Brazil, for example, these death squads operated at a time when the country saw tremendous economic development. The cleansing of the cities was a necessary reflection of the country's assumed prosperity (Inicardy and Suratt 1998). Indian cities do not have an innocent history in this department either (Patel 1990). Recently, during Ivanka Trump's 2017 visit to Hyderabad, the city authorities rounded up as many beggars as they could find and confined them to temporary shelters (Burleigh 2018: 300–301).

The municipal authorities in *Lubdhak* had the task of ridding the city of its stray animals. In a post-globalisation world, cities around the world seem to have developed a compulsion to mimic their most prosperous counterparts (Mayer 2000: 141–156). Even a teeming, largely unplanned patchwork of a city like Kolkata must rid itself of its unwanted, humans and non-humans alike to project an image of unblemished prosperity. The animal protagonists of *Lubdhak*, in fact, recognise this as the root cause for the proposed animal-genocide (Nabarun 2010: 399). The proposed methods, however, are quite disturbing. Nabarun presents these proposals as arguments and counterarguments, evaluating their merits and demerits. The proposals include shooting the dogs, dropping poisoned meat in different parts of the city so that the stray dogs can eat them and die and routine culling of the pups in order to curb the escalation of stray population. This third 'solution' comes straight out of the playbooks of the death squads and paramilitary juntas of Latin American countries (Nabarun 2010: 390–391). These proposals, however, are shot down because the authorities do not want to disturb the sentiments of the citizens in any way. Bullets cost a lot of money and the noise disturbs the peaceful atmosphere of the 'respectable neighbourhoods', the poisoned meat can be consumed by the beggars and the homeless, the people in charge of killing puppies might take pity and not kill them. At one point, it is suggested that such operations should happen on days when the schools remain closed in the city so that children do not get affected (Nabarun 2010: 392, 399).

Yet another rejected solution involves putting the animals in the gas-vans, and slowly injecting carbon monoxide into the chambers containing the animals, suffocating them to death. To burn the carcasses, the authorities propose the construction of furnaces that will function for as long as it takes to turn every carcass into ash. Appreciative as they are of the merits of this proposal, the authorities recognise the similarities with Adolf Eichmann's 'Final Solution' and reject this plan, determined to avoid bad press (Nabarun 2010: 392). In the end, though, the proposal that gets selected is the one involving capturing dogs using large tongs, and then putting them in *pinjrapoles* (shelter for old and, often abandoned, animals), designed by the former British government. Here, dogs will be kept without any food and water and, the authorities hope, will eventually die on their own (Nabarun 2010: 393).

As the animal-culling operation escalates, news also spreads through non-human grapevines. Years of living with humans, and surviving their whims and gratuitous violence, has given the animals the necessary grip on human language. While the humans continuously struggle to fathom the intentions of stray animals, animals have no problem in understanding the speech of humans.

In one scene, an SUV stops by the dirty yard where Kan-gojano and Gypsy are staying. On the radio, the evening news is being broadcast, with the newscaster giving details of the dog-catching operation that is sweeping across the city. Gypsy and Kan-gojano overhear to comprehend what the human newscaster is saying (Nabarun 2010: 398–399). This also acts as a catalyst for overcoming the natural inter-species rivalry, as the cats and dogs forge an alliance.

The animal-protagonists of *Lubdhak* find themselves at a critical point of animal-history—a narrative that blends animal mythology and the history of the animals' survival in a human-governed environment. While humans remain unaware of this, entities from animal-myths start shaping the course of the story. Shadow-dogs, in all probabilities the spirits of the dogs that have lived in the city before, sprint across the sky, bearing the news of the animal-catching operations that the authorities are planning in earnest, and animals being confined in *pinjrapoles* that function as evil places in animal urban legends where they are kept in terminal captivity. Facing this non-natural threat to their existence, animals use their own version of language in order to form a working resistance against human cruelty.

As it is, dogs and cats possess hearing ranges that are far superior than what humans can access, along with superior olfactory abilities (Miklosi 2007: 3–5; Heffner and Heffener 1985: 85–88). This physiological ability forms the basis of metaphorical language that the non-humans use in *Lubdhak* to communicate amongst each other, and organise against their human oppressors. However, this language is inaccessible to humans not merely because of its 'non-humanity', but also because humans cannot imagine that animals can use language to forge emotional bonds within their own communities. This is where Nabarun flips the power-structure of linguistic advantage. Dog-volunteers travel through the city, risking their own lives to alerting others about the dangerous turn of events. Groups of dogs and other stray animals gather in abandoned parts of the city, where humans do not venture, apart from the homeless of the city (Nabarun 2010: 406–407). Dogs also confuse the civic authorities by 'camouflaging' whatever information they were supposed to convey or comprehend.[7] Aged dogs assemble in large groups at crossroads throughout the city; every time a dog-catchers' van appears, they calmly amble towards the humans and start giving themselves up (Nabarun 2010: 402–403). Confused animal-behaviour experts start debating if this is a natural response of a community of animals who have made peace with their fate, or if this is an acquired, 'unnnatural' response to a situation (Nabarun 2010: 402–403). A sense of unease spreads amongst humans as the behaviour of dogs start altering throughout the city. Used to delimiting the scope of canine linguistic abilities to a few basic gestures, humans become extremely confused when they find that once the aged dogs are thrust into the *pinjrapoles*, they simply sit quietly without trying to defend themselves (Nabarun 2010: 404). While the human scientists and zoologists agree on observing these dying animals for a few days, the machineries of the modern, rationalist state start buckling under the pressure of the collective actions of a community they can no longer comprehend. The scientists observe dogs in *pinjrapoles* are gazing upwards at the sky, concentrating on the dog-star Sirius. For a while, they even flirt with the idea that the dogs are praying (Nabarun 2010: 405). This idea, though, is quickly discarded as too fantastical. Scientists petition the government to provide some food and water to the dogs in *pinjrapole* 1 so that they can study their behaviour for a little longer. Everything, they insist, is for the betterment of science only.

The dogs, it seems, are indeed praying to someone that the humans do not expect, though this is a god of their own making. A terrifying figure of a huge black hound, with tall pointed ears, terracotta skin and flaming red eyes that appears in *pinjrapole* 1. Panic spreads amongst the scientists when observers start reporting frequent sightings of this demonic figure in various dog-gaols in the city. Some speculate that this is Anubis, the ancient Egyptian deity of afterlife. Scared scientists urge the authorities to open the *pinjrapole*s, but dogs just refuse to

7 Camouflaging information is a common practise during war and conflict. As contact between two language-using communities intensifies, so does the use of codified language, that allows communicators to withhold information. Camouflaged language essentially pretends to be something else, thereby, deferring the decoding of meaning. See Footitt and Kelly, *Languages at War: Policies and Practices of Language Contacts in Conflict* (2012).

come out. At any rate, most of the dogs in *pinjrapole*s 2 and 3 have died by this time, and those in *pinjrapole* 1 refuse to come out even after the gates are opened. They just stand inside and keep on praying to Anubis (Nabarun 2010: 414–415). The international scientific community initially tries to dismiss the sightings of Anubis as hoax, concocted by the addled brains of Third-World hacks, but the embassies of the US, the UK and Germany start evacuating their officers from Kolkata (414–415). Undetected by the limited capabilities of human language or scientific faculty, the Shadow-dogs start sprinting across the city, led by the legendary Soviet dog, Laika—the first animal sent to space and left to die in a burning capsule. As this is the final signal for the dogs and cats waiting in various hiding-spots, the final exodus begins. Non-human animals start abandoning Kolkata. They have seven hours to get out of the range of impact of the planetoid that Sirius has sent hurtling towards Earth, and its target is Kolkata (Nabarun 2010: 414).

In Adam Roberts' *Bête* (2014), a novel that explores similar themes, talking animals try to tell their human captors and executioners about the pain that they are inflicting upon them. In *Lubdhak*, though, such an option is foreclosed because for years, non-humans have tried to tell their human counterparts about their problems, but they have only been ignored. Their bodies are mutilated in the name of science, and eventually humans have applied the findings of those scientific studies upon other humans. That barrier of patience, therefore, has already been broken. The only time non-humans contact the humans in this novella is when the outbound silent procession of stray animals choke the roads of the city. As humans stand helplessly in this sea of non-humans, with helicopters from various international news agencies whirling above, covering this strange exodus, little puppies walking alongside their mothers address the humans one final time in a chilling monologue. They tell them that it is because of the injustice inflicted upon them that the animals were now being compelled to evacuate the city. 'You can remain here, with your city, shops, hotels, knives for killing chicken … keep your *pinjrapole*s, and go there for holidays if you want to. Thank you, but we are leaving' (Nabarun 2010: 412). The puppies remind the humans that it is their enormous hatred, ignorance, greed and heartlessness that have destroyed everything. Humans have betrayed the planet: they are traitors to the living beings for the way they have destroyed the planet through various polluting mechanisms. But, of course, the humans are so busy with their 'superior rational intelligence', that they can never hear what the animals are saying. Now, everything is over. Humans can live on as much as they want in this world; the animals want to be out of it (412). As the humans stand dumbstruck in front of this great procession, the non-humans of Kolkata proudly exit the moribund city. In the sky, across the empty expanse of space, the planetoid keeps hurtling towards Kolkata.

What *Lubdhak* presents in front of us is a description of an organised resistance, carried out by the non-humans against an occupying force that is vastly superior to them in technology and firepower. Nabarun borrows extensively from the history of resistance movements to create the communication methods of the animals. During the Nazi occupation of Warsaw, for example, couriers carried messages between various divisions of the Warsaw Resistance using codes (Rotem 1994: 66–67). However, resistance fighters were by no means the only people to use coded messages for communication and evading the authorities. In Soviet Russia, where the entire society was shrouded in one of the most sophisticated and elaborated network of censorship ever devised, the general populace learned to communicate in codes, often in whispers. Using language in order to bypass the censors became a way of life.[8] More recently, during the ongoing 'Umbrella Movement' in Hong Kong, the protesters have developed various sophisticated methods of coded communication in public spaces and on social media (Lee et al. 2017: 457–469). Persecuted, hunted and standing on the brink of certain arrest and torture, resistance fighters and civilians had perfected the art of subverting everyday language to avoid the clutches of the law. These are also example of weaponisation of language, not merely for using it for armed resistance, but also for survival, for letting others in the community know where to find the safehouses for hiding, for protecting others who might be less able to stay beyond the reach of the authorities. In *Lubdhak*, the animal protagonists do not use their

---

8 For a more detailed study of private life in Soviet Russia, see Olando Figes, *The Whisperers: Private Life in Stalin's Russia* (2008).

own coded language to attack their human counterparts, but they certainly use it to collectively reject the senseless authorities of their human occupiers.

IV

The germinal idea behind *Lubdhak*, as explained by Nabarun in an introductory note to the novella's first appearance in the Puja issue of *Disha Sahitya* magazine in 2000, lay in Fran Trutt's attempt of bombing the offices of US Surgical Corporation in 1989. While US news outlets were quick to brand Trutt as an ecoterrorist and hater of capitalism, Trutt herself maintained that she was moved by the inhumane ways in which dogs were experimented up at US Surgical's research and development facilities.[9] More often than not, the main excuse behind this has always been the pursuit of knowledge, and the desire to actually 'know' animals for what they are (Seligman and Maier 1976: 3–46). Yet, in this short-sighted pursuit of asserting themselves over the world, humans never really tried to comprehend what the animals were trying to say. In *Lubdhak*, the animals turn the assumed human linguistic superiority on its head. Language becomes a vehicle that allows the animals to eventually reject the superiority of humans. Here, animals did not need a human vigilante like Trutt. They could take matters in their own paws, and eventually carry out a coup of epic proportions that rocked humanity.

References

Baker, Gordon P. and Katherine J. Morris (2002), *Descartes' Dualism*. London: Routledge.

Bamford, Samuel ([1905] 1967), *Autobiography*. London: Frank Cass & Co.

Bentham, Jeremy ([1789] 1888), *An Introduction to the Principles of Moral and Legislation*. London and Oxford: Clarendon Press.

Bhattacharya, Nabarun. ([2000] 2010), 'Lubdhak' in *Upanyas Samagra (Collected Novels)*. Kolkata: Dey's.

9 For a detailed account of the Fran Trutt incident, see Deborah Rudacille, *The Scalpel and the Butterfly* (2014).

Borges, Jorge Luis (1964). *Dreamtigers.* Austin: University of Texas Press.

Breuil, Brenda Carina Oude and Ralph Rozema (2009), 'Fatal imaginations: death squads in Davao City and Medellín compared', *Crime, Law and Social Change.* 52 (4): 405–424.

Burleigh, Nina (2018). *Golden Handcuffs: The Secret History of Trump's Women.* New York: Simon And Schuster.

Certeau, Michel de. (1984), *The Practice of Everyday Life*, translated by Steven Rendall. Berkeley: University of California Press.

Cottingham, John. (1978), '"A Brute to the Brutes?": Descartes' Treatment of Animals', *Philosophy.* 53 (206): 551–559.

Diogenes. (2012), *Sayings and Anecdotes: with other popular moralists*, translated by Robin Hard. London: Oxford University Press.

Doyle, Catherine (2017), 'Captive Wildlife Sanctuaries: Definition, Ethical Considerations and Public Perception', *Animal Studies Journal.* 6 (2), 55–85.

Figes, Orlando (2008), *The Whisperers: private life in Stalin's Russia.* London: Penguin.

Footitt, H. and M. Kelly (2012), *Languages at War: Policies and Practices of Language Contacts in Conflict.* London: Palgrave Macmillan.

Harriosn, Peter (1993), 'Animal Souls, Metempsychosis, and Theodicy in Seventeenth-Century English Thought', *Journal of the History of Philosophy.* 31 (4): 519–545.

Heffner, Rickey S. and Henry E. Heffner (1985), 'Hearing Range of the Domestic Cats', *Hearing Research.* 19: 85–88.

Heidegger, Martin. (1962), *Being and Time*, translated by John Macquarrie and Edward Robinson, Oxford: Blackwell.

—— ([1983] 1992), *The Fundamental Concepts of Metaphysics: World, Finitude, Solitude*, translated by William McNeill and Nicholas Walker. Bloomington: Indiana University Press.

Hough, Susan Elizabeth (2016), *Predicting the Unpredictable: The Tumultuous Science of Earthquake Prediction.* Ithaca: Princeton University Press.

Hribal, Jason (2011), *Fear of the Animal Planet: the hidden history of animal resistance.* California: AK Press.

Inciardi, James A and Hilary L Surratt 'Children in the Streets of Brazil: Drug Use, Crime, Violence, and HIV Risks', *Substance Use And Misuse.* 33 (7): 1461–1480.

Johansen, Thomas Kjeller (2012), *The Powers of Aristotle's Soul.* Oxford: Oxford University Press.

Kim, Claire Jean (2017), 'Murder and Mattering in Harambe's House', *Politics and Animals.* 3: 1–15.

Kirschvink, Joseph L. (2000), 'Earthquake Prediction by Animals: Evolution and Sensory Perception', *Bulletin of the Seismological Society of America*, 90: 312–323.

Klaits, Joseph (1985), *Servants of Satan: The Age of the Witch Hunts*. Bloomington: Indiana University Press.

Lee, Francis L. F. et al. (2017), 'Social media use and university students' participation in a large-scale protest campaign: The case of Hong Kong's Umbrella Movement', *Telematics and Informatics*. 34: 457–469.

Lefebvre, Henri ([1970] 2003), *The Urban Revolution*, translated by Robert Bononno. Minneapolis: University of Minnesota Press.

Lewis, Simon and Mark Andrew Maslin, 'Defining the Anthropocene', *Nature*. March: 171–180.

Mayer, Margit (2005), 'Urban social movements in an era of globalisation' in *Urban Movements in a Globalising World*, edited by Pierre Hamel, Henri Lustiger-Thaler and Margit Mayer. London: Routledge.

Miklósi, Ádám (2007), *Dog Behaviour, Evolution and Cognition*. Oxford: Oxford University Press.

Rainey, Hugo J. et al. (2010), 'Survey of *Raphia* swamp forest, Republic of Congo, indicates high densities of Critically Endangered western lowland gorillas *Gorilla gorillagorilla*', *Oryx*. 1 (3): 124–132.

Roberts, Adam (2014), *Bête*. London: Gollancz.

Rotem, Simha (1994), *Memoirs of a Warsaw Ghetto Fighter*. London and New Haven: Yale University Press.

Rudacille, Deborah (2015), *The Scalpel and the Butterfly: The War Between Animal Research and Animal Protection*. New York: Farrar, Straus and Giroux.

Seligman, Martin, and Steven F. Maier. (1976) 'Learned Helplessness: theory and evidence'. *Journal of Experimental Psychology: General*. 105 (1): 3–46.

Sharkin, Bruce S. and Lisa A. Ruff (2011), 'Broken Bonds: Understanding the Experience of Pet Relinquishment' in *The Psychology of the Human-Animal Bond: A Resource for Clinicians and Researchers*, edited by Blazina, et al. New York and Heidelberg: Springer.

Sluka, Jeffery (2010), *Death Squad: The Anthropology of State Terror*. Philadelphia: University of Pennsylvania Press.

Sorabji, Richard (1993), *Animal Minds and Human Morals: The Origins of a Western Debate*. Ithaca: Cornel University Press.

Tributsch, H (1982), *When the Snakes Awake: Animals and Earthquake Prediction*. Boston: MIT Press.

Wilby, Emma ([2000] 2011), 'The Witch's Familiar and the Fairy in Early Modern England and Scotland', *Folklore*. 111 (2): 283–305.

Machine, Bio-Politics and Death in Nabarun Bhattacharya's Fiction

Arka Chattopadhyay

This chapter examines Nabarun's portrayal of machines in the order of late-capitalist bio-power. I will complicate the problematic network that exists in bio-political capitalism between the omnipresence of machines, on the one hand, and a growing catacomb of the dead, on the other. Bio-power, as we know it today, is not just a way of managing life, but it also entails the other dimension of taking care of the dead. Does it take any good care of the dead? As global capitalism creates increasingly stratified domains of social inequality across the world, are we not improving lives of a few by making human lives of a humungous number expendable? Nabarun uses the expression, 'surplus humanity' ('*udbritto manush*') to refer to these expendable lives. Judith Butler highlights these surplus and unwanted lives in *Frames of War*: 'when such lives are lost they are not grievable, since, in the twisted logic that rationalizes their death, the loss of such populations is deemed necessary to protect the lives of "the living"' (Butler 2016: 31). This exposes a nexus between bio-politics and thanato-politics in which death of a few is the cost for preserving life of a so-called 'majority'. Global capitalism that has taken charge of *bios* or human life, thus, has an equally important liaison with death. What role does machine have in this? I will explore this political triad of machines, bio-politics and death in Nabarun.

Dipesh Chakrabarty, discussing the Marxian discourse of man, labour and machine, observes how capitalist machinery has an inextricable relation with death:

> It [machine] transfers the motive force of production from the human or the animal to the machine, from living to *dead labor*. This can only happen on two conditions: that the worker be first reduced to his or

> her biological, and therefore, abstract body, and that the movements of this abstract body be then broken up and individually designed into the very shape and movement of the machine. (Chakrabarty 2000: 57; emphasis mine)

As Chakrabarty suggests, machine works in tandem with the human body as another labouring machine. The non-human machine accentuates human body as machine and, in the process, converts human labour into 'dead' labour. For me, this is a bio-political and capitalist mode of deadness. In Nabarun, we find something more than this capitalist deadness of machines. We spot a human death as resistance to the bio-political reduction of death to machine. This is a death that thrives in crafting its own individual and subjective pathway of dying. It situates itself as a form of resistance against capitalist deadness.

Though he is a committed political writer of the political left, Nabarun is not a copybook Marxist. In a 2000 interview, he says that he has no trust in the 'mechanical materialism' (*jantrik jorobad*) that Marxist practice gets reduced to. He also observes that there is a human-oriented philosophy, somewhere outside the grasps of traditional Marxism and that is where his interest lies (2016: 132). Even though his work shows a fascination with the machine in its varied bio-political and capitalist incarnations, as we shall see, it is a human-centric philosophy of machines that finally emerges through his narratives. Though human-centric, this philosophy does not make masters of the human. With a tinge of irony, death in all its subjective ramifications upholds this human perspective on capitalist machinery.

Necro-Politics from Human to Post-Human: Mbembe, Bataille and Braidotti

Before coming to Nabarun, let me briefly set up our theoretical development on necro-politics vis-a-vis late-capitalist mechanicity. Drawing on Georges Bataille's coupling of sovereignty with death, Achille Mbembe in his piece 'Necropolitics' characterises contemporary politics as 'the work of death' (Mbembe 2003: 16). Extending Alexandre

Kojeve's Hegelian formulation, admired by Bataille, Mbembe declares that politics is 'death that lives a human life' (15). He argues that contemporary notions of sovereignty are anchored on the violation of the limit that prohibits killing. Going back to Mbembe's source, in Bataille's text, we read:

> [...] sovereignty is essentially the refusal to accept the limits that the fear of death would have us respect in order to ensure, in a general way, the laboriously peaceful life of individuals. Killing is not the only way to regain sovereign life, but sovereignty is always linked to a denial of the sentiments that death controls. (Bataille 1997: 318).

For Bataille, though death features in the world of the sovereign, it exists there only as a limit to be negated. In other words, the sovereign can overcome the fearful limits of death. Sovereign bio-power must acknowledge necro-politics because death in its framework is no longer a frightful zone, never to be stepped into. In this politics of sovereignty, it is an actual reality rather than an apprehended possibility. The experience of death comes close to sovereignty in their shared accent on unknowing. Just as our own dying is essentially an exercise in unknowing, insofar as death as an experience of the self is impossible; for Bataille, 'only un-knowing is sovereign' (308).

Mbembe derives from Bataille, a definition of politics as transgression of bio-power in the necro-political horizon:

> By treating sovereignty as the violation of prohibitions, Bataille reopens the question of the limits of the political. Politics, in this case, is not the forward dialectical movement of reason. Politics can only be traced as a spiral transgression, as that difference that disorients the very idea of the limit. (Mbembe 2003: 16)

Mbembe studies the function of necropower in late modern regime of colonial occupation, his example being Palestine. He also explores the varied phenomenon of contemporary global terrorism as a 'war machine' in which death takes the cake over life. He discusses the figure of the suicide-bomber in the context of martyrdom and sacrifice. Mbembe's position on necro-politics is negative and critical. He evokes necropower to point to the insufficiency of biopower. But, for him, necro-politics is destructive; it creates 'death-worlds' in which entire populations are 'subjected to conditions of life conferring upon them the status of living dead' (40).

Let us now turn to Rosi Braidotti for a more positive view of post-human necro-politics as a subversion of *bios* (human life) with *zoe* (all lives, human and non-human). Braidotti articulates a politics of *zoe* that effectively obliterates the difference between life and death and opens up a post-human philosophy of death that is anything but anthropocentric. She builds on Mbembe's insights into what he calls a 'new semiosis of killing' and talks about post-human warfare that creates new machinic ways of dying. '"RISE", a six-legged robo-cockroach that can climb walls' is such an agent of what Braidotti terms 'techno-bestiary' (Braidotti 2013: 124). She notes that while political thought around bio-power continues to proliferate and diversify, the concept of death remains somewhat frozen as a 'unitary' and 'un-differentiated' phenomenon (128). With a materialist, vitalist turn on *zoe* as endless cosmic energy, Braidotti constructs an affirmative ethic of death from necro-politics. An awareness of death is written into the temporal script of human life and this pushes it back into the past. She falls back on Deleuzean 'impersonality' of death to establish it as a matter of the past:

> [...] death is behind us. Death is the event that has always already taken place at the level of consciousness. As an individual occurrence it will come in the form of the physical extinction of the body, but as event, in the sense of the awareness of finitude, of the interrupted flow of my being there, death has already taken place. (133)

Personal death is subsumed within a larger flow of *zoe* as life force. Braidotti's clinching claim rests on the 'productive differential nature of *zoe*' as a continuum of life and death (132). According to her, the desire to live and die are two aspects of *zoe* and there is no tension between Eros and Thanatos. Death is the mark of the inhuman that passes into never-ending *zoe*, as an immanent flow of intelligent and self-organising matter. Braidotti's move is to incorporate death into the energetics of life as *zoe*. She suggests that within the desire to live, our 'innermost desire is for a self-fashioned, a self-styled death' (135).

This is not simply a nihilistic death wish but an affirmative desire to style, craft and stage one's own death. The uniqueness of each life rests on this uniqueness of how the person dies. As we shall see, this labour of constructing a particular way of dying is crucial in Nabarun's 'surplus humanity'.

Nabarun: Death-Machine between Dying and Death

These interconnected discourses acknowledge necropower as the reality of contemporary bio-politics. They attempt to take this reality onboard and construct an affirmative post-human ethic of death. These discourses foreground the relation between machines and death in a war-like horizon of the political. With these links established, let me now come to Nabarun whose work uses necro-politics to make a statement of resistance. I will argue that this stress on thanato-politics (necro-politics as politics of corpse-management being one specific part of a larger politics of death) as resistance is Nabarun's contribution to the aforementioned theoretical edifice. Nabarun's entire body of work shows consistent interest in the operativity of machines in our contemporary post-human world. But the nuances shift from one text to another. Can death resist the statist paradigm of bio-power?

Nabarun's most famous novel *Herbert* (1994) asks this question in its penultimate scene, wherein, we see the protagonist's corpse, exploding in the crematorium. The sleeping dynamites, hidden long back in Harbart's mattress by his Naxalite nephew Binu come back to life and his death becomes a politically subversive event. To evoke Braidotti's point here, Harbart's personal death is subjugated under the larger energetics of *zoe*. This *zoe* includes dynamites as non-human matter that organises itself and returns to life after decades. The post-human *zoe* that continues after Harbart's individual death casts a shadow on the final chapter that is written in a speculative and futuristic mode. This chapter describes the scattering of Harbart's dead person's belongings like the death-ritual of scattering ashes. Apart from Harbart's explosive mattress, there are these objects that present *intelligent* and *self-organising* matter. This matter redistributes itself into yet another generative cycle after the destruction of death. The things in Harbart's room, from his assortment of books, notepads, the signboard declaring his profession as a necromancer, to his clothes, are all given away to various people. Nabarun's narrator focuses on a balloon-shooting stall owner who takes Harbart's signboard (1993: 79). The narrator speculates if someone will ever see Harbart's name, written on the other side of what becomes a balloon shooting board. Who knows, if by some occult turn of magic, integral to Harbart's practise, the balloon shooting gun may become a dissident machine at some future point. In these memorial traces of Harbart's after-life, Nabarun uses non-human *matter* to evoke the *Zoe* that transcends individual death. The being of machine, in this case, the shooting gun, falls under this category of non-human or shall we say, post-human matter. This *Zoe* is not transcendental but immanent. Harbart's post-mortal and post-human remains do not need another world to situate themselves. They are redistributed in the very world, he lived in. Intelligent and self-organising matter that re-organises itself *ad infinitum* incorporates death as a passing phase of dissolution in its larger continuum.

Harbart, who was never an explicitly political person in life, becomes political in death as the mysterious explosion assumes the radical character of a revolutionary political event. It leaves state-machinery in utter confusion and announces the absolute unpredictability of revolutionary dissidence. Cremation is not death, but it is the cultural ritual that enfolds death. Let me note that it is the machinic site of this ritual, that is, the crematorium that is blown out of existence by this explosion. Is this death's attack on the machine that ritualises death? Let us keep this question in suspension and navigate from the 1994 *Harbart* to the 1997 short story 'Cold Fire'. In this story, crematorium moves indoor to become a private property, commoditised by global capitalism. The story is written in the form of a commercial dialogue between a potential buyer and a salesman who wants to trade an indoor machine that performs the last rites. The machine is a coffin-like box for the body to go in with red lights flashing. Once the lights turn blue, two shining bowls, labelled 'ashes' and 'navel' come out. Going by the salesman's persuasive words, this machine offers an exclusive and private death-experience for users. It helps them avoid the putrid state of affairs in the burning ghats. The salesman who claims to have attended classes on thanatology as part of his sales training programme is successful in making Mr Sarkar buy the machine. But Nabarun's ironic narrator notes that immediately after its installation, two of the oldest servants (the old gardener and the janitor) quit their jobs, frightened by the possibly occult powers of the machine. The class-dimension of this 'techno-thanatological' object is, thus, put under critique. The underclasses do not understand the technocratic prowess of the death-machine. All it generates in them is fear at the face of the incomprehensible. The funeral machine works as an emissary of bio-political global capitalism. At one point, the salesman says, 'you had to wait eighty-four years for the fall of Communism. And only in six years, you get "Cold Fire" whose gentleness and amazing company fits you and people like you alone' (2010: 181; my translation). There is discussion about the polarisation of the rich and the poor in a post-communist social order assuming *logically absurd* proportions (182; English in the original).

The story ends with a convergence of life and death as it describes what happened to the first buyer of 'cold fire' in Kolkata. The man in question, Chandramadhab Chatterjee, enters the machine the very next day after a gala party of his granddaughter's first birthday. This convergence registers the bifidity of biopolitics and necro-politics as two aspects of the same *zoe*. The machine tries to commoditise death into the bio-political scheme of capitalism. But the unpredictability of death as an event that does not mind coming seconds after a festive occasion, creates its sovereign rule over the machine. The machine can only be an inert observer of this radically contingent event. One can buy the exclusivity of one's funeral rites and make the process of cremation as sophisticated and personal as possible. But it does not alter the masterful accidentality of death as an event. Though Braidotti would insist on the consciousness of death as a matter of the past; for Nabarun, the death-event, when it actually happens, holds the key to political resistance in its emphasis on chance. We observe two different but striated iterations of this resistant thanato-politics in *Herbert* and 'Cold Fire'. As the famous line from *Herbert* suggests, 'when and how the explosion will happen and who will make it happen is something the state machinery is yet to have any clue about' (78; my translation). This sentence that refers to the accidental explosion during Harbart's cremation, is testimony to the contingency of the death-event. 'Cold Fire' taking its first user's life in days is a sardonic reminder of the same aspect of contingency that underpins death. In both cases, a machine situates this contingent dynamic of death but fails to master it in any way.

In a Youtube lecture on the Bengali alternative filmmaker, Ritwik Ghatak, talking about the 1970s Naxalite movement in Bengal, Nabarun emphasises the passion represented by the ultra-left movement. More importantly, he dwells on the specific machineries and techniques of warfare that the Naxalite historical sequence taught its next generation. In this context, we may remember the Chinese revolver in the story 'Amar Kono Bhoy Nei Toh' ('I Don't Need to Fear, Do I'). Biren, who finally gets killed by this machine in a mistaken act of casual violence, is a disposable common man. He is always in the grip of an anonymous fear of the social, as articulated in the title. He becomes the unfortunate victim of a horrific game played by local hooligans. They taunt him by tapping into his fear-psychosis and ask him to point the gun at himself. Contrary to their expectations, when Biren pulls the trigger, there is an actual gunshot though the revolver does not have a magazine. The last lines of the text explain this quirk by historicising the machine:

> Hari Dutta gave Salman the Chinese Revolver to keep it. Hari Dutta did not know this. Neither did Salman. Even if you take out the magazine from those models, a bullet is always stored inside. Many such revolvers entered Calcutta during 1971–72. (2010: 267; translation Sourit Bhattacharya)

The historical reference signals how the Chinese revolver operates as a Naxalite trace in the story. For us, more interesting is the logic, peculiar to the machine that leads to Biren's suicidal or homicidal death. The Chinese revolver's machinic logic is such that even when one takes the magazine out, a bullet always stays inside. Moreover, as the above passage clarifies, those who were using this relic from the 1970s, in the early 2000s when this story is written, did not know this idiosyncratic logic of the machine. So, there is something enigmatic in the logic of the machine that stumps the users' human understanding here. As the story suggests, there is a direct causal continuity between this machine's peculiar functional logic and the event of death. It is the machinic order that gets calcified into the hard reality of death. In the 1970s, this bullet might have been the last resort of a radical to eliminate the class-enemy. But as farcical repetition of a potentially tragic history, in this story, it comes back to take the life of an innocent who had increasingly become surplus and insignificant in what Nabarun calls the 'acquisitive society' (2010a: 520). Bio-politics shows its necro-political alter-ego here. Nabarun does not simply evoke a Naxalite nostalgia but comes at its historical trace in a critical mode. The return of Naxalite violence produces injustice here. Biren's death at the hands of the machine is a sad reminder of how countless human subjects do not count anymore in the bio-political logic of governmentality. But at the same time, this death installs a striking example *of techno-thanatological* victimisation.

In the 1994 story 'Toy', the eponymous child kills fishes in the aquarium by designing a death-machine with a pencil and a miniature immersion heater. The child, indicatively pet-named 'Toy' (toy-machine for techno-capitalism?), puts a little pencil, diagonally over the aquarium after lifting its lid and hangs a small immersion heater from the pencil. This electrocutes all the fishes in the aquarium. The calm and quiet kid does this when his parents leave him alone at home for a while. There is no given machine but the capitalist subject is invited to assemble a death-machine from the given elements. The death-trap Toy sets up is a machine indeed. It is a machine he himself makes to kill the fishes. Here, not only does Nabarun question the sadistic aspects of this death-drive but he also takes a dig at the normativist social discourse that makes acts like these seem perfectly acceptable. When Toy's parents, shocked at what he has done, take him for counselling, psychiatrist Dibyendu Mukherjee finds him absolutely normal. He comments that the act might have been caused by a 'sort of curiosity.... [A]lmost scientific' (2010: 145; English in the original). This cold diagnosis of scientific curiosity is corroborated by an article that Toy's father Mithil reads in an international magazine. This article by a French psychologist posits the criminal inclination in children in England and France as an extension of their scientific interest. The article argues that the calm with which these children are able to describe what they have done is an unmistakable sign of their scientific normalcy. Mithil reads this to his wife, Mimi. The final line of the story declares: 'Toy's parents finally became assured about their son' (145; my translation). Nabarun's critique is directed at this positivist social belief in the scientific that normalises violence in this case. Capitalism and its so-called 'scientific' machinic logic are artificial supports for the toy-child's aggressive fascination here. The non-human machine comes into being for the work of delivering death to another avatar of the non-human—the fish. Here, death and machine operate together in a completely negative light, unlike the Chinese revolver, wherein, revolutionary nostalgia came back but only to produce social injustice in the present.

To move to a narrative that gives a positive inflection to both death and machine vis-à-vis political resistance, let me briefly turn back in time to Nabarun's second published story, 'Steamroller', from 1970. 'Steamroller' unifies the old human labourer with his machine as they put up a joint fight. But the inevitable destiny of this political fight is death. To remember Braidotti's point, the old man who runs the steamroller in intolerable heat decides to fashion his unique way of dying when the rest of the construction process fails to pass the cue. The old, hungry, rickety man does not know which part of the road must be levelled as others before him have not done their job well. As he descends from his steamroller to find out, the searing sunlight plays its part. He almost collapses with a presentiment of death. The text has a long meditation here on serial images of death as the poor old man grapples with his mortality. To quote a few images from this extensive, specular ode to death: 'Death is the horrific face that burns in the tamarisk row, lit up by numerous tussles between joy and pain … Death is the meaningless smoke-ring of fear, lost in the coal breath of the sky, after the train goes under the over-bridge … Death is the sensation of sound when night's black water hits metal and wooden decks on a jetty' (27; my translation). The old man's fear that his death is round the corner gives him the defiance to revolt. Fear and anger propel him into a necro-political act of resistance. He whistles again and again but no one comes out of adjacent houses. He interprets this non-response as indifference and enmity (28). He targets the series of cars, standing in a procession in front of him. Sitting tight on his own machine, the steamroller, he makes an onslaught into these other machines. He tells himself that if he can get rid of these cars from the road, his work of levelling can happen without disturbance.

As the steamroller strikes against the series of cars, fire spreads across the horizon. There is mayhem that leads armed forces into the scene. The man is taken to be a terrorist and ultimately killed off in a spectacle of statist violence, in response to his own necro-political resistance. When thousands of bullets pepper his body, the old man does not fear death but relishes the onward movement of his steamroller against the black van of armed forces. Though it is a premonition of impending death that initiates the revolt, there is no fear when actual death presents itself to the man. By that time, he has incorporated death into his life-world by generating the aforementioned series of poetic and affective images on death. These images signal his assimilation of death into a continuum of life and death and a resultant sublimation. They indicate a generative and sublimating function of aestheticising death. This is the psychic self-fashioning of a uniquely individual death. This self-fashioning happens through another kind of machine, that is, the mind and its cognitive images. This mental imagery is yet another machinery. But in its creative slant, this aesthetic machinery is irreducible to bio-politics and its technocratic form in global capitalism. After this process of aesthetic assimilation has taken place, there is no fear when death as an event offers itself to the human subject.

Nabarun uses anthropomorphic images to unify the steamroller with its human operator. He compares it with a mad elephant on prowl (28). In the final scene when the man's blood-smeared corpse slides down its surface, the steamroller has blood all over its body. The faint smoke that comes out of its chimney is analogous to the old man's angry breaths. The tremble in its body echoes his anger. It is a surplus common man who perishes while fighting the statist system, and the system has no other way than branding him a terrorist. The steamroller comes across as a positive incarnation of the machine that goes hand in hand in establishing death as an event of resistance. While this story is not post-humanist in any simple sense and has multiple humanist throwbacks, 'Steamroller' returns to the mysteriously anonymous figure of the dog. The story began with the image of a dog, not mentioned by its name (25). It decided not to sleep under a blue car due to old age and apprehensiveness that 'anything might happen any time' (25). The narrative comes a full circle when we return to the dog, again not named as such. The dog had a foreshadowing of things to come and in this final image, we see it coming back to the blue car. It inspects the spot where the old man's corpse had slipped down the steamroller. After a moment's reflection, it pensively looks up 'into the cloudless sky, at the sad moon' (29). This non-human figure, not named as such, activates a dialectical tension between the human and the post-human tropes in the story. The anonymised old dog echoes the nameless old man. While the latter did not see it coming, the former could smell that something was amiss. This tension marks Nabarun's consistent stress on the contingency of the political event of resistance. A self-fashioned death in which the human and machine join hands is the horizon of this resistance. In this story, we, thus, see a harmonious relation between human and machine in enacting death as a resistant political event.

In the novella *Auto*, titled after auto-rickshaw, Chandan has an affectionate relationship with the machine he drives. The *auto-maton* is invested with humanist energy as Nabarun's narrator compares Chandan's washing the auto with a care-giver's act: 'he wipes the seat just like children are wiped' (2007: 14; my translation). Chandan lost his sexual ability in a showdown with goons when he performed the heroic deed of stopping a cab of criminals with his auto. He is teased as an impotent man. The impossibility of his becoming a father finds a compensation in his bond with the machine. Nabarun implies an internal hierarchy of machines. Auto is a marginal machine here, compared to taxi and bus. Bus drivers call Chandan's auto 'a tin of puffed rice'. Auto emblematises Chandan's impotence and solitude. Nabarun signals this stylistically, by placing the signifier 'auto' in isolated one-word sentences: 'It went that way. Auto' (32) and again: 'It is silently awake outside. Auto' (59). In one scene, when Chandan's wife Mala has an affair with Vicky, he complains about his failed masculine pride. The only entity that inertly listens to his suffering is the auto. As Chandan asks the machine, 'can't you cure me?', the narrator humanises it: 'Auto does not reply. Remains silent. As if it can't speak in shame' (45).

In the climax, when Chandan kills Mala's lover in jealousy after receiving the news of her pregnancy, he commits the crime with the auto's help. Vicky's body falls, touching the auto's exterior. Chandan surrenders himself at the police station. The last two sentences read: 'After this, behind the police station, just touching the wall, stood silent for many days. Auto' (64). In *Auto*, Nabarun marks the machinic inertia of the auto. But, his narrative does not fail to underline an affective relation established between man and machine. Capitalism might hold up machine in all its material inertia, the human subject cannot help anthropomorphise it. Death in the form of murder becomes the destiny of the machine. It is by committing this crime that Chandan's impotent masculinity reclaims his subjectivity. The machine, thus, has this double valence. It offers human company to the solitary, impotent man but it also becomes instrumental in this man's criminal act of self-establishment.

To conclude, though Nabarun's insights into man-machine-death in capitalism is manifold, his work gives an affirmative value to necro-politics by emphasising a subjective way of self-generated dying. Death becomes a well-wrought resistance against the capitalist dead order of machines that tries to reduce death to a matter of bio-political management. Harbart's uniquely explosive death becomes his political and subjective signature. 'Cold Fire' fails to master death's absolute contingency for the consumer. Toy's death-machine is fetishised as scientific curiosity in capitalist culture. The Chinese pistol that kills Biren remains a testimony to the sudden violence, built into the logic of machines, however revolutionary its past use may have been. Nabarun's work seems to gesture towards the non-human, if not the post-human, but remains humanist (without human exceptionalism) in its humane characterisation of the human–machine rapport. Be it the steamroller or the auto, the man-machine duo puts up a fight for life by way of dying.

References

Bataille, Georges. (1997), *The Bataille Reader*, ed. Fred Botting and Scott Wilson. Oxford: Blackwell.

Bhattacharya, Nabarun. (1993), *Herbert*. Kolkata: Dey's.

———.(2015), 'I don't need to fear, do I?', trans. Sourit Bhattacharya, *Sanglap* 2:1: 165–170, http://sanglap-journal.in/index.php/sanglap/article/view/98/87 (accessed 12 April 2019).

———. (2014), 'Nabarun Bhattacharya talks about Ritwik Ghatak', Youtube, https://www.youtube.com/watch?v=VIuC9Gv-R2o (accessed 12 April 2019).

———. (2010), *Sreshtho Golpo*, Kolkata: Deys.

———. (2010a), *Uponyash Shomogro* (*Complete Novels*), Kolkata: Deys.

———. (2016), *Kathabarta* (*Collected Interviews*), Kolkata: Bhashabandhan.

———. (2007), *Auto o Bhogi* (*Two Novels: Auto and Bhogi*), Kolkata: Deys.

Braidotti, Rosi. (2013), *The Posthuman*, Cambridge: Polity.

Butler, Judith. (2016), *Frames of War: When is Life Grievable?* London and New York: Verso.

Chakrabarty, Dipesh. (2000), *Provincializing Europe*, Princeton: Princeton University Press.

Mbembe, Achille. (2003), 'Necropolitics,' in *Public Culture* 15 (1): 11–40.

#Animalosa: A Study of the Theroid Cosmic in Nabarun's Fiction

Dibyakusum Ray

In 2012, I interviewed Nabarun Bhattacharya at his 'Bhashabandhan' office in Kolkata—headquarter of a Bengali literary magazine founded by the author. He described the 'Life-world' of his writing as this:

> My world has a sundown, as I don't quite believe in toiling for an indefinite cause. My world is also a 'Life-world', as I think this [world] is a complex network of all things breathing, how they communicate ... you know ... survive with each other, which is not a matter of choice. This embargo that we are in now, this darned structure being imposed on us ... it is on this Life-world to reject it. We only think in humanistic terms, but rejection, resistance, rebuilding can come from any kind of sentient Life. It's the action that matters, not who's acting it out. (Interview with Nabarun, 3 April 2012)

Structure. Rejection. Resistance. Clear yet onerous, Nabarun's credo has been the dorsum of several essays during the past half-decade (Sourit Bhattacharya [2016], Priyanka Basu [2015] and Dibyakusum Ray [2016], to name a few) attempted to evaluate Nabarun's works in the urban resistance as well as the ecocritical frame. What this emergent—and already sizeable—Nabarun-scholarship seems to point out is circa what the author himself suggested: 'rejection, resistance, rebuilding can come from any kind of sentient Life', outspread through variant thematic analyses, such as marginal spaces in postcolonial cities, radical ideas about literary performativity, anthropomorphic politics in Nabarun's animal characters, etc. Rebellion—precipitate, upsetting and often self-serving—has been the favoured theme of Nabarun, and scholarship around his oeuvre has attempted to validate an alacritous 'space-of-alternation': how Nabarun's philosophy can be read and applied to several resistive approaches to the social–

cultural mainframe: citizenship, performance, eco-criticism, urban development, etc. This is directly aligned to Nabarun's *recusant-ad-infinitum*, to maintain a marginal existence and engage the normative society combatively for as long as it takes. This network has its own validity. This essay, however, attempts something else as it focuses on the third point the author himself mentions in the quotation above: 'Rebuilding'.

My argument is that the 'animal collective' in Nabarun's oeuvre—which I term *#Animalosa*, borrowing an Instagram animal-awareness hashtag trend that ironically surfaced in the year of Bhattacharya's passing: 2014—is somewhat foiling Nabarun's oft-discussed *láppel du vide*: his fondness for a strongly cavalier mode of resistance that fosters infinite warping without any perceivable conclusion. Or, it can be read as a furtherance—an inevitable next-step of resistance, a 'what now' after the rebellion is staged (like in 'Andho Beral' [The Blind Cat] or *Lubdhak* [Sirius]—two stories I have specially analysed in this essay). My argument abounds the theroid world created by Bhattacharya where animals constitute a parallel universe that has its own, unfathomable misanthropically austere 'restarting' of the world-order. I propose that Nabarun's animals—even when they are not talking and thinking in a humanly legible format like in *Lubdhak* (*Sirius*) (Nabarun's dystopic novella depicting the woes of anthropomorphic dogs)—serve more than the purpose of narrative scaffolding; they are never the 'other' in the millennial critical sense (a point that I will discuss in greater detail); not in the sense where '[T]he Other manifests itself by the absolute resistance of its defenceless eyes. [. . .] The infinite in the face [. . .] brings into question my freedom, which is discovered to be murderous and usurpatory' (Levinas 1990: 294). In other words, what Levinas talks about here—and what I argue to be the foundation of the millennial criticality—is a constant recognition and reparation for the 'other'. The 'I' has to admit that there are 'irreducible' beings outside its immediate periphery, and a never-ending responsibility towards that 'other' can bring lasting communication between the two. Instead of this innate 'ethicalism', Nabarun's *#Animalosa* thwarts the slightest attempt to mutuality. They, if analysed through a cluster of representative texts, progressively retrocede into a cold, disinterested, abstruse cypher, consisting of cosmic wisdom and disengagement. Before I move further, two things beg explanation: the established criticality about the 'other' and how the cosmic other differs from it.

It comes dangerously close to a self-luring critical trap to have a soiree of 300 years' critical argument involving ideas and limitations 'self' and ontology, especially when the likes of Kant and Heidegger are—temporally and methodologically—quite apart from Nabarun. Hence, I will be brief about the first explanation. I will then explore the last through direct references from the texts I have chosen as case studies. The Western *outré*—in its millennial form—is the result of a ponderous critical development that starts with Kant, and here I am focusing strictly on the chapter 'Critique of Aesthetic Judgment', the first part of *The Critique of Judgment*, where Kant makes his argument in favour of universal perceptions of pleasure, judgment and goodness (1987: xxx–xxxix). The matrix of the 'other' is Nature—and Nature is perfect, distant and unknowable by sentient mortals. The subject—the 'self'; basically the foil of the 'other'—might be able to grasp a mere representation of 'otherness' through its sensuous faculties—yet that 'judgment' remains imperfect, ergo to live as the 'self' *is* imperfect. What we—the human selves—can best hope for is an endless struggle of knowing the 'other', an endeavour fated to fail. Yet, this struggle is important for Kant, as it delivers the way to *pure reason*: the sublime whole and possibility, goodness and spiritual fulfilment, infinitely possible and worth living in, where everything makes sense. The essence of wholeness—a holistic network where 'self' and 'other' remain in perfect consonance—rests in the fractured pattern of infinite trial and error. You have to *strive* to know the other even if such striving is futile, and therein lies the secret to the honing upto perfection.

One can continue infinitely about this, but the bedrock of the 'other' established criticality is already upon us. There is an 'I' and there is the 'other'; the 'other' is natural and supra-sensory, and to attempt to know it is to strike harmony with *everything*: 'the greater good'. *#Animalosa* and (this is where I make my insertion into the second important critical point of this essay) the *philosophy of cosmicism* in general—I argue—wrangles with this holism. Before I go deeper into the 'cosmic', allow me a further look into the evolution of continental aesthetics.

The inter-war scenario in philosophy had a furtherance of the Kantian 'other' in *Being and Time* (1927), where Heidegger, rather than searching for the answer beyond the physicality of the subject, focuses on the internal machinations of consciousness within. Can a harmony be reached between the 'I' and the 'other'? Heidegger's answer would presumably be affirmative by way of *Da-sein*. To put it simply, *Da-sein* is the centre of Heidegger's cognitive universe—a centre the Being originated from the being, but transcends it, and connects the multitude of beings. It cannot be questioned or negotiated with, because it itself knows the answer to its own question. Undoubtedly, there is a subversive element in Heidegger's idea of holism: *Da-sein* is not above the conflicts, *Da-sein* is the conflict. The *outré* is not asunder; the 'I', the 'other' and the severance between the two—all are part of the same, sentient neither-me-nor-thou *Being*: *Da-sein*. Can we see slivers of warmth around the cognitive horizon here? You may not ever know, but you know that you may not ever know. The unattainable is distant, but never without possibility, and certainly not foreboding or frigid towards the attempt of knowing it. This is—and I am afraid if this sounds linear—a 'benign' other which faces severe challenge within *#Animalosa*, and the post-millennial critical spectrum I would like to align it with: Cosmicism.

Let us consider this section from *Lubdhak*:

> The rain is playing an essential part in decomposing and bloating the dead dogs, along with the sun, sultry air, flies, rats and bacteria. See, the dead puppy that was born and dead at the same spot; its eyes still unopened [...] see, the ants have eaten away the postnatal layer over its eye, thus helping him to finally see. That small, and dead eye is too insignificant, glassy too. Now see, reflected on that eye, is the space. That single dead eye, like a dead glass is capturing the Milky Way, the galaxies departing elsewhere ... many asteroids, comets and lifeless mechanical satellites [...] look at the south eastern side of the Orion. You can see Canis Major. Look within, and you see the extremely beautiful brightest star of the night sky. It is called Lubdhak or Sirius ... It has given its verdict. It cannot be revoked. But we have seven hours left still. (Bhattacharya 2010: 384)

Calcutta—a massive and dystopic metropolis in some unspecified future—is about to be destroyed by a stray comet on a collision course with Earth. This is unbeknownst to the citizens, who are busy in the latest updates from the city-wide Dog-annihilation programme. In an almost cinematic style, Bhattacharya's vision widens to reveal heaps of dog carcasses lying all over the out-of-order stable, strewn throughout Calcutta. The heaps of dead bodies consist of all forms of canines: domesticated, half domesticated, pregnant, young and old, belligerent or docile or simply stoic. This macabre vista is interspersed with the constant reminder that these bodies will lie inert for the next seven hours, the seven hours that are never passed in the course of the novel. For me, this denotes the continuing suffering of the dogs; on the other hand, it makes us stop on the brink of something with cosmic importance, constantly deferring the climax, allowing us space to laboriously reach and speculate what it should be. The dogs can 'finally see', while the humans cannot as yet.

This might be an ideal time to delve into Cosmicism, and how it is different from the millennial criticality surrounding the 'other'. The strain from Kant and Heidegger has a robust presence in contemporary literary criticism, augmented later by Levinas: 'The idea of the infinite is found in my responsibility for the other' (Levinas 1979: 238). An avenue into the infinite is always possible. Levinas repeatedly describes the 'other' as a supreme responsibility, the 'unmasterable' face making us conscious of anthropogenic traits like altruism, sympathy and divinity. Admittedly, Levinas does say that a total replacement of the self by 'other' would certainly result in the death of the consciousness; hence, it exists in relation to the totality but remains within itself, separated from the totality. Still, this challenge is not without a certain comfort. Nature is unknowable, but you *know*—as a warm, reassuring gesture to *your* humanity—that you cannot know it. The subject crawls out of the prison of selfish appreciation to discover that Nature can be pleasing universally. Nature, however, does not aim to please, nor does it create awareness of its perfection and harmony—the human subject can only strive for coherence for the supreme knowledge, the ultimate beauty beyond reach. Ergo, even at its full unreadable aura, Nature does submit itself to our sensual appreciation: that is supposedly contra-discernment lending itself to fancy; the 'irreducible' can be apropos of 'responsibility'; and we are assured that we are allowed to try to understand the mystique.

This invitation is what is missing from Nabarun's theroid cosmicity. 'Cosmicism'—sowed deep within late Renaissance science and occult (by the likes of Heinrich Agrippa)—is not necessarily about the physical cosmos; what it chiefly talks about is the defeat of Enlightenment rationality. There are acreages of no-knowledge, Cosmicism says, that are and will forever remain untouched by cognition, and the icy vastness of outer space is but a potent metaphor for it. In the *Horror of Philosophy* trilogy (2011–2015), Eugene Thacker traces a long tradition of cosmic philosophy of literature abounding Lord Dunsany, H. P. Lovecraft, Graham Harman. Thacker talks about a reading of the extant critical tradition recast into a drift between Knowledge and no-Knowledge. This lacks the starkness of good/evil, holy/unholy or even Life and Death, especially because nature—as Cosmicism argues—is the sentient quiddity which was and will be. Reason is just an upshot that reaffirms its negative. We, the conscious beings, perennially stand at the precipice of comprehension, looking out at the darkness beyond comprehension—the vertigo and/or the dread. Its removal from the Kantian comfort—and proximity to Bhattacharya's *#Animalosa*—is also perspicuous from its claim to the essential nonchalance this idea pursues. H. P. Lovecraft, possibly the first dedicated theorist of Cosmicism, describes how nature does not give a 'damn one way or the other about the especial wants and ultimate welfare of mosquitoes, rats, lice, dogs, men, horses, pterodactyls, trees, fungi, dodos, or other forms of biological energy' (Joshi 1929: 483). Nabarun's Cosmicism, I argue, is an exiguous version of this. Instead of the cosmic abandon of nature, the focus here is on the animal world, and how it has transcended the barriers of relentless resistance. Instead of nature, the animals do not *care* about the human cognition of them. The reader of Nabarun's theroid literature is not privy to the theroid cosmic knowledge. His animals are not trying to make a political statement by jettisoning the anthropocene. This is rather *pure* desertion of the human and an atavism into know-not-what. You may not know. You may never not know.

Here, we make a comeback to *Lubdhak* (*Sirius*). Nabarun—to avoid the structural and linguistic barriers of a published novel—mixes rational dialogues and chimeric elements in subsequent chapters. The dogs do speak Bengali, but they talk about things beyond men's purview. The novel is initiated through three instances of random cruelty inflicted on stray dogs in Calcutta. This, in turn, serves as the initial point of a lengthy and meandering dialogue between several stray dogs and cats that reveals the real nature of systematic animal cruelty by the metropolitan authority. It also casts a premonition of a subsequent bigger 'change', something the animals can sense but cannot define. We meet three characters of the novel—Ear-sprout, Whitey and Brownie (my translation), all victims of deadly or semi-deadly and unnecessary assaults by human beings. Whitey does not survive the onslaught of a speeding car, but both Ear-sprout and Brownie survive long enough to witness the intricately planned dog annihilation programme, unleashed by the city about to enter a new millennium. Several ingenuous ideas of ridding the city of dogs—each crueller than the other—in the name of extensive beautification are toyed with. Finally, the civic authority zero in on covertly kidnapping the dogs and throwing them, sans food and water, into the unused stables. While this planning takes place inside the heavily guarded strong rooms of human authority, the dogs and cats of the city talk among themselves, all scared of the impending doom, a news first secretly served by the crows. The animals talk of their past and plan for the bleak future, while their comrades are ceaselessly caught and thrown into the stables. In the overall gloom, another stray-dog called Gypsy brings the news of an impending paradigmatic shift that, apparently, cannot be stopped:

> —Within two days we will have to leave the city. Something deadly is about to happen. What precisely I cannot tell. The moment the word is spread, we shall leave this city in scores. You better join us. Ear-sprout has also requested the same.
> —So you say it is better to leave?
> —Whatever I have heard till now, that is the impression. Come down. Let's go.
> —Well, but what is this deadly event?

> —It's all a rumour. Some say it will be a war. Some say an earthquake. It might be something coming out of the beyond in order to save the dogs. Nothing can be stated specifically. Let's go, we will tell you the rest on the way. (Bhattacharya 2010: 404)

While this discussion continues, the narrator's gaze shifts to the cosmic machinations occurring somewhere deep inside the cosmos. The humans discover through telescope and other sensors that an immense asteroid is on a collision course with earth, originating from the Canis Minor. Bhattacharya's imagination takes us straight into the legion of 'shadow-dogs' ethereal, mythological and divine bodies flying over the Bay of Caninus. While zooming through the clouds, Laika, the spirit of the iconic Russian astronaut dog addresses Anubis, the dog-faced guardian of the netherworld of Egyptian mythology. They engage in a discussion of when precisely to strike, and how far the dogs' exodus shall proceed by the time the attack is initiated. Their concern is answered by the repeated statement—'There are still seven hours to go' (Bhattacharya 2010: 414). The dogs in Calcutta, meanwhile, suddenly abandon their commotion in the black holes of the abandoned stables, and suddenly sit in strange formations as if to welcome the canine-faced asteroid, approaching like the Judgment from cosmos. As the elderly dogs engage in strange pagan dance, and their claws emit sparks from the friction with the stone floors, the city authority, now in throws of consternation and panic, opens the gates of the stables; the elders do not budge, but the small dogs and puppies leave with their mothers, halting traffic throughout the city pouring from every corner:

> [...] we are leaving [...] We leave in strides. You may guard your assets in this cursed city that we rejected, like blind Golems [...] Your cruelty, ignorance, greed, callousness are all coming back to you like boomerangs [...] if the police sergeant moves one bit, his feet will hit us and he will never ever reach home tonight. All the trucks [...] beware! Your wheels must not move an inch, for this placid, vast, sea of canines might turn into a gaping shark [...] Woof! Woof! (Bhattacharya 2010: 412)

And, thus, it continues. Bhattacharya's gallery of beasts keeps on frustrating human cognition in favour of a rejection, without the promise of comeuppance or redemption. Rebecca Raglon and Marian

Scholtmeiger define environmental literature to be frequently oriented toward a 'big picture' view—concerned with nature's processes as a whole, or with ecosystems. 'In such works, writers can be found frequently chiding themselves to be more emotional about nature's ways and not remembering the "processes" they are a part of' (Raglon and Scholtmeiger 2007: 122–123). Theroid Cosmicism furthers this view: even the author cannot be cognizant of the animal's cypher to the cosmos; it is a unique appraisal, an attitude that baffles and defeats the human mind. For example, consider 'Andho Beral' or 'The Blind Cat', published in 1997 in the magazine *Pratikshan*. Not much dialogue happens in this story, and certainly no anthropomorphic canines. There is no narrator even; all that happens, disjointed as ever, and is basically spun around the consciousness of either a non-human presence, or no presence at all. The eponymous blind cat—very importantly—cannot *see*. The story comes to the reader as a purely instinctive impression of a world centring on the sole figure of non-human entity that has nowhere to go, nothing to do, nothing to aspire for—*cognisably*. The only humanly coherent idea about the story is survival, but that may not be the only pure drive for the blind cat, that sits almost unmoving under a derelict table in a derelict small town beside a river, and refuses to budge from its position upon the destruction of the building; as if in a cryptic conversation with the cosmic paraphernalia that nobody ever understands. No other concrete information of the setting is ever provided in the story. All we know is:

> … in this hotel, on some random noon in the year 1972, a man with a pair of cracked glasses ate some daal and rice, then left after paying the bill. He had a revolver near his waist. He was, however, not a robber. He used to write poetry for people. This was before the time the blind cat had started residing under the table […] when that man died after puking blood, and was duly cremated, most of those who cried 'we won't forget you' started forgetting about him very soon. From that respect, the chances of anybody remembering the blind cat are extremely few. Many people lived, dined, committed suicide, seduced foolish girls by lying to them of/marriage, murdered, counted the money of fish business in that hotel. Many, many people—all of them so busy with themselves that they never realized towards the slope of

> the floor in some gap amongst the crooked tables and chairs the blind cat was sitting, ears upright. He couldn't understand all the words, the events, the sounds of shattering glass, that sound of the burning cigarette stubs touching the river's surface, songs, belching, shards of laughter, halting sobs. There is a difference between hearing and understanding. (Bhattacharya 2006: 185)

The blind cat is just an aural witness who shall never turn into an actor. I would certainly not call this the archetypical fence-sitting behaviour, because the machinations or purposefulness of the blind cat's mind is never revealed. The hotel is also an important aspect of the story as it is structurally incumbent towards the river. The blind cat survives by some mysterious realisation that here food shall never run out. He was right, and there was no dearth of residual fish bones. The unexpected suicide of the young couple upstairs, the subsequent raid of the police, the three unknown people on their way to a murder, the self-satisfied bourgeois elites who came to the town in order to organise a workshop involving the village peasants—all either saw or completely missed the inert blind cat under the table, thus, momentarily converging their individual stories with a chance of overlap; then went off to their respective ways. Bhattacharya builds hundreds of such chances of separate narratives, never chasing one of them in the hope of fruition, perhaps, because there is nothing called a fruition. Another important aspect is the interplay of myriad emotions triggered by the presence of the cat—sympathy, nonchalance, heartbreak or simply innocent and evasive curiosity, all encircle fruitlessly the pure survival instinct of the blind cat—nothing makes any difference the way he spends each moment.

The story's heart is forlorn. Melancholia as an essential device to grasp a fleeting impression of the nameless, faceless entity that sits in the centre: it is not sadness of/for anything specific; rather, this melancholia only guides us to the realisation that the icy vastness of the network of beings is something which is not necessarily concerned with personal tragedies. Meanwhile, Nabarun reveals that there will be a tremendous thunderstorm in the next few days. The river shall rise by several feet, and if the pressure is too much the dam will certainly break. Even the blind cat's guardian angels—the kids and their mother—will not be able to visit him in such situations. It is very likely that the entire hotel will shake and will bend towards the river dangerously as its base pillars weaken. Bhattacharya predicts if the water breaks into the hotel, the best the blind cat can do is to climb up a little towards the opposite side of the room; but it will certainly not go out. The story ends with two possibilities: first, the water shall engulf the entire room or the hotel itself will submerge in the river, thus, spelling doom for the cat; and second, if the storm is not that intense, then the hotel shall survive and the blind cat shall remain in the darkness under the table. 'When the kids will come in the morning, they will discover him sitting silently in the familiar place' (Bhattacharya 2006: 189). In short, Nabarun doesn't know what the animal would do, and we'll never come to see what fate shall befall the hotel. There is a certain defeat for us, and for the blind cat, 'we-know-not-what'.

I will approach the conclusion with a cluster of examples, and a brief echo from earlier paragraphs. Nabarun's *#Animalosa* is a next step from his most celebrated thematic axis: resistance. While all of his texts can and will be read as the furtherance of a central stance, I argue that animals and animality, which contrive a significant part of Nabarun's much-discussed 'life-world', constitute 'cosmicity'. It can be read as contra-redemption; not 'resistive' because it shuns alternate possibilities, and also 'defeatist' in the sense that it cares little about the humanly attempts to understand it. It is the building of a cypher between the animals and the natural equipage that consists of civilisations, forests, dust, stars, sun, water … basically, the whole cosmos. It's a robust anti-criticality: you-know-not-what. 'Steamroller' (1970)—story of a mad anarchist who terrorises an urban commercial district with his violent Kamikaze—opens with a stray dog that runs away once the carnage begins, and reappears at the close for some unreadable purpose: 'It looks at the place the Steamroller ran over the old man, hangs its dry snouts momentarily before looking up at the pensive moon in the clear sky for a long, long time' (Bhattacharya 2006: 29). Sympathy? Melancholia? Some random gesture? 'Korai' ('The Cauldron') (2005) speaks of the eponymous urban roustabout who dies a nondescript death after lifelong poverty and neglect. His only capital—an enormous iron cauldron which he used to lease out to cheap restaurants—reminds the author of a blind leviathan tortoise, at the base of the cosmic ocean that holds the earth and countless other celestial bodies. In this narrative strand, which is virtually unconnected from the main story, the author imagines the doom when the colossal leatherback will raise its head over the ocean, destroying nebulae and galaxies. He also imagines the enormous cauldron to be the shell of an Aldabra Giant restless, blind, powerful. Is this a warning? A symbol of the suffering proletariat? Or is it just a random yearning for a dark, unfathomable catastrophe?

The last example is from 'Shob Shesh Hoye Jacche' ('It's All Ending') (2004). Having no legible narrative at its core, this is obviously a perfect continuation of 'The Blind Cat', not only in its constant reminder of a bleak future, but more so in its indecisive, uncompromising universal network ever on the brink of apocalyptic destruction. In fact, the process has already started—'It's all ending! It's all ending' (Bhattacharya 2006: 273). Why, how, when—all remain unanswered. The resolution lies in some unspecified 'out there' into which human cognition is unwelcome. It is not even a knowledge; rather, an innate wisdom:

> The obvious time we are talking about might not contain any writer or any reader, although the possibility cannot be ruled out. The rivers and ponds, snails, smaller snails, tadpoles, small fishes—will these exist then? Will the worms, flies, mosquitoes or centipedal insects that can or cannot fly, unicellular organisms be living at that time? Will the dried body of a spider hang with the drier bodies of other insects from the web? Will the sea dry up to give space to saline foam?... The mummified Lenin in Russia, The Eifel Tower, the destroyed statue of Buddha in Bamian, Borobudur, the Taj Mahal, the third-fourth-fifth Howrah Bridge and the dry mud flowing beneath them, the waves in photographs, the deep-sea diver's grotesque suit, the skeleton of a crocodile—these will not carry any meaning. It's all ending! It's all ending. (Bhattacharya 2006: 273)

What-you-may-not-know. A wisdom beyond sense or language. A cypher between the animal and the world, beyond the Anthropocene. Such is #*Animalosa* in Bhattacharya.

(All passages from Nabarun are translated by the writer.)

References

Basu, Priyanka. (2015), 'Texts of Power, Acts of Dissent: Performability and Theatricality in Nabarun Bhattacharya's Short Stories,' *Sanglap: Journal of Literary and Cultural Inquiry*, 2(1): 70–89. Available online: http://sanglap-journal.in/index.php/sanglap/article/view/72 (Accessed 30 May 2019).

Bhattacharya, Nabarun. (2006), 'Andho Beral,' in *Sreshtho Galpa*, 184–189, Kolkata: Dey's.

——. (2006), 'Steamroller,' in *Sreshtho Golpo*, 25–29, Kolkata: Dey's.

——. (2006), 'Shob Shesh Hoye Jacche,' in *Sreshtho Golpo*, 273–277, Kolkata: Dey's.

——. (2006), 'Korai,' in *Sreshtho Golpo*, 282–287, Kolkata: Dey's.

——. (2010), 'Lubdhak,' in *Upanyas Samagra*, 381–416, Kolkata: Dey's.

Bhattacharya, Sourit. (2016), 'The Margins of Postcolonial Urbanity: Reading Critical Irrealism in Nabarun Bhattacharya's Fiction,' in *Postcolonial Urban Outcasts: City Margins in South Asian Literature*, M. Chakraborty and U. Al-Wazzedi eds, 51–67, Abingdon, New York: Routledge.

Heidegger, Martin. (1962), *Being and Time*. Grand Rapids: Wiley-Blackwell.

Joshi, S.T. (1929), *H.P. Lovecraft, a Life*, 483, Rhode Islands: Necronomicon.

Kant, Immanuel. (2001), 'The Critique of Judgement,' in R. Kearney and D. Rasmusseneds, *Continental Aesthetics*, 5–42, Grand Rapids: Blackwell.

Levinas, Emmanuel. (1990), 'Signature,' in *Difficult Freedom: Essays on Judaism*, trans. S. Hand, 291–295, Baltimore: Johns Hopkins University Press.

——. (2007), *Entre Nous*, London, New York: Viva-Continuum.

Raglon, Rebecca and Martin Scholtmeijer. (2007), 'Animals are not believers in ecology: Mapping Critical Differences between Environmental and Animal Advocacy Literature,'*ISLE: Interdisciplinary Studies in Literature and Environment*, 14 (2), Summer 2007, 121–140, Available online: https://doi.org/10.1093/isle/14.2.121 (Accessed 27 May 2019).

Ray, Dibyakusum. (2016), 'The Mute, the Stoic and the Rebel: Animals in the Works of Mikhail Bulgakov and Nabarun Bhattacharya,' in *Rupkatha Journal on Interdisciplinary Studies in Humanities* 8(3): 42–51, Available online: http://rupkatha.com/mute-stoic-rebel-animals-works-mikhail-bulgakov-nabarun-bhattacharya/ (Accessed 1 June 2019).

Thacker, Eugene. (2011), *In the Dust of this Planet: Horror of Philosophy*, Vol 1, Hants: Zero Books.

——. (2015), *Tentacles Longer Than Night: Horror of Philosophy*, Vol 3, Hants: Zero Books.

Toxic Ecologies of the Global South: The Ecogothic in Nabarun Bhattacharya's *Toy City*

Sourit Bhattacharya

In an interview translated in this collection as 'There's an Uncanny Pluralism in Marxism', Nabarun Bhattacharya spoke about his long-term interest in science fiction. The 20th century for him 'was the cruelest century in history' where millions of human and non-humans were obliterated, first in the World Wars and then in the postcolonial, ethnic, and territory war. What has made these wars the cruelest is the unprecedented use of weapon-technology, which has now 'merged' science fiction with scientistic productions and given birth to a deep existentialist crisis as to what 'man thinks of himself as omnipotent is nothing but a pure fallacy' (Bhattacharya 2016: 13–15). It is from this sense of crisis Nabarun wrote his dystopian novel, *Khelna Nagar* or *Toy City* (2004).[1] Here, Nabarun's main concern is the apocalyptic nuclear warfare. This theme is repeated in some of his latter writings. For instance, the short story 'Nuclear Winter' (2014) begins with a terrifying description of the impact of an impending nuclear winter upon us. At the end of the story, the old, disabled mother of the main character, Jyotish, dies helpless on the roof because of Kolkata's (mild) cold weather. The narrator wonders if we are so vulnerable to the current cold, how do we plan to survive the nuclear winter, the last of which had managed to obliterate even the dinosaurs from this planet? This idea of the imminent destruction of our planet appears in the dog-novel *Lubdhak* (*Sirius*, 2006) too, where the dogs of Calcutta in order to avenge human violence on them hatch a cosmic conspiracy with legendary and planetary dogs,

1 For convenience, I'm using *Toy City* throughout. All translations are mine.

such as Sirius, of mass-leaving the city, which is told to be on the verge of annihilation. In *Toy City* (2004), a tiny working-class area surrounding a now-defunct toy city factory is destroyed, partly by capitalist greed and partly by nuclear detonation. Borrowing from environmental literary critics like Lawrence Buell, Rob Nixon, Sharae Deckard and others, in this chapter I will discuss the toxic ecologies of the Global South through Nabarun's *Toy City*, which, I argue, takes up the form of an ecogothic with fabular dimensions to reflect the 'disposable' nature of life and living in this part of the world.

A few recent examples may set the context for us. In May 2019, a news report in *The Guardian* went viral on social media that South-East Asia had decided to return mountains of toxic and waste materials to the North American, European and First World countries (Hannah Ellis-Petersen 2019). The President of the Philippines, Rodrigo Duterte, threatened to sever diplomatic ties with Canada if the latter did not vow to take back its waste routed to the Philippines. In another report of around the same time Malaysia spoke of sending back thousands of tons of plastic waste to Australia. Malaysia's environment minister, Yeo Bee Yin, declared that Malaysia would not be treated as the 'dumping ground' of the world (*The Guardian* 2019). These declarations came in the backdrop of the recent GAIA meeting of South-East Asian leaders where the severe national health and economic problems, conditioned by plastic and toxic waste from the West, such as crop death, contamination of water, respiratory issues and others were brought to critical purview. As India declared in March 2019 that it would not import plastic any longer from the West for recycling, a report in *The Independent* read that it had, thus, become difficult for the developed, First-World nations to find suitable alternatives for 'dumping' their toxic materials (Cockburn 2019).

These examples offer a 'toxic' picture of life and living in the Global South, which has long been the destination of the Global North for dumping hazards and waste. While the Global South as the developed (read, the colonising and imperialist) world's dumping ground has strong connotation of world-colonialism and imperialism,[2] the ground for the current situation, however, began more specifically in the mid-1970s. Jennifer Clapp tells us that from the early 1980s, it 'became apparent that hazardous wastes generated in industrialized countries were being shipped to developing countries for final disposal' (2001: 3). The power structures of the global economy, Clapp notes, allowed the International Monetary Fund (IMF) and the World Bank, controlled chiefly by ex-colonising and industrialised nations, to impose stringent structural adjustment schemes including deregulation on free trade and investment in the developing, ex-colonised debt crisis ridden nations (11). Along with it, fluidity of trade, globalisation of production processes and weak environmental and economic regulations in developing nations in the Global South had paved the way for global toxic and hazard transport in the poorer nations. It is in this context that the notorious words of Lawrence Summers, chief economic advisor of the IMF in 1991, need be understood:

> [S]houldn't the World Bank be encouraging *more* migration of the dirty industries to the LDCs [less developed countries]? ... I think the economic logic behind dumping a load of toxic waste in the lowest wage country is impeccable and we should face up to that ... I've always thought that under-populated countries in Africa are vastly *under*-polluted'. (Arestis 1992)

This context is clear in Nabarun's *Toy City*, where the eponymous derelict city now includes a mountain of radioactive and chemical hazards. One of the characters, Bamon tells Windcheater, the catalyst for Toy City's final destruction, that this mountain was built by thousands of trucks carrying and dumping hazards and toxic materials in the past years. He came to know from one of the truck drivers that 'our country has bought these hazards from richer countries for money. The rich people may make these hazards but do not like to store them

---

2 Terms such as 'toxic colonialism' or 'environmental racism' have been widely used by NGOs and academics since the 1990s. See for instance, Naguib Pellow's use of 'garbage imperialism' in Pellow 2007; For understanding the discourses of poison and toxicity in colonial India, see David Arnold's chapter on 'embracing toxicity' in *Toxic Histories*, 144–175.

in their own countries, they transfer them to the poorer ones. He was saying that this was the way of the world now. Is that so?' (2004, 199). In Bamon's puzzled query, there is both curiosity and wonder as to how the world could run in this way. He is barely able to understand the conspiratorial structures of global economy. Ironically enough, he was himself part of this economy as an accountant in the toy factory which used to supply toys to richer countries in North America and Europe. Like many in the Global South who sell their cheap labour to work in outsourced operations of the Multinational Companies (MNCs), he is unknowingly part of the global capitalist structures. And like many whose safety and security are not the concerns of the middlemen or of the owners of these companies, he is also a victim of the sudden closure of the factory after a massive fire. Like the workers in the Bhopal Gas Disaster in India (1984) or of the Rana Plaza Disaster in Bangladesh (2013), who died of safety issues because of the callousness and irresponsibility of overseas-based capitalists and local supervisors, most of the people in this novel died because of no fire safety regulation in place (196–197). A few surviving families continued to live in the hope that the owner would come back and re-open the company, which would hardly happen. So, when the civil war began in the last years (it isn't clear though who is battling who), the effects of this war came to be seen through the import of toxic materials. The materials were dumped here because this place was considered 'empty'. And soon toxic liquid from the mountain poured into the nearby river Pāri and poisoned its water, killing not only the fishes and other aquatic organisms but also the non-aquatic living beings, such as insects, reptiles or even birds. Drinking water from this river, for lack of other sources, the inhabitants suffered the immediate toxification: there were bluish dabs on their skin, they felt exhausted all the time and could not stand for longer hours and people have now begun to die from the consequences. Here, it would not be entirely wrong to think that the factory owner who bought this arid land very cheap had now sold it to MNCs dealing with dumping toxic waste in the Global South. In either way, there is hardly an escape from the structures of global economy where people like Bamon participate either by selling cheap labour to produce luxury materials for richer countries or by digesting and 'embodying' the hazards produced in faraway richer places. It is a selective killing in which, as Kevin Bale (1999) writes in a different context, some humans are rendered 'disposable' in the logic of globalisation and, thus, killable.

These socio-economic and physio-ecological conditions—characteristic of the Global South—are understood in this chapter as toxic ecologies. Such ecologies, however, have made the question of aesthetic or discursive representation increasingly difficult. As Lawrence Buell notes in his essay 'Toxic Discourse' (1998), while toxicity has clearly shaped modern life and politico-economic practices, the discursive strategies to represent it and to turn it into an urgent public agenda have varied significantly. Reading Rachel Carson's classic *Silent Spring* (1962) and the eco-populist movements in the 1980s and 1990s North America, Buell points at three major strategies used by activists/writers in this context: a betrayal rhetoric of the pastoral, a totalising narrative ridden with deep anxieties over impending eco-catastrophes of global nature and a moral melodrama of pastoral sanctity versus corporate greed (647–651). Since Buell's essay, which urges us to note the metaphorical use of toxicity in literary works, not only have issues of toxicity, radioactive waste, and eco-catastrophe received more literary-critical attention, literary studies has also ventured to understand the stylistic strategies adopted by writers-activists to engage with the issue. Thus, speaking about the Nuclear detonations in the Pacific islands and their hyper-visualisation in photography and cinema, Elizabeth DeLoughrey informs of a contemporary 'dystopian nuclear modernity' characterised by 'radiation ecologies' (2009: 469). Reading fictional works from the same region, Anthony Carrigan writes that 'regional militarization and neocolonial power consolidation have combined to produce what can be termed as *disabling environment*, in which disability and disaster operate as processual terms' (2010: 256; emphasis in original). For Carrigan, this disablement is often invisibilised because of its nature of, what Rob Nixon influentially terms, 'slow violence' (2011). Nixon defines slow violence as a violence that is accretive, long-term, delayed and magnified in nature, such as malnutrition, hunger, toxic drift, radiation, etc., as opposed to 'spectacular' violence, such as earthquake, cyclone, flood, etc., which hogs all media and public attention for its focused time and body-bound nature. Nixon is interested in knowing how we can make the non-visible in the peripheral (for instance, a delayed eco-catastrophic outcome of a decision taken by core capitalist countries decades ago) visible, and how we can give rhetorical and medial potency, that is, 'figurative shapes' to 'formless threats' in an age of resurgent imperialism (2011: 10).

One such potent figurative shape could be that of the 'ecogothic'. While the gothic genre deals with horror and romance in periodic or enclosed settings where supernatural events and characters abound, gothic's link with nature and ecology has been widely discussed. In a volume devoted to exploring this link, Andrew Smith and William Hughes (2015) note the emerging critical focus on the 'ecogothic' in the context of drastic climate change and environmental anxiety: 'Gothic seems to be the form which is well placed to capture these anxieties and provides a culturally significant point of contact between literary criticism, ecocritical theory and political process' (5). Sharae Deckard's use of the term comes closest to our context. While Deckard's essay in the above volume points to the socio-ecological crisis brought over by extractive capitalism in the peripheries of the world, she also reminds in another essay that the 'ecogothic form offers a powerful method of yoking *courte* and *longue durées*, in which longer histories outside the capacity for memory of individual human protagonists manifest as apparitions that disturb the present' (2015: 288). In a more recent essay, Deckard has explored the link between the toxic and the ecogothic (although it is helpful to remember that such a link was passingly mentioned in Buell's essay on 'Toxic Discourse': 653). Following a reading of Robert Barclay's Nuclear and toxic fallout novel, *Melal* (2003), Deckard notes that it is not the natural world that is terrifying here, but rather 'degradation and extinction—the unravelling of the whole web of life as a result of nuclear colonialism' (186). Speaking of 'telesthesia' as a moment that is able to reveal the periodicity of different moments of history, Deckard argues that the use of mythological or native cultural belief-systems works as a form of resistance to 'imperial cultures of governance'. The ecogothic, in this context, 'offer(s) a portal into the contemporary imagination of compound ecological crises with complex temporal antecedents, to materialise with an uncanny immediacy those revenants of "undead" processes in the past that continue to shape contemporary environments' (186). These contexts and readings appear particularly relevant for Nabarun's *Toy City*. Although we never know where Toy city is located, Nabarun's use of characters, setting, language and context, as well as the governing politics that the city is buying and dumping toxic materials from richer countries, points at its postcolonial location in the Global South. I will argue here that Nabarun blends ecogothic with fable genres to remind us of the essential paradox of the postcolonial life: that the current situation is both as improbable as a gothic/fable and yet as quotidian as an everyday embodied reality in the Global South.

Toy City begins on 4 December 2004 with a section called 'Martya sharir' or 'Earth body'. The city looks desolate on a wintry afternoon. The narrator, after bringing to our attention the radioactive mountain and the poisoned river in the city, tells us that a couple of nuclear bombs were dropped in this region two years ago which have cumulatively killed more than 17 million people. We are then informed of some of the surviving inhabitants of Toy City, who are all dead on the day of narration (4 December). We would know later that most of them died because of a fire in the factory, while the rest were killed by nuclear bomb testing on the day before the narration day, that is, on 3 December. From here, in a new section called 'Jogagni sharir' or 'Fire body', the novel does an analepsis and begins from 18 November 2004, building up the context for the nuclear explosion and then finishing with a confession by the catalyst character, Windcheater, about the necessity of these experiments for securing borders and showcasing power to enemy countries. What strikes our immediate attention is the apocalyptic nature of the narrative. This element of the apocalypse is managed not only by the production of 'disabling environment' through a neocolonial military-industrial complex, but also by the setting itself. The toxic mountain and the poisoned river and their effect on the bodies of the population already anticipate their impending death. There is no living ecosystem in the city because of the radioactive elements, pointing at the rather ironic reverse of a fable in the postcolonial, post-apocalyptic aftermath. Toy City is mostly deserted now. Equally, a desertification has picked up from the nuclear fallout—there is no vegetation around except for thorny weeds. There is no electricity in the city. After the factory was burnt, the state decided to terminate electricity supply. Indeed, it may appear that the state, following its military logic of using this space as a profitable ground for nuclear experiments, has stopped identifying the inhabitants as capable of exercising rights and duties—aspects that make living beings humans. Here, the nights are dark, and people have begun to drink an addictive coughing medicine called Coughidryl to forget their physical pain as well as the horrors of the dark. Whatever houses had survived the fire are currently in tatters, and because these houses are made of asbestos and the area has a toxic, tangy smell all around, they have combined to doubly toxify the inhabitants, rendering the border between the living and the dead meaningless. As Bamon tells Windcheater, 'What has remained of Toy City (after the fire) is actually the ghost of the old city' (198). Poisoned and depleted of labour-commodity value, these inhabitants of this toxic city are what Michael Edelstein (2004) calls in his book 'contaminated communities'—surviving with a bleak hope that things will turn otherwise, but only to be used as 'lab-rats' by the state and then quarantined at will.

The active production of this death-world by the state, which Achille Mbembe has influentially called necropolitics in the modern world (2003), has greatly affected our surroundings and our ecology. The cosmic references in the narrative accentuate the ghostly and contaminated nature of the atmosphere, suggesting what Sharae Deckard has elsewhere called 'an enduring nuclear'—the different temporalities of radioactive decay and the sense of blocked futurity in the literary genres of post-apocalyptic catastrophe (2018: 1). The narrator tells us in the beginning that the sun is 'dumb' today, and the road has a 'metal chill' (186). Later that night, the sky is 'choked with smoke', the moon appears 'sick', the 'trembling wind' turns into 'invisible mincemeat', while the cloud is 'bandaged here and there' (188). Nature is anthropomorphised in these images through pathetic fallacy. At the same time, there is a clear indication of the literalisation of the metaphorical: that this is what humans in the Anthropocene have turned nature into a sickly wounded body choked with blood and fear. In this 'dystopic nuclear modernity', what ensues is an enduring cold. The clear gothic elements of the setting are then re-energised in the description of the three witch-prostitutes who can foretell the events using a doll in a tiny pot of water. They believe that if the spinning doll comes to the centre of the watery pot, something fatal is bound to happen. The night before they all died, the witches had seen such a pattern. To be sure, they are considered crazy; but people seem to also retain faith in their words and haven't kicked them out of society. It's a society that is markedly coeval where capitalism's injunctions onto human life appear unevenly juxtaposed with everyday, native cultural belief systems. Indeed, Windcheater, who will soon gain the trust of the inhabitants of Toy City by his discovery of fresh water, tells them that these imaginings are true and need to be believed (of course, it is ironic considering his pivotal role in bringing them to destruction). This use of different temporalities, beliefs and practises point to a telescoped time, a telesthesia, that is able to capture the periodicity of compounded crises—radioactive explosion, war, toxicity, global capitalism, indigenous sociocultural beliefs and others—of our current times.

While the gothic elements reinforce the magical realist or critical irrealist style of the narrative—characteristic of Nabarun's fiction—*Toy City* appears to, however, also exploit the fable genre, albeit in an inverted fashion. If the fable genre, for instance, is known for its features of anthropomorphised non-human beings, plain storytelling style, short dialogues and a moral message—these features are either undermined or inverted in this dystopic tale of socio-ecological crisis through a radical use of narratorial interventions composed of omniscient exposition, short, raspy dialogues, fragments from books and maps, confession statement, etc. While the expository narrative shuttles between objective description of place and events and emotive appeal, the concision and brevity of the dialogues between strangers recall the communicational crises in post-war European drama. For instance, here is a section (the second paragraph of the novel) of expository narration:

> After the initial anxiety regarding the huge damage caused by two nuclear bombs, which were dropped in the Northern and Western

> sides of the country a couple of years ago, was over, scientists predicted that our climate would encounter remarkable changes. But while the bombs weighed 1 megaton each, the cloud of the nuclear winter wasn't too long and enduring. The first bomb had killed 9 million people, and the second vanquished 8.93 million. Toy City faced a severe winter in 2004. The North side was open. So, the chilly wind flew unhindered. It brushed past the City, pushed against the waste mountain, and then left. The toxic and heavy bluish dust on top of the mountain was for a while disturbed by it and then fell back in place again, quietly. (185)

One can hardly miss the calm, scientific tone of the narrator and the report-like narration here. The description of the bombs and the exact number of killings, reported in objective solemnity, produce a chilling effect—of how humans and places are turned into death worlds by the state. The commentary on the anxious repercussions in the scientific world regarding the bombs and the relatively weaker actual after-effects give us a clue into the deeply concerned yet sharply satiric mind of the narrator–author. The next and abrupt shift to Toy City from the country holds clear the synecdochic element in the novel—Toy City standing for the country as well as for the cities and regions in the Global South. The next fast-paced use of anthropomorphic imagery both questions the calmness of the narration above and the fear of desertification, while its humanness of action (the wind annoying the dust) and the post-apocalyptic sense of place are a reminder of our catastrophic damages of nature and climate.

Such calmness and objectivity, however, disappear in the dialogues between characters which are short, raspy and pointed, creating a sense of aesthetic disjunction. Consider, for instance, the introductory discussions between Bamon and Windcheater in Windcheater's shack on a 'poisoned moonlit night':

> Who are you?
> Me? I am no foreigner. I arrived today.
> Name?
> I take whatever name people choose to give me.
> Vagabond?
> You can call me that. Would you like to sit on the packing box? Bamon sits. Windcheater takes off his glasses, folds them.

> I have no weapon on me.
> What?
> Your pocket is small. So, I can see it. Bamon places a hand on his side pocket.
> Keep it there, no problem as long as you don't take it out. It can be a folded knife. But I assume it's rather a razor.
> Bamon changes the topic.
> What book is that? I have not seen an English book for a long time.
> Windcheater hands over the book. Bamon reads the cover—'The Nuclear Winter'
> What do you gain by reading this book now?
> There's no gain, but there's no loss either. (197)

The conversation goes on with the narrator informing us then that Bamon tells Windcheater the history of the city, which also forms part of the next section. Throughout the novel, conversations comprise either short and direct questions and/or mystifying responses like above, reminding us of their uses in modernist European writings by such writers as Samuel Beckett, Harold Pinter or Italo Calvino. Writing in the aftermath of a long war (the Second World War), these writers have used conversations in their work to conjure up an everyday world of miscommunication, fear, anxiety and distrust. It is not surprising that post-war European writings have often been found surrealist or fabular in style for their curious juxtaposition of the irreal and the real, or rather for their attempt to tease out the bizarrely extraordinary from within the banally ordinary (indeed, this argument can be extended to writings from a decolonised Global South using magical realism or critical irrealism as a powerful tool to explore and challenge received notions of history and truth).[3] After a long narratorial exposition or plot description, these abrupt, matter-of-fact exchanges create an aura of puzzle and mystery. The aesthetic bewilderment is heightened in another section where Windcheater tells people of Toy City of the possible presence of fresh water around. Here, his language, tone and rhetoric about water's self-preserving, curative and protective elements elevate his persona to that of a saint:

3 European post-war drama or fiction is increasingly understood as having absurdist, surreal, postmodernist elements; in the context of Nabarun, see my essay, 2016.

> Yes, water speaks. If water didn't speak, trees, animals, humans, nothing could ever exist. Water is a medium between the humans and the infinity. When you touch water, you don't know how many different things are also touching you in return. What do you think, water is dead? Water does not have life?
> Water has life?
> Yes, water has life. This water here wants to get rid of poison. And it is doing so on its own. It is so close to you, yet you can't hear it speak. But I can. (209)

Since he discovers fresh water very soon, clearly his position as a visionary as well as a messiah within the Toy City is firmly established (a saint or a messiah discharging moral instructions is at the heart of parables and fables as well). With this discovery, readers will also be puzzled as to whether Windcheater does actually have the visionary powers, until he explains his method in chilling calm in the end. But the use of a pedantic, mystic and bemusing language of a soothsayer after a matter-of-fact plot description and brisk dialogues between inhabitants adds to the aesthetic effects of disjunction. If fable is a story where the non-human being is anthropomorphised in a language characteristic of ancient storytelling manners for a moral message, the modern fable brings these features back only to deconstruct it and to remind us that the ethics and aesthetics of a fable are consciously manufactured to serve a purpose: either to unify humanity on a class-caste-gender axis, or to anthropomorphise/demonise non-human animals and living beings, or, in the context of our current nuclear modernity, to bring vulnerable humans and non-humans to self-destruction. Fable in the contemporary context adopts its more modern meaning in the narrative: that of falsehood.

This falsificatory side is ratified by the abrupt use of book or map excerpts which hold details about nuclear winter or thermonuclear fission. For instance, after 8 and 9 (the surviving Marxist–Leninist factory workers in Toy City) have spoken of a necessary revolution, Kumar finds a fragment about thermonuclear fission. Using free-indirect-discourse, the narrator describes the details in the fragment such as how much heat is needed to generate nuclear power, how much energy the Hirsoshima and Nagasaki explosions had carried, how many people died as a result, and that since then newer and more efficient and damaging bombs have been manufactured. This detailing ends with the note that 'it is funny that the more people know, the more they want to know more. They have no interest in knowing well things that they already know about' (204). This sophisticated, self-reflexive and satirical use of narration is characteristic of Nabarun (the narrators either chastise us for our lack of knowledge about basic/everyday things or speaking in an esoteric manner anticipate something fatal). This is not only a narrative hint of nuclear fear, but also a signal of the literalisation of nuclear modernity in everyday life. We live with these fragments and these truths and are extremely vulnerable and powerless to them. After describing with scientific precision, the effects of such bombs, the narrator reverts to the story. To be sure, these are not self-serving fragments. The narrator focalises on them strategically to remind us that we are reading a narrative of nuclear war and toxic ecology. This fragment takes up the role of a fuller confession narrative in the end when Windcheater tells us of his ulterior motive, that is to work for the state for 'Operation Vulture' to find out about such places and peoples who can be dropped bombs on and killed with impunity. Here the narrator's tone is report-like or journalistic—one of studied objectivity:

> To cut short, my work was to set up the business at a microlevel, and to make sure that things went well without anyone getting to see or know about it. [...] Known as Enhanced Aviation Warhead, these weapons are completely dependent on nuclear fission. The heat and the sudden tremor resulting from the explosions remain limited to relatively smaller regions. But the huge wave that arises from the Gama and the neutron radioactive explosions can pierce through any hard shell or any thick cover and vanquish any kind of living organisms in a moment. They however do not damage natural resources and such things. (227)

Such an ending not only pieces together the nuclear references into a coherent post-apocalyptic narrative but also amply points to a post-human, toxic habitat of 'enduring nuclear' that we live in. While there is resistance to this modernity from the margins (such as that of the factory workers which made Windcheater's task difficult, as he himself admits in the confession), people like Windcheater are deployed so as to neutralise such resistances by playing the role of either efficient collaborators or pseudo-resistant voices from within—a classic capitalist strategy. Though Windcheaters need human, emotive appeal to be part of the vulnerable population groups (so successfully done by him in the narrative), they are not allowed human emotions in real life. This is clear when he ends the confession with the note that the corpses of the couple, Jisha and Kumar, who he established an emotional relationship with and promised to rescue, are sent wrapped in plastic to be studied in a lab. The caustic, subversive and farcical aspects of the narration come full circle in the use of this deeply scientific, terse and dehumanised prose that ensures that humanity has lost all humanist values in a world of extractive capitalism and permanent war.

In the same interview quoted in the beginning of the piece, Nabarun added despite the prospect of a nuclear warfare and impending annihilation, he believed surrendering was not an option: 'we have a world to win. This is something I still believe in, and I write these thoughts because I believe in socialism. I am an out and out political person and an unrepentant radical' (Bhattacharya 10). His writings would continue to empower the poorest of the poor, who would snatch power from the rich and give birth to a socialist egalitarian world. While this aspect, what Pablo Mukherjee in a different context calls 'the transpersonality and collectivity in response to the toxic degradation of the postcolonial environment' (2015: 228), makes Nabarun into such a fascinating writer, in *Toy City*, however, such a possibility is missing. People are made vulnerable and then tricked by 'messiahs' of death like Windcheater. The slowly dying are ensured extinction through post-human machineries of the state, such as the camera-driven vultures, bombs, helicopters, etc. This is where I believe the narrative achieves the power of an ecogothic fable where gothic elements of haunting and telesthesia are compounded with the storytelling and moral traditions of fables—where the fable is only its contemporary avatar, enabled by a dystopian nuclear modernity. Here multiple temporalities and belief systems exist, here animals, machines and humans struggle against each other and vie for supremacy, here everyday life of slow violence often encounters spectacular and specular forms of violence and here ways of telling a story or giving hope to a dying community is actually used by the storyteller against the vulnerable community themselves. In this post-apocalyptic fabular world, unfortunately for Nabarun here, there is no escape from a toxic genocide.

References

Arestis, Phillip (1992), 'Furor on Memo at World Bank', *New York Times*, 7 February, accessed on 16 September 2019, https://www.nytimes.com/1992/02/07/business/furor-on-memo-at-world-bank.html.

Arnold, David (2016), *Toxic Histories: Poison and Pollution in Modern India*, Cambridge: Cambridge University Press.

Bale, Kevin (1999), *Disposable People: New Slavery in a Global Economy*, Los Angeles: University of California Press.

Bhattacharya, Nabarun (2011), 'Khelna Nagar' in Nabarun Bhattacharya, *Upanayas Samagra*,183–228, Kolkata: Dey's.

—— (2014) 'Nuclear Winter' in Nabarun Bhattacharya, *Angshik Chandragrahan*, 9–16, Kolkata: Dey's.

—— (2016) 'Marksbader Modhye Ekti Aschorjo Pluralism Achhe' in *Aro Kathabarta (A Collection of Interviews and Monologues by Nabarun Bhattacharya)*, 9–27, Kolkata: Bhashabandhan, 2016. (Translated in this book as 'There's an Uncanny Pluralism in Marxism').

Bhattacharya, Sourit (2016), 'The Margins of Postcolonial Urbanity: Reading Critical Irrealism in Nabarun Bhattacharya's Fiction' in Madhurima Chakraborty and Umme Al Wazedi (eds.), *Postcolonial Urban Outcasts: City Margins in South Asian Literature*, 39–55, New York: Routledge, 2016.

Buell, Lawrence (1998), 'Toxic Discourse', *Critical Inquiry*, 24 (3): 639–665.

Carrigan, Anthony (2010), 'Postcolonial Disasters, Pacific Nuclearization, and Disabling Environments', *Journal of Literary and Cultural Disability Studies* 4 (3): 255–272.

Clapp, Jennifer (2001), *Toxic Exports: The Transfer of Hazardous Wastes from Rich to Poor Countries*, Ithaca, NY: Cornell University Press.

Cockburn, Harry (2019), 'India Bans Imports of Waste Plastic to Tackle Environmental Crisis', *The Independent*, 7 March, accessed on 16 September 2019, https://www.independent.co.uk/environment/india-plastic-waste-ban-recycling-uk- china-a8811696.html

Deckard, Sharae (2015), 'Ghost Mountains, Snow Maidens: Ecological Imperialism, Compound Catastrophe, and the Post-Soviet Ecogothic' in

Elizabeth DeLoughrey, Jill Didur and Anthony Carrigan (eds.), *Global Ecologies and the Environmental Humanities: Postcolonial Approaches*, 286–305, New York: Routledge.

——— (2018), '"The Future is Behind Them!": Post-Apocalypse and Enduring Nuclear in Pos- Soviet Russian Fiction'. Unpublished. Academia.edu, accessed 16 September 2019, https://www.academia.edu/33390677/Post-Apocalypse_and_the_Enduring_Nuclear_in_Post-Soviet_Russian_Fiction.

——— (2019), 'Ecogothic' in Maisha Wester and Xavier Aldana Reyes (eds.), *Twenty-First-Century Gothic: An Edinburgh Companion*, Edinburgh: Edinburgh University Press.

DeLoughrey, Elizabeth (2009), 'Radiation Ecologies and the Wars of Light', *Modern Fiction Studies* 55 (3): 468–498.

Edelstein, Michael R. (2004 [2018]), *Contaminated Communities: Coping with Residential Toxic Exposure*, New York: Routledge.

Ellis-Patersen, Hannah (2019),'Treated like Trash: South-east Asia Vows of Return Mountains of Rubbish from West', *The Guardian*, 28 May, accessed on 16 September 2019, https://www.theguardian.com/environment/2019/may/28/treated-like-trash-south-east-asia-vows-to-return-mountains-of-rubbish-from-west.

Mbembe, Achille (2003), 'Necropolitics', *Public Culture* 15 (1): 11–40.

Mukherjee, Pablo (2015), '"Tomorrow There will be More of Us": Toxic Postcoloniality in *Animal's People*', in Elizabeth DeLoughrey and George B. Handley (eds.), *Postcolonial Ecologies: Literatures of the Environment*, 216–234, Oxford: Oxford University Press.

Nixon, Rob (2011), *Slow Violence and Environmentalism of the Poor*, Cambridge, MA: Harvard University Press.

Pellow, Naguib (2007), *Resisting Global Toxics: Transnational Movements for Environmental Justice*, Cambridge, MA: MIT Press.

Reuters (2019), 'Philippines Threatens to Dump Rubbish Back in Canadian waters as Row Deepens', *The Guardian*, 23 May, accessed on 16 September 2019, https://www.theguardian.com/world/2019/may/23/philippines-threatens-to-dump-rubbish-back-in-canadian-waters-as-row-deepens.

Smith, Anthony and William Hughes (eds.) (2015) *EcoGothic*, Manchester: Manchester University Press.

'The Unknown Something': Objects beyond the Economy of Use in Nabarun's Short Stories

Samrat Sengupta

'Where the world of objects is no longer taken seriously, the seriousness of the world of the subject must vanish with it.'

—George Lukács, 'On Walter Benjamin', (Lukács 1978: 88)

Nabarun Bhattacharya, a Bengali writer from India coming from Marxist lineage, wrote in a style that deviates majorly from traditional concepts of realism. In this chapter, I delineate his departure from conventional realist depictions of difference and alienation in society through his use of objects in short stories. In the modern realist form of thinking, objects generally appear either as background of the human world or as a part of man's own economy of use, his phenomenological experience of being and belonging. Objects are no longer enchanted or magical or carry some deep inexplicable meaning in modernity. They are understood only in terms of human experience and ways of looking. The word 'object' also leads to the word 'objectivity', where man can measure his relationship with his non-self dispassionately and in terms of what value they carry to man's experience and knowledge. Looking from a western enlightenment tradition objective, knowledge can lead us towards progress and a better form of existence. Marxist thought follows the same trajectory of understanding the real relationship of man with other things to move towards a more just society. Both socialist and critical realism appear to affirm the role of human mind in understanding reality as objective artefacts. My point is to show how Nabarun's stories employ objects not in terms of human use and understanding, but as wasted things inexplicable to human understanding. They effect the form of his writing as well as content. The shifting importance of things as they become more than a setting gives the form of his works an unreal character with respect to the 'real' human world. In terms of content, the description of objects as wasted pushes them out of human economy of use and creates a crisis of interpretation. Nabarun does not write in the tradition of orthodox Marxists who would prefer a transparent understanding of the world in terms of class struggle or a description of the capitalist crisis. In one of his short pieces titled 'Ojana Bostur Akar' ('The Form of Unknown Object') (2010a: 101), Nabarun refers to a dialogue between Arnold Hauser and Georg Lukács where Hauser comments on how great art is a way for responding to the crisis of life and cannot be equated with any social theory. Form is only a gateway to such response. His works show how instead of transparency and understanding, inscrutability of things that are unusable in the capitalist economy of use and exchange poses a threat to the structure of power. In Nabarun, men, animals, muted bodies and wasted things often take the form of unusable objects or get alienated by the economy of use and exchange. They sublimate into another alternative paradigm beyond our realist phenomenological thinking. To elaborate on this, I have chosen to focus on his short stories, though similar concerns frequently appear in his novels and poems too.

Nabarun started his literary career in a moment when the Naxalbari movement, a radical Maoist movement, was at its zenith. Looking into the revolutionary literature of the period one can find socialist realism that consciously portrays the revolutionary cause of the marginalised peasants or the urban poor as the preferred genre of writers. Dedicated activist and radicalised poets and fiction writers from Saroj Dutta, the leader of Naxalite cultural front, Birendra Chattopadhyay, a prominent sympathiser of the movement, up to activist storytellers like Utpalendu Chakrabarty or Jayanta Joardar formed this canon. One may also find the thick phenomenological description of the world in the way it is, or the way things may happen in writers like Samaresh Basu, Samaresh Majumdar or Mahasweta Devi (who is Nabarun's mother) among others. Both the objectivity of the onlooker and the subjectivity of an activist writer, however, keep faith in the vision of a human subject who can think, analyse and describe the world outside. Nabarun's stand is more precarious in this paradigm as he describes the objective world not as a totality, but as contingent, volatile and supposedly unreal. He is emotionally attached to the marginalised and the subjugated and does not remain an objective onlooker of human history and its flow. Marginal men occupy his stories as mundane and uneventful. It makes one doubt the status of those stories as meaningful, complete narratives. His world is a perfectly thingified (Lukács 1971: 83–110) world where non-human objects are placed alongside human and non-human beings, making the situation precarious for delineating their supposed difference. However, such 'reification' is not actively denounced with the subjective intrusion of human explanations or a promise of emancipation from alienation of the human essence. Rather, the entanglement of the beings and things creates an anxiety in the reader trained to think them as different. Nabarun's writings seem to challenge not only this reification of the human world but also the reduction of things to objects of human consumption and interpretation. While the Marx–Lukács paradigm of thought would suggest an objectively real world of things which are alienated from their natural essence, Nabarun would seemingly represent that circuit of alienation of both objects and subjects that are appropriated and subjugated to the capitalist process of *thingification*. Nabarun's works, instead of exposing an economy of use and exchange, precipitates an economy of waste and trash. Wasted or unusable objects as well as animals and men become the core of his worldview. Walter Benjamin's role of the artist as a collector of relics and objects from the past and the present to create history (Benjamin 2003: 389–400; Sontag 1979: 16–17) appears impossible in Nabarun, as both men and objects in his stories are ousted from the economy in the capitalist culture of commodity fetishism.

Several of the titles of his short stories speak about things that are nothing in the capitalist economy of use. Stories like 'Steamroller' (Bhattacharya 2006: 25–29), 'Kaktarua' (Scarecrow) (61–68), 'Cold Fire' (181–183) or 'Korai' (Cauldron) (282–287) are about objects which are ineffectual but which often become a tool for resistance towards the dominant paradigm of power. There are other stories like 'Chapor Marlei Se Ghum Theke Jege Uthbe' (A Slight Slap Will Wake Him Up from Sleep) (Bhattacharya 2014: 105–111) or 'Andho Beral'

(The Blind Cat) (Bhattacharya 2006: 184–189) whose titles are about dead bodies or animals. The story 'Chapor Marlei Se Ghum Theke Jege Uthbe' is named after the freshly killed body of an Iraqi soldier in the Iraq–America war. The story is a montage of scenes. There is the scene of a war zone in Iraq where the soldier gets killed by bullets from the US army which merges with the city of Baghdad in the middle of bombing where a blind orphan boy and an old man are trying to survive in a shelter, and the scene of excitement around a world cup cricket match in the city of Kolkata in India. The apparent safe zone from where the spectators of the match are casually gossiping about the Iraq war merges with the actual war zone to expose the precarity of people against an apparently safe world. The story ends with the body of the Iraqi soldier lying as if it can wake up any moment. The apparent safe life of the spectators of the cricket match placed alongside people in Iraq, dead or about to die gets reversed, as the dead body of the soldier is ironically described as one which can wake up by a slight probe. The expendable body-objects of the old man, the blind boy or the dead soldier are separated from the living spectators of the match by a thin screen. The frequent references to precarious life (Butler 2004), thrown out of the circuit of human meaningfulness and cast out as useless objects, correspond and supplement things in Nabarun's works. Similarly, non-human entities are pushed out of their status of beings, as they are abused in the human economy of things. In the story 'Ekta Lok o Ekta Kukur' (A Man and a Dog) (Bhattacharya 2010b: 27–29), we witness an old man and a dog as central objects of the story. They are not lives that matter and lives that can be put to use in a machine-like capitalist arrangement. In the story, they turn into dead bodies and get washed away by a flood together. The mattering of beings and things comes together to produce a new philosophy of objects, exposing the precarity of all things as they are in the process of becoming thingified, losing their status of an entity—the thing as such, that Heidegger defines with the definite article 'this' (Heidegger 1968:1–54). Similarly, in 'Chita manush' (The Leopard-Man) (Bhattacharya 2006: 121–125), animal, human and object become mutually exchangeable as we see an economically impoverished person entertaining children of rich people, wearing robes that makes him look like a leopard. The figure of an energetic violent animal becomes an entertainer in the restaurant Hot Breads—like a toy. A toy is often a thing which can be used as well as considered expendable, if needed. Beneath the false skin of the apparently happy animal-object, the suffering labourer stays hidden, whose humanity is devalued and rendered unknowable. He is unlike the traditional labourer in the Marxian paradigm. In traditional Marxism, a labourer is likened to his tool, but through class-consciousness could be separated from his tool. In a post-Fordist economy of service industry, man becomes a tool by himself. Like all tools, the person who plays leopard-man is also expendable. But the object leopard-man shall remain. The thing becomes no-thing as it loses its particularity—it's this-ness. But that is how a thing is thingified—by losing its identity to become one among many things that are exchangeable. The author asserts:

> If Dipaiya dies, it won't make any difference to the leopard-man's slough. Rather, someone else will wear it and become the leopard-man. He'll play with the children. There shouldn't be any dearth of people who'll dress up as leopard-men for three hours everyday. (Bhattacharya 2006: 221–225)[1]

Nabarun's stories are full of uneventful, useless things or beings that are transformed into things, and things that are usable and expendable. They are also full of descriptions of objects that are wasted. In post-enlightenment thinking, a conceptual separation is maintained between the consciousness-bearing subject and the object dependent on the understanding of such subject. Even in Marxian and Lukácsian frame of thinking it is as if the subject is vulnerable to become an object under capitalism which 'he' must resist. The anxiety of becoming an object looms large and our intellectual practises resist such possibility. Resistance to the process of being reduced to an 'object' indicates that the conscious individualistic subject of modernity rests on a structural separation of subject and object. Thus, under this structure, the subject

1 The page reference is drawn from the original Bangla text. This translation is included in the present volume, done by V. Ramaswamy.

is always haunted by the horror of losing the conscious individualistic subjecthood of modernity.

Nabarun's marginal characters mostly become a part of the world of objects they belong to and with which they are hermeneutically chained. These objects are not fetishised objects of capitalism which have a commodified sense of enchantment in terms of value. They have an unreal enchantment of a mystical world of the past where objects hold secret meanings and particular associations with people. Yet these objects, as we have discussed, are beyond the economy of use and exchange values, even though they are not in a world beyond the limits of these values. Rather, they refer to a world of economic abuse, a world where consumption is inextricably linked with waste, value with meaninglessness and life with death. Dead bodies become a central preoccupation in the oeuvre of Nabarun, both in his short stories and novels. Objects perform a threat to the human world of meaning in their wastefulness. In 'Ekta Lok o Ekta Kukur', for example, the difference between the background and the main characters becomes enmeshed by a strange singularity of death and uselessness. Not only the dog and the man but also the spatiality of their belonging is characterised by this wastefulness as the author describes:

> The shop, where the old man used to sit usually, did not prepare jalebis except during those two days of fair ... All the jalebis fried during fair could not be sold as well. After fair, those jalebis remained stuck against a dirty stained box. Some flies got caught in it as well. Their scattered bodies remained stuck onto the jalebis after death. (Bhattacharya 2010b: 27–28; translation mine)

The description suggests a world and things which remain shrouded by meaninglessness. So are the man and the dog lying dead and unattended and getting washed out by water. Such descriptions challenge our notion of a story with separation of plot and setting. It unsettles what matters to us.

The word 'matter', in Judith Butler's concept of mattering, suggests that bodies and entities become meaningful through an act of mattering that is the way we imagine and think of matter (Butler 1993: 3–27). Wasted objects and human subjects who resemble those wasted objects for being not usable in this world of commodification and consumption posit a threat to such mattering. Useless characters also become things—thick and inscrutable with impenetrable boundaries and not accommodable to the economy of use. Marx, while delivering his concept of capitalist alienation, talked about a fundamental alienation of the natural world (Marx 1976: 283; Marx 1973: 489; Clark and Foster 2010: 124–138). The obsessive consumption and appropriation of the natural world to suit the smooth flow of world capitalism rests on a metabolic rift. Objects of natural world in this rift get alienated from the natural metabolic process. Self-maximisation of profit and relentless expansion of capitalism require appropriation of all objects into its economy of use. But that is also an active forgetting of the objects as objects, the thing as thing-in-itself. The concept of historical time of modernity becomes meaningful by alienating the thing. In Nabarun, the thing returns as thing with its inscrutable thingness to unsettle our comfortable course of thinking. This thingness appears in the form of alienated things—as wasted humans, animals or objects. They signify the effects of the human economy of consumption. In Nabarun's works, frequently, the mythopoesis of a possible end of civilisation happening as a result of relentless human consumption and exploitation gets delivered.

For instance, a story titled 'Nuclear Winter' (Bhattacharya 2014: 9–16) begins with the description of a civilizational threat of annihilation of creation and a fundamental precarity that hovers through nuclear warheads ready to be fired by a callous push of button. The story, however, descends immediately from the global to the mundane and quotidian life of an ordinary man called Jyotish (the name literally means an astrologer) whose old and ailing mother passed away because of his neglect. She was helped by Jyotish to reach the open space in the rooftop where she was forgotten. She tried to come down by herself, lost control, pissed and died out of cold, as Jyotish fell asleep. The apparently unconnected nuclear winter hinges on the logic of an imminent and ominous futurity committed by neglect and alienation. The transformation of the human thing into a forgotten nothing is comparable to the neglect of the objective world in determining it absolutely by an economy of use. Nabarun wrote a series of stories with the character Baby K, who is a whore (could be called a Baby Ho in English as K suggests the word *Khanki* which in Bangla slang means a whore) and who drinks petrol (Bhattacharya 2013). The stories often end in an explosion or a possibility of it, as any combustible object can turn Baby K into a human bomb, a Molotov Cocktail. The sinister relationship between the combustible human or object of use with the possibility of a total annihilation, the human-object being an impending threat of violence and terror, is hinted upon here. The object can be of use and also outside the circuit of use. When it is outside the economy of use and the structure of exchange, it is either waste or an unknown threat, or perhaps both in a singular logic of resistance against global capitalism. Baby K is at the same time thingified, a person with marginal existence as a sex worker and a potential explosive. She becomes a threat not only for the petty womaniser Parijat who is fatally attracted towards her and as a result incurs petroleum in his blood, but she is also an explosive for the American soldiers who kidnap her to make her dance for their entertainment and tries to light a cigar on her lips. In a world of normalised terror of making humans expendable as dead bodies and usable as entertainers measured by exchange value, the unknown thing returns beyond the horizon of human measuring tools. US anti-terror warfares, their quest for controlling the oil repositories of the Middle East and their emergence as cultural imperialist across the world comes together in these stories in terms of the singular logic of use and wastefulness in the economy of consumption. Baby K, the feminine object of desire and appropriation also becomes the unknown other. She is a machine that is usable but also explodable. The wastefulness of Dipaiya in 'The Leopard-Man' as an entertainer comes back in another shape in Baby K. Her reduction to a machine that is fed oil and used for entertainment can any moment yield to an explosive human-object, that can turn the American soldiers into ashes along with her own self like a suicide bomber. The sphere of wasteful things haunts the living and the meaningful paradigm of life.

Unused objects mark the limit to the known world just like men who are outside the economy of consumption. We can relate it to the way Kant defined *noumena* or 'things-in-themselves' (Kant 1999: 354–365) which are not defined by the circuit of experiences and happen to be 'a concept setting limits to sensibility' (363) and the 'unknown something' (363) and can be only 'answered negatively' (364) with respect to the world of things in experience—of *phenomena*. However, in Kant, a tussle between the things-in-themselves as a limit concept to phenomena and one which 'serves, like an empty space' (365) remains. It stays inscrutable 'to limit empirical principles, without containing or displaying any other object of cognition beyond the sphere of the latter [empirical principles]' (365). In most of Nabarun's stories and novels, scattered objects mark the limit of the human cognitive world united with the *apriori* logic of global capital and its economy of use. The story 'Fakirer Jibone Kono Ekti Shonibar' (A Certain Saturday in Fakir's Life) (Bhattacharya 2014: 17–27) describes the marginalised existence of a contract labourer Fakir who was fighting for workers' rights against the shutdown of a factory where he used to have permanent employment once. The story is based on a detailed description of a random Saturday of Fakir's life when he used to meet with his comrades of protest. The world of Fakir is marked with wasted or poorly used objects which merge with Fakir's shadowy figure resembling a useless object, less than a human. The day ends with Fakir taking out a book containing quotations of class struggle by Marx and Mao. Before that the author describes the horizon of things where Fakir is implicated:

> Fakir could hear someone drawing water from tubewell far away. Silently, he switches on the ten-watt bulb of the kitchen space after finishing his smoke. He was in his underwear, casting a tall, skin and bone ghostly figure. He pulled the plastic tool and moved the useless Janata brand stove, the broken plastic tumbler, the effigies of God lying there for years, the shoe box and families of cockroaches and spiders, he grappled to find out and take it [a book] down. (Bhattacharya 2014: 26; translation mine)

This is how he found the book containing quotes on class struggle amidst the heap of wasted objects. Can we compare this wasted array of things with the shadowy figure of Fakir and ideas of class struggle, cast away in an age of withering revolution? Perhaps they form the sphere of the 'unknown something' and unsettle the world of phenomenon governed by the structural logic of the capital—the economy of use and exchange.

Nabarun's oeuvre provides an alternative to the paradigm of progressive and positive movement of time where all objects, human and non-human, living and non-living become meaningful by virtue of an economic logic of use. He raises a fire alarm to the progressivist ego of human history. The objects fall on the other side of human use and meaningfulness. Humans and animals also seem to be like those impenetrable objects. We can never know those objects objectively. In the story 'Andho Beral' (The Blind Cat) (Bhattacharya 2006: 184–189) the central character is a blind cat doubly removed from human consciousness in terms of being an animal and being blind at the same time. Its blindness reflects upon the blindness of the human cognitive apparatus structured by the economy of use. The biopolitical regime of power attempts to map each and every being in terms of its needs and aspirations to manage and mediate them. The 'unknown something' resists that biopower (Foucault 2009: 1). It rather exposes the security of being safely 'human' as contingent and precarious in a world where humans are subjected to the logic of use and exchange and valued in terms of usable objects or commodities. They are as much expendable as things, as the inanimate world outside, that has been trashed by what environmental Marxists like Clark and Bellamy Foster (following Marx's theorisation of social metabolism mentioned before) calls the metabolic rift (Clark and Foster 2010:124). The revolutionary literature usually places human consciousness at the centre of thought. But here an impossible world of non-passage guided by the primordial logic of usability and expendability working in tandem with objects come at the centre of resistance. In the story 'Kaktarua' (Scarecrow) (Bhattacharya 2006: 61–68), the human-like object scarecrow witnesses the murder of a *harijan* (a term for lower caste people) activist by hired goons of an upper caste landlord. This was the beginning of a caste and class struggle in the small locality of Bihar. The scarecrow in the story becomes an object which can feel but whose feelings can never be known. A police encounter kills some *harijans* when they try to march into the upper caste village with the dead body of their leader, Nirbhay Pasowan; many were arrested after that. The government did not acknowledge Nirbhay to be dead as he was beheaded, and the headless torso was not identified by the authority. The headless torso of the dead leader becomes comparable to the human-like object scarecrow. The lower caste people in the Indian system of caste are dehumanised, associated with filth and dirt, and are not allowed to be touched. They are equivalent to trashed objects. The transformation of this incident of violence was made into corner-page news in an esteemed daily and it never got attention of a city like Kolkata. In the story, a Marxist agro-economist with a Jawaharlal-Nehru-University-degree writes a theoretical article where he denounces this *harijan* movement as not having the potential for revolution. The human paradigm of explanation gets silently mocked by dehumanised objects like the existence of lower caste people like Nirbhay and the silent witness, *kaktarua*. The author suggests that both are unaware of their photograph featuring in a weekly magazine. Nirbhay's son puts on the tattered shirt that Nirbhay was wearing when he was killed on the top of the scarecrow. The story ends with the air of an upcoming election and the statement that scarecrows never vote.

Dead bodies that are inaccommodable to human structure of meaning and significance occupy an important place in Nabarun's work. They are more akin to unused objects than to a living body that has suffered demise. Dead body of Nirbhay like the scarecrow cannot vote and is outside the logic of biopower. Like the scarecrow, therefore, it is an undecidable object which is unknown to the modalities of power. Similarly, in 'Karai' (Bhattacharya 2006: 282–287), which literally means a large cooking vessel similar to a cauldron, a man was returning with his cooking cauldron which he gave out for rent but was not eventually paid for. Ironically, the man who rents his *karai* is also named Karai. He is one of the several nameless urban poor who pass away unattended owing to lack of money and proper treatment. He died of throat cancer. In the middle of the story, the narrator who is an auto driver, tells us that Karai is already dead and he was telling only a dead man's story. The large cauldron becomes an inaccommodable object in his little room where he was ailing. His friend Ram Singh chained it to a nearby lamp post to stop it from being stolen. After a detailed description of how poor people are constantly being dispossessed, disenfranchised and pushed out from their existence, the story ends with the chained karai—the cauldron that stays as a remainder of its owner Karai, just as in 'Kaktarua' we see the scarecrow wearing the shirt of dead Nirbhay. The karai remains chained in the lamp post as human-objects are phenomenologically and historically chained to their surroundings through an *apriori* meaning. Yet the useless objects posit a threat of throwing away those chains because we do not know their real meaning. The inner emptiness of the *karai* is like the jug Heidegger described to illustrate the thing (Heidegger 2001: 161–184). It is a thing characterised by a presence which cannot be fully accessible to human knowledge. The *karai* is described in the last few lines as a turtle which is trying to free itself from the chains and move away somewhere else.

In the end, we may want to invoke Latour's questioning of a disenchanted world of modernity where beings and things are separable (Latour 1993). The imaginative world of Nabarun is one where beings and things are not only connected in an anthropological cycle but are also mutually transferable. They can undergo metamorphosis. This metamorphosis is not simply anthropomorphic as it happens in fables but occurs through the mediational logic of mattering or how matters acquire meaning, becomes meaningful matters. It does not follow the logic which tells that the humans are becoming like matters and assumes them to be two separable categories where one is unduly imposed on the other. Nabarun's stories instead talk about boundaries between beings and things. The logic of boundaries constitutes both as mutually exchangeable. If the economy of things is to separate the usable and the waste, the productive and the unproductive, then the same rationale interpellates the human world. The boundary of human world is also set in terms of the valuable and the expendable, meaningful bodies of citizens that matter and the lives that are simply disposable. The precarious lives are *actually* understood as precarious things in a world where beings become meaningful by virtue of their usability to world capitalism, that is, by becoming usable objects. The logic of use produces value and puts it into a larger circuit of exchange. It also forms the shadow of suspension, of being trashed any moment when it is considered extraneous and useless to the system. Things that are useless form the waste, which though is a product of consumption, is a threat to its logic. This logic of consumption has to be protected from wasteful things. In human civilisation, useless things have to be thrown or kept out of sight to manage. Dominant forms of literature and literary reading also do not feature in any of these useless things except as a background or as explained as a condition of human existence. In Nabarun, it occupies a place that is more than a background. Things become the uncanny exposure to the reality of how things are made. Things are made into things by pushing out their actual thingness which could not be determined by some *apriori* knowledge or system. They are made a part of the capitalist world order, based on consumption. Consumption produces the alienation of matter that is inconsumable and beyond the economy of use and exchange values. This alienated thing is what does not matter and unsettles the mattering of things and beings. Thus, the function of literature in Nabarun is not a positive portrayal of life or rendering the negations of history meaningfully. He doubts meaningfulness and its immediacy and throws his objects beyond the economy of the meaning-making apparatus and human phenomenology. His artistic function is rather the experience of the extraneous, useless and meaningless things which cannot be sublated to any higher form and accumulate as waste in the horizon of human history.

References

Benjamin, Walter. (2003), 'On the Concept of History', in Michael W. Jennings (ed.), *Walter Benjamin: Selected Writings, Vol. 4,* 389–400. USA: Harvard University Press.

Bhattacharya, Nabarun. (2006), *Sreshtho Golpo(Best Stories),* Kolkata: Dey's.

——— .(2010a), 'Ajana Bostur Akar' (The Form of Unknown Object), in *Aquarium*, 101. Kolkata: Bhasabandhan.

———. (2010b), *Mahajaner Ayna (Mirror of Mahayana),* Kolkata: Bhasabandhan.

———. (2013), *Baby K Parijat*, Kolkata: Saptarshi.

——— . (2014), *Angshik Chandragrahan* (*Partial Lunar Eclipse*), Kolkata: Bhasabandhan.

Butler, Judith. (1993), 'Bodies That Matter,' in *Bodies That Matter*, 3–27. London and New York: Routledge.

——. (2004), *Precarious Life: The Powers of Mourning and Violence*, New York: Verso.

Clark, Brett and John Bellamy Foster. (2010), 'The Dialectic of Social and Ecological Metabolism: Marx, Mészáros, and the Absolute Limits of Capital', in *Socialism and Democracy 24.2*: 124–138.

Foucault, Michael. (2009). *Security, Territory, Population: Lectures at the college de France, 1977–1978*, London: Palgrave Macmillan.

Heidegger, Michael. (1968), *What is a Thing?*, trans. W. B. Barton, Jr. and V era Deutsch. Chicago: Henry Regnery.

Heidegger, Martin. (2001 [1975]), 'The Thing', in *Poetry, Language, Thought*, trans. Albert Hofstadter, 161–184. New York, Perennial Classics.

Kant, Immanuel. (1999), *Critique of Pure Reason*, trans. Paul Guyer. Cambridge: Cambridge University Press.

Latour, Bruno. (1993), *We Have Never Been Modern*, trans. Catherine Porter. Cambridge, MA: Harvard University Press.

Lukács, Georg. (1971), *History and Class Consciousness*, Trans. Rodney Livingstone. Cambridge: MIT.

——. (1978), 'On Walter Benjamin', in *New Left Review* 1/110:83–88.

Marx, Karl. (1973), *Grundrisse*, trans. Martin Nicolaus. New York: Vintage.

——. (1976), *Capital, Vol. 1*, trans. Ben Fawkes. New York: Vintage.

Sontag, Susan. (1979), 'Introduction by Susan Sontag', in Walter Benjamin, *One Way Street and Other Writings*, 7–28/ London: NLB.

'*Fyant Fyant Snai Snai*'—The Clarion Call of the Masses and Bengali Entertainment

Arnab Banerji

In a documentary based on his life and some of his iconic creations, author Nabarun Bhattacharya (1948–2014) criticises the complacency of the Bengali middle class and their obsession with efficient mediocrity. Bhattacharya with his unkempt beard, fierce bespectacled look and the wardrobe of a Bengali clerk was a far cry from the Waterman toting, cotton-kurta-pajama wearing, storm-in-a-teacup, Bengali bhadralok intellectual. The deliberate avoidance of intellectual gimmick is evident in Bhattacharya's body of work that put the squalor and grime of Kolkata's underbelly squarely in the centre of attention and gave it wings to explore the organic chaos of the unkempt metropolis and its continued sprawl. Bhattacharya maintains that he has achieved neither fame, nor money or even cultural influence in the 'culturally conscious, cheesy, and pretentious ghetto' (Bhattacharya 2015: 214) of Kolkata. In spite of his claim to the contrary, Bhattacharya has achieved iconic status amongst Bengali intellectuals for his chilling depictions of the Bengali social underbelly. Beyond the elite circles, however, no other work of Bhattacharya has resonated more with the average Bengali than his iconic creations—the human flying machines, the Fyatarus. The Fyatarus made their literary debut in 1995, an event that Bhattacharya celebrates as a 'memorable event in mine as well as in the life of Bengalis' (214). In this chapter, I chronicle the journey of the Fyatarus from the social margins to counterculture icons, thanks to popular culture adaptations in the form of popular plays and films. I will demonstrate in the ensuing discussion that the theatrical and cinematic adaptations of not only Bhattacharya's iconic creations, but his work in general has downplayed the characteristic subversion of Bhattacharya's oeuvre, reducing them to commodities for mass consumption.

It is perhaps important to note here that Bhattacharya's fiction was published primarily in small literary magazines grouped under the umbrella moniker—Little Magazines. The little magazines 'were typically published, with less rather than more regularity, on the cheapest paper imaginable, on presses run by printer's devils, on tiny budgets which usually came out of someone's personal savings. Their editors, who had no particular publishing expertise, ran them on pure fire, for want of anything better. They wanted to change the world, you see' (The Little Magazine n.d.). Bhattacharya, in spite of his cultural legacy (he is the son of the celebrated playwright Bijan Bhattacharjee and Magsaysay award-winning author and activist Mahasweta Devi) steered clear of major presses and chose this forum for his literary output. This must have been a conscious decision to stay away from the cynosure of media and critical glare. The stage and screen adaptations of his work, however, contrapuntal to his writing take place in the centre of the Bengali cultural bastion and are shepherded by Bengali cultural celebrities, the directors Debesh Chattopadhyay and Suman Mukhopadhyay. The precarity of Bengali theatre and Bengali independent cinema might carry over the cultural subversion at the heart of Bhattacharya's writing but the social and cultural capital symbolised by Chattopadhyay and Mukhopadhyay along with other fallacies, as this essay will demonstrate, subvert the political process of Bhattacharya's prose.

Let us begin with the example of Fyatarus. The magic-real characters cannot be explained adequately:

> What exactly are Fyatarus then?
>
> —I don't know what exactly they are. But Fyatarus are really special. Get it? If you look through history, you will see that several wise men have suggested several new tricks to reinvent humans. I think that Fyatarus are what they have finally settled upon after all this digging around (Bhattacharya 2015: 10).

These magic-real characters recruited from among the social underbelly after checking 'proper credentials' are inherently disruptive.

Bhattacharya notes that Fyatarus are his response to the status quo. He writes, 'I don't like witnessing this status quo, the many mischiefs of the rich and the elite. But I can't do anything about it. I can't get into a five-star hotel and wink at them in derision. But I can make four Fyatarus enter this space. And give them a free rein' (Bhattacharya 2015a). Bhattacharya tells us that there are several different kinds of Fyatarus from different walks of life. But in his stories on these characters he focuses on initially two and subsequently three Fyatarus—a failed share broker DS, an unemployed middle-aged man Madan and the failed poet Purandar Bhat. The three Fyatarus meet for the first time in the short story 'Kabi Sammelane Fyataru' ('Fyatarus at the Poetry Convention'). The meeting merits a retelling here. Madan and DS meet in Central Kolkata's Curzon Park. Madan reprimands DS for offending the rats who live in Curzon Park by throwing a banana peel at them after eating the banana himself. DS is sent away by Madan to buy snacks for the rodents as retribution.

There are several subversive political messages in this otherwise simple episode. Madan extols the might of the rats who live underground but seem to have the city under their grip through their extensive tunnel networks. The rats have dug tunnels that connect the administrative (the Writers' Building, the erstwhile seat of the State Government), communications (GPO or the General Post Office), law enforcement (Lalbazar Police headquarters) and ground transportation (Koilaghata, the Eastern Railway headquarters) centres of the city and give the rats control over these units. The innocuous rats are, therefore, reimagined as possessing great power that they can and have exercised when provoked to do so. In his true style, however, Nabarun centres the power of the rats on their preferred mode of attack—dismembering the male penis. While DS is gone looking for snacks to offer to the rats, Madan notices a man resembling a scarecrow and drenched in sweat reciting lines of a poem. The two strike up a conversation and soon is joined by DS. The three develop an immediate camaraderie over Purandar's poems and before long embark on their first adventure to ensure Purandar's participation in the poetry convention of the title.

In the play *Fyataru*, Debesh Chattopadhyay left the moment of their introduction intact. Unfortunately, however, in performance, the audience's attention seemed to be drawn to the phallic joke from the episode and DS's over-the-top reaction in response to it over the political commentary evident in Nabarun's writing. In the stage version, a ragtag Purandar recites 'Ghumole hobe na klanti dur/Oi dekha jaye Borobudur…' (Sleeping won't dispel the weariness/Borobodur is seen yonder…) when Madan spies on and befriends him (Bhattacharya 2015b: 60). During their initial conversation, Purandar observes that Madan must be from a history background. The observation is made with reference to Madan's carefree retelling of the history of the rodents and their abode Curzon Park in the heart of Kolkata. Nabarun's casual disregard for the formal history of the neighbourhood as signified by Madan's retelling of it with a conviction of a seasoned historian is yet another political act—subverting conventional histories. Just like the episode concerning rats, however, the political significance of Madan's reimagining of Kolkata's history seemed to be lost on the audience who regale at DS's homophobic reference to the park being a gay cruising spot.

The three Fyatarus embark on several adventures across a wide spectrum of Kolkata landmarks and cultural events, creating constant havoc and disruption to the staid mediocrity of Bengali life. And yet Fyatarus are fiercely ordinary. Madan's wife has left him, DS lives in a house that is barely held together and Purandar has no prospects as a poet. The three regularly get drunk on cheap local booze and survive one day at a time. But the precarity of their existence on the urban margins does not dissuade them from their ultimate goal—to constantly provoke the outrage of the Bengali bhadralok culture. Purandar's poems are serious creations in the world of the Fyatarus. The simple lines and the simpler message resonate with Madan and occasionally DS, who marvels at Purandar's poetic prowess to improvise on his feet and about any subject. Chattopadhyay's direction, with its emphasis on the melodramatic, transforms DS from the ruffian that he is on page to a jester on stage. As the ruffian, DS often provides the necessary push to the narrative that betrays his association with the city's underbelly—like the time he threatens one of the organisers of the poetry convention or whenever he questions Madan having some extra cash. In spite of his rough edge, DS balances out the connivance of the street-smart

Madan in Bhattacharya's text, keeping the mediocrity of the Fyataru enterprise intact. As a comic relief, however, as he is on stage, DS seems to lose that political agency and is little more than a rabble rouser who navigates audience response almost like a live laugh track.

The world of the Fyatarus, located below the surface of what meets the eye in Kolkata and Bengal, is an unmarked parallel reality to life in the metropolis. Eviatar Zerubazel notes how 'marked identities carry greater semiotic weight, it is nevertheless the unmarked ones that tend to carry greater political weight' (Zerubazel 2018: 32). The political weight from being unmarked is a result of the unmarking being conflated with 'normal', the non-deviant middle ground that is accepted as representative of the general. In the Indian context, and more specifically in the context of the present discussion, however, the unmarked represents the subaltern other. An identity, that in India, is often unaware of its political weight. In Bhattacharya's milieu, the marked identity of the bhadralok carries the semiotic as well as the political weight being as it is in the cynosure of attention as bearers of cultural and social values. Bhattacharya's writing, therefore, deliberately steers clear of the marked identity of Bengali gentleness. His narratives like his characters draw inspiration from the 'sickening hospital wards, chaotic crematoriums, buzzing country liquor holes, corrupt government chambers and scheming political party offices' (Bag 2016). And in doing so, Bhattacharya inspires subversion by forcing us to see '*the ordinary as extraordinary [and] the familiar as strange*' (Zerubazel 2018: 62). Bhattacharya's tactic echoes Zerubazel's, '[u]nmarking the hitherto marked' to blend in the extraordinary world of the Fyatarus with the normalised world of the bhadralok (87). But given the political and the semiotic weight of the marked category of the Bengali gentle folk, Bhattacharya's iconic Fyatarus work towards '*backgrounding the hitherto marked while simultaneously foregrounding the yet unmarked*' (87). By doing so, Bhattacharya creates literary as well as semiotic subversion. In this subversive reality, the Fyatarus are the protagonists who give Bengali gentleness a run for its money.

In their stage adaptations, however, which undoubtedly celebrate Bhattacharya's foregrounding of the unmarked subversive world of the Fyataru, the actions of subversion are highlighted devoid of the author's political finesse. The resulting political dissonance reduces the plays to populist cheap thrills instead of the radical tool that Bhattacharya's work is meant to be. When Fyatarus take flight in Bhattacharya's writing, the inhibited dissatisfaction of the Bengali subaltern takes flight with them—'let them commit foul play, let them break things—there is a satisfaction in spoiling things. I feel that there is a provision for the insulted to exact revenge here' (Bhattacharya 2015a). Similarly, when Bhattacharya proposes a mutiny armed with brooms, human refuse and a rusty old *nunu-kaman* (tiny canon, the word *nunu* being a slang reference to a tiny flaccid penis) in *Kangal Malshat*, he is demonstrating the subaltern potential of reversing the status quo. *Kangal Malshat* is a particularly difficult text to adapt for the stage and, as we will demonstrate later, film. The novel not only chronicles the impossible subaltern revolution spearheaded by Fyatarus and Choktars, it also frequently includes social commentary from Bhattacharya. For example, the seventh instalment or chapter seven of the novel starts with Bhattacharya's scathing critique of the Durga Puja special editions of Bengali literary periodicals and their contributors. The same chapter continues with a series of supposed letters to the editors that either celebrate or (largely) decry Bhattacharya's novel in real time as it is being written (Bhattacharya 2013: 272). Bhattacharya offers a parallel criticism of the ineffectual intellectual and literary environment around him and then immediately locates himself within it to hint at how, in spite of obvious differences with the multitude, his work is somehow part of the continuum. It is almost impossible to capture these critiques without derailing the narrative integrity of a stage play. But the novel masterfully weaves its way through this treacherous territory, bringing its focus back to the revolution in preparation. Therein lies the brilliance of Bhattacharya's writing, which Aveek Majumdar calls a binocular, offering both macro and micro analyses of the society depending on which end of the tube you look through (Majumdar 2017). However, in their stage adaptations, we can witness how the flight of the Fyatarus is reduced to a demonstration of stage gimmicks, and the subaltern revolution is cheapened by the audience's uproarious reaction to the word *nunu* at the expense of the canon that the word signifies in this context. Especially, since these performances are taking place in the bastions of Bengali bhadralok culture. Unlike his writings, the plays don't generate discomfort among the audience about their meek acceptance of the status quo. The cathartic experience of hearing slangs spoken out loud and the rich being ridiculed is contained within the performance space and celebrated as expert craftsmanship. In a way, theatrical adaptations of Bhattacharya reinforce the status quo by taking the politics out of Bhattacharya's semiotic subversion of foregrounding the unmarked world of the Fyatarus.

Film adaptations of Bhattacharya's work, on the other hand, have been able to exploit the political possibilities of the original works better. The 2005 Suman-Mukhopadhyay-film *Herbert* is based on Bhattacharya's 1993 novel of the same name. *Herbert* is Bhattacharya's most celebrated and decorated work, having received several state and national awards. The novel's protagonist, Harbart Sarkar, played admirably in the film by Joyraj Bhattacharjee (young Harbart) and Subhasish Mukhopadhyay (older Harbart), lives a life that offers a subaltern lens to the first four decades of independent India from the 1950s to the 1990s. Harbart is an urban outcast who fights hard to find a corner for himself in a system that seems firmly rigged against him. The film is a 'mad, messy, and frequently amazing epic [...]chronicl[ing] several decades' worth of social and political tumult in Calcutta [sic]' (Lee 2008). One major difference, however, between the novel and its silver-screen counterpart is the loss of the novel's immediacy in its screen avatar. True to his signature style, the world of Harbart that Bhattacharya paints in his novel is ordinary: 'the house of Dhanna-dada was neither too big nor was it too small. Two storied. The roof had a room for the family deity, and a tank for Ganges water on the roof of this small room' (Bhattacharya 1993: 19). Like Purandar Bhat, a decade later and perhaps foreseeing the Fyataru Purandar's poetic prowess and failure, Harbart wrote poems while idling away his time on top of this small room. The poems trace the creative development of an ordinary mind as much as they chronicle Harbart's ordinariness.

In his screen adaptation, Suman Mukhopadhyay gives Harbart and his milieu a more universal canvas to play. This is in contrast to the ordinariness palpable in the novel, which is what perhaps sets it apart. In the film, Harbart's ancestral home is reminiscent of a zamindar's mansion, decrepit in its current avatar but resplendent, nonetheless. In the novel, Harbart's childhood friend, Robi, commits suicide by drowning in a municipal reservoir. Robi's loss is the protagonist's first conscious encounter with death. The mundane fact of suicide in a putrid municipal reservoir is replaced by Robi drowning in the river Hooghly in the film. Harbart's guilt-ridden face framed in a close-up, drawing our attention firmly to Harbart, as opposed to his being one of the many in a crowd as Bhattacharya described the episode in writing. Similarly, the choice of the celebrated Presidency College campus as Harbart's cousin Binu's place of education over the more modest Asutosh College campus of the original allows cinematic grandeur made possible by the grand staircase of the Presidency to take the place of the urban ordinariness of the Asutosh College campus. In spite of these deviations and other narrative liberties, the film aptly comments on the social underbelly that is the focus of Bhattacharya's novel. *Herbert*, the novel, never romanticises its protagonist's predicament. The mundane and yet fantastic reality of Harbart Sarkar is reported in a matter of fact way—the way perhaps we talk about an intriguing mysterious neighbour. The film, on the other hand, invokes nostalgia. Mukhopadhyay's narrative with its minor deviations from Bhattacharya's novel, looks at Harbart's milieu as a lost Edenic past complete with its many failures. Mukhopadhyay's film initiates the 'mourning, longing, and attempts to retrieve or recreate (in memory or reality) the desired prelapsarian condition' (Sprengler 2009: 72). Mukhopadhyay's narrative strategy to depict Harbart's childhood and adolescence also lends the film a mnemotopic identity. Sprengler explains, citing Purdy (who draws on Bakhtin) that a mnemotope is a 'chronotopic motif that manifests the presence of the past, the conscious or unconscious memory traces of a more or less distinct period in the life of a culture or an individual' (74). Mukhopadhyay's film prompts the audience to revisit the past, thus, shifting our interpretation of the present. The cultural past of Bengal is invoked continually in an effort perhaps to affect our reading of it in the present. Likewise, music in *Herbert* functions as a mnemonic device. The soundscape, score and the occasional song in the film forcing audiences to be 'located somewhere else' away from their present and in a nostalgic past

(76). *Herbert*, the film, represents Suman Mukhopadhyay's nostalgic retelling of a lost time through a freewheeling adaptation of a Bengali literary classic. The film draws its life blood from Bhattacharya but the translation from the page to the screen weakens the politics at the core of this celebrated novel.

Suman Mukhopadhyay's *Kangal Malshat* (2013), also adapted from Nabarun Bhattacharya's 2003 novel of the same name, however, turns the political satire at the heart of the novel completely on its head. The novel, serialised in 2003, is a scathing criticism of the Government of West Bengal. Although leftist in its official moniker, the government and its latest machinations had proven to be anything but progressive, twenty-six years after being sworn into power in 1977. By the time Mukhopadhyay made his film in 2013, however, the leftist government had been summarily voted out of power from local, municipal and state administrations along with returning embarrassing results in the federal general elections of 2009. Mukhopadhyay's cinematic criticism, therefore, was not only levelled at the erstwhile Communist regime but also at the new administration of the Trinamool Congress led by Mamata Banerjee. The government did not take the criticism lightly and tried to stifle the release of the film regionally (Banerjee 2013). The film finally received the requisite nod from federal agencies and was in wide release across Kolkata and its suburbs in August 2013 (Sengupta and Mukherjee Pandey 2013).

The film, like its stage predecessor, also directed by Suman Mukhopadhyay, makes several significant departures from Bhattacharya's text. Let us start with one of the most basic differences that demonstrate the departure from Bhattacharya's intended subaltern reality to Mukhopadhyay's comic hilarity. As part of the preparation for the subaltern revolution, Bhodi's assistant, Sarkhel, starts digging a hole in the courtyard of his house. To keep Bhodi, the leader of Choktars, abreast about the latest status of the dig, Sarkhel and Bhodi establish a primitive communication mechanism between their two houses. The primitive technology in Bhattacharya's fiction ensconces the reader further into the world of the Fyatarus and Choktars at a considerable distance from that of middle-class comfort, a constant object of derision in Bhattacharya's writing. In Mukhopadhyay's stage and screen adaptations, the actors playing Bhodi and Sarkhel mimic the nasal tone when they communicate with each other, using this children's contraption. The false nasal tone giving their exchange a comic ring which is not only inessential but belies the political significance of the conversation between the two principal instigators of the revolution giving it a rather strange comic bent.

In a similar manner, the characterisation of Dandobayosh, the primordial talking crow, takes a very interesting turn on stage and screen. In the novel, Dandobayosh serves as a guardian to the revolution. He is a literal crow, with sagely and pertinent advice. On stage and on screen Dandobayosh portrayal, in spite of the respective actor's best efforts, amounts to little more than a forced caricature. On screen, Mukhopadhyay imagines Dandobayosh as an apparition rather than the actual crow that he is in the novel. It is an understandable deviation to accommodate the anthropomorphism which is perhaps executed more easily on page rather than on screen. For his film, Mukhopadhyay seems to have given in to the temptation to include a song from Kabir Suman. Incidentally, the iconic singer-songwriter also plays Dandobayosh in the film. Suman's song, 'Jhinchak chhara kichu thakbena' (Nothing but the flashy will survive), as a standalone piece captures the mood of Bengal in 2013—transitioning to a period of political naivete after three decades of leftist government. It is a foreboding reminder of the stark political quagmire that the state was stepping into. In the world of the novel and even in its screen version the song is, however, startlingly out of place. The sagely Dandobayosh of the novel and even his less wise screen avatar breaking into a techno-rock number, replete with a rather inconsistent dance performance of the Fyatarus, betrayed the conviction in the subaltern revolution that the talking crow and the Fyatarus have in the novel.

Mukhopadhyay also makes a drastic departure in the closing moments of his film from that of Bhattacharya's novel—both in representing the revolution of the masses and in the way the government and the revolutionaries arrive at a peace resolution. In the novel, the positional warfare led by Marshall Bhodi is a serious business. It puts the police, in spite of no casualty, on the backfoot and forces them to reimagine and rethink their battle preparedness.

Bhattacharya cuts a very sorry figure of the Kolkata Police and the administration that governs it. And the battle itself is serious business, in spite of the primitive weapons used. Bhattacharya's description of the aerial assault of the Fyatarus under the cover of the roving discs or *chaktis*, the myriad combination of cannon balls fired from the restored *nunukaman* under the supervision of the retired Army Officer Major Ballabh Bakshi and the army of painted tin tanks that infest the streets of Kolkata are a multi-modal assault on civic institutions that have failed civilians. The warfare on stage and screen are, however, significantly tamer. Interspersed with scenes of refuse raining on police stations, frantic phone calls between various police personnel, a single shot firing off the *nunukaman* and an attack launched by cockroaches is an ever-expanding montage of popular uprisings from across the globe. Mukhopadhyay wants to locate the revolution of the Fyatarus and Choktars on a global canvas of popular uprisings. And while the effort is certainly laudable, it perhaps misses the point of Bhattacharya's work. *Kangal Malshat* plays out in the narrow lanes surrounding south Kolkata, its dingy crematoriums and red-light districts. The universal message of the text lies in Bhattacharya's fierce familiarity of every nook and cranny of this decrepit underbelly that rivals the world of shopping malls, fancy hotels and secret power brokering. Spivak writes:

> Outside [though not completely so] the circuit of the *international* division of labor, there are people whose consciousness we cannot grasp if we close off our benevolence by constructing a homogeneous Other referring only to our own place in the seat of the Same or the Self. [...] To confront them is not to represent (*vertreten*) them but to learn to represent (*darstellen*) ourselves (Spivak 1988: 84).

Mukhopadhyay's screen adaptation and its tendency to equate and conflate the localised revolution of the Choktar–Fyataru alliance with those of the global struggles of oppressed people seems to be an attempt to forcibly create and then grasp the consciousness of oppressed people everywhere at the expense of faithfully reproducing the local struggle of the oppressed masses of a specific geopolitical identity. Bhattacharya in his writing understands that it is naïve to seek to represent every subaltern subject position and, therefore, focuses on the local while being fiercely conscious of not only the global but also his own problematic position between and betwixt the populations he seeks to represent and the intellectual cadre that he can very easily slip into. His conscious disavowal of the mainstream and constant reminder of the same is a political position that Mukhopadhyay seems to assume but fails to in this instance.

Mukhopadhyay faithfully replicates the moments of war declaration in his stage and screen versions of the novel. Bhodi calls the Police Commissioner and declares war on the city. After terrorising the civic authorities, the situation is brought under control when the city's intellectuals deploy themselves to write a declaration of pacifism. Bhattacharya's master stroke now shifts its target from the failed civic institutions and leftist ideals of the government to the intellectuals of the city who value their rest a little too much—'sangram jemon darkar temon bisramero darkar. Seshokto proyojonti amader khub beshi' (Just like the class struggle one also needs rest. And we need the latter much more) (Bhattacharya 2013: 377). In the stage and screen versions, several intellectuals are shown talking over each other as they jointly draft the pacifist proposal. The ensuing cacophony blunts the political edge of Bhattacharya's prose which did not seem to mince any words and was written as a direct and targeted attack on the vagaries of the city's intellectuals. The cacophonous rendering of the intellectual's declaration is an interesting creative choice from Mukhopadhyay. One cannot help but wonder if the artistic consciousness of the director superseded his politics at this moment. Mukhopadhyay, after all, is counted amongst the city's intellectual elites. He is the recipient of several civic decorations and was a prominent figure in the anti-left coalition floated by the city's intellectual leaders protesting the excesses of the erstwhile Left Front led state government in West Bengal. Without insinuating malevolence, it is perhaps not wrong to conjecture that Mukhopadhyay cannot totally disavow the community that he belongs to with as much élan as Bhattacharya does in his writing.

Bhattacharya ends *Kangal Malshat* with a temporary hold on the revolutionary instincts of the masses. Bhodi is promised the chairpersonship of the corporation that gets to control the oil reserves which is the supposed target of Sarkhel's endless digging. He is also assured that all his associates would also be hired in this corporation. Assured of the success of this arrangement, Bhodi and his team of revolutionaries agree to a ceasefire. And then the fierce cadres of the revolution recede into their ordinary lives.

For the ending of his screen edition of the novel, however, Mukhopadhyay chose to take a dramatically opposite route to the one in Bhattacharya's novel. All of the principal characters find refuge in what can only be described as middle-class comforts. A newscaster announces DS buying a flat, Purandar becoming a regular in poetry conventions and Bhodi vacationing in Shantiniketan. Mukhopadhyay may have attempted to suggest that all people are eventually sell outs and choose personal comfort over a collective revolution. But in doing so, the film echoes Spivak's warning of an essentialist historiography that lends credence to locating ourselves as opposed to representing the subaltern Other.

Writing about American stand-up comedian and late-night TV host Stephen Colbert and his faux conservative television show *The Colbert Report*, Jonathan Rossing observes, 'one of humor's greatest contributions is educative error correction' (Rossing 2016: 73). He continues, 'When the borders people construct become too rigid, too constraining, or too oppressive to prove valuable, humor points out the flaws and models creative new modes of thought and action that might inspire ways to transform those borders' (73). Rossing, however, also warns that excessive caricatures which reinforce problematic beliefs belie humour's potentially positive effects. Mukhopadhyay's cinematic adaptation of Bhattacharya certainly attempts to create fissures in what was becoming an increasingly stifling political climate. But instead it resorts to caricatures of the social underclass in Kolkata rather than celebrating the subaltern. In the novel, the subaltern in the city seize a seat in the table and force the civic administration to give in to their demands. In the film, the portrayals of the subaltern by popular matinee idols Kaushik Ganguly et al. make for excellent entertainment but have been divested of the political potential. The clarion call of the masses that Bhattacharya imagines, thus, reduced to a jester's yelp during its transition from the page to the screen.

Nabarun Bhattacharya died on 31 July 2014, two months after the Indian electorate elected a right-wing Hindutva government. He died away from public glare in a small suburban cancer hospital, battling pancreatic cancer. His death, like his life, was a quiet affair. The quiet, unassuming and yet fiercely political was his rhetoric. In stage and screen adaptations, however, this rhetoric frequently became a populist tool minus the political vitality underscoring his cheeky poetry. The lack of political depth also plagues Q's documentary, *Nabarun*, released after the death of the author in 2018. The director wanted to capture the dynamism of his personal interactions with the author rather than, 'Contextualising Nabarun-da', which 'would take a lot of time, and then the film could not concentrate on the dynamism of my personal interaction with him' (Ghosh 2018). An academic study is not at the heart of the project and the director acknowledges being a 'fanboy' but nevertheless the documentary suffers from celebrating the cult that seems to have been forming around Bhattacharya much to his chagrin. Bhattacharya may have made conscious attempts to steer clear of being at the centre of fandom and to put his political objective of 'a democratic socialist order beyond the rigid Marxist theory [where] people will get enough to eat, their health and lives will be looked after and children educated. Till then, I'll protest.' Bhattacharya did not get to realise his dream of a democratic socialist order, but he continued protesting until his death. It is a pity that the protest at the heart of his work lost its teeth on stage and screen. Bengali group theatre's failure to capitalise on the political edge of Bhattacharya's work is especially unfortunate. The Kolkata-based-group-theatre stage has suffered from a chronic lack of original content, a lacuna that has often been filled with random and indiscriminate borrowing from below par Western texts besides an overreliance on the Western canon.

Bhattacharya's disdain for the contemporary Bengali theatre rings true when looking at the stage versions of his work which overlook the political, the struggle and aim straight for simply the festive. And yet, as Priyanka Basu demonstrates, Bhattacharya's writing is inherently performable—'sketch[ed] through dark humour, slapstick, and parody' (Basu 2015: 85). Under right maneuvering, Bhattacharya's fiction certainly holds the spark to reinvigorate the Bengali group theatre stage. This possibility, however, can only be realised if Bengali theatre practitioners and screen directors look beyond the cheap thrills that abound in Bhattacharya and aim to recreate and reflect on the political in his work.

References

Bag, Shamik. 2013. 'Nabarun Bhattacharya: Offence given and taken'. *Live Mint*. March 16. Accessed November 2019. https://www.livemint.com/Leisure/hVBrf6IjV1TGHigZRNj7GP/Nabarun-Bhattacharya--Offence-given-and-taken.html.

Banerjee, Monideepa. 2013. 'Bengali Film, critical of Mamata Banerjee, blocked by Regional Censor Board'. *NDTV*. February 25. Accessed 2 November 2019. http://www.ndtv.com/article/cities/bengali-film-critical-of-mamata-banerjee-blocked-by-regional-censor-board-335125.

Basu, Priyanka. 2015. 'Texts of Power, Acts of Dissent: Performability and Theatricality in Nabarun Bhattacharya's Short Stories'. *Sanglap: Journal of Literary and Cultural Inquiry* 2 (1): 70–89.

Bhattacharya, Nabarun. 1993. *Herbert*. Kolkata: Dey's Publishing.

———. 2013. *Upanyas Samagra*. Kolkata: Dey's.

———. 2015a. 'January 2001-e Proma Prokashona theke prokashito 'Fyatarur Bombachak' boitir Mukhobondho'. In *Fyataru Bingshoti*, by Nabarun Bhattacharya, 214. Kolkata: Bhasabandhan,

———. 2015b. 'Kobi Sammelane Fyataru'. In *Fyataru Bingshoti*, by Nabarun Bhattacharya, 59–74. Kolkata: Bhasabandhan.

———. 2015c. 'Sadhu Samagame Fyataru'. In *Fyataru Bingshoti*, by Nabarun Bhattacharya, 109–118. Kolkata: Bhasabandhan.

Chattopadhyay, Debesh. 2017. Phataru: Reaction by Nabarun Bhattacharya and Avik Mazumdar. April 18. Accessed 1 Novemeber 2019. https://youtu.be/yY6m8i_deVs.

Ghosh, Devarsi. 2018. 'In Q's "Nabarun", a look back at the Renegade Bengali Writer with a Cult Following: Q's Documentary Celebrates the Iconoclastic Bengali Writer Nabarun Bhattacharya'. *Scroll*. June 24. Accessed 25 October 2019. https://scroll.in/reel/883520/in-qs-nabarun-a-look-back-at-the-renegade-bengali-writer-with-a-cult-following.

Ghosh, Madhusree. 2016. 'Kangal Malshat Movie Review'. *The Times of India*. May 17. Accessed 26 October 2019. https://timesofindia.indiatimes.com/entertainment/bengali/movie-reviews/kangal-malsat/movie-review/21622033.cms.

Lee, Nathan. 2008. 'Storm Advisory: Cyclone of a Life on the Horizon'. *New York Times*. December 10. Accessed 27 October 2019. https://nyti.ms/2NdTnIY.

Rossing, Jonathan. 2016. 'Humor's Role in Political Discourse: Examining Border Patrol in Colbert Nation'. In *Crossing Borders Drawing Boundaries: The Rhetoric of Lines Across America*, by Jonathan Rossing. Boulder: University of Colorado Press, 60–75.

Sengupta, Ratnottama and Jhimli Mukherjee Pandey. 2013. 'Kangal Malsat cleared by Tribunal with Cuts'. *The Times of India*. March 5. Accessed 28 October 2019. http://articles.timesofindia.indiatimes.com/2013-03-06/kolkata/37499388_1_kangal-malsat-kangal-malsat-film-certification.

Spivak, Gayatri Chakravorty. 1988. 'Can the Subaltern Speak?' In *Marxism and the Interpretation of Culture*, edited by Nelson, C. and Grossberg, L. Basingstoke: Macmillan Education, 271–313.

Sprengler, Christine. 2009. 'The Nostalgia Film in Practice and Theory'. In *Screening Nostalgia: Populuxe Props and Technicolor Aesthetics in Contemporary American Film*, by Christine Sprengler. New York: Bergahn Books, 67-92.

Zerubazel, Eviatar. 2018. 'The Politics of Normality'. In *Taken for Granted: The Remarkable Power of the Unremarkable*, by Eviatar Zerubazel. Princeton: Princeton University Press, 32–59.

Index

M

List of Contributors

Editors:

Sourit Bhattacharya is a Lecturer in Postcolonial Studies at the University of Glasgow. His research interests include postcolonial literatures (especially South Asian writings), food crisis, catastrophe and ecology, literary form, translations studies and Marxism. His works in these areas are either published or forthcoming in such journals as *Ariel, Textual Practice, Irish University Review*, and in edited books such as *Cambridge Critical Concepts: Magic Realism* (forthcoming), *Aesthetics and Politics of Global Hunger* (2018) and others. His first monograph, entitled *Postcolonial Modernity and the Indian Novel: On Catastrophic Realism*, has been published by Palgrave (2020). Sourit is a founding co-editor of *Sanglap: Journal of Literary and Cultural Inquiry*.

Arka Chattopadhyay is an Assistant Professor of Humanities and Social Sciences in IIT Gandhinagar, India. He has been published in books like *Deleuze and Beckett* and journals like *Interventions, Textual Practice, Samuel Beckett Today/Aujourd'hui* and *Psychoanalysis, Culture and Society*, etc. He has co-edited *Samuel Beckett and the Encounter of Philosophy and Literature* and a Bengali compendium on Nabarun Bhattacharya. Arka is the co-editor of the online journal *Sanglap* (http://sanglap-journal.in/). He has guest-edited the SBT/A issue on *Samuel Beckett and the Extensions of the Mind*. His first monograph, *Beckett, Lacan and the Mathematical Writing of the Real* has been published by Bloomsbury in 2019.

Samrat Sengupta is an Assistant Professor and Head of the Deptartment of English at Sammilani Mahavidyalaya under University of Calcutta. His doctoral work is on ethico-politics of postcolonial resistances focusing on the Naxalbari movement, a radical Maoist insurgent movement in Bengal. His research interests include Gender

Studies, Post-structuralism, Memory Studies and Posthumanism. His recent important publication is on Stiegler and Derrida's take on teletechnology and power published in an anthology from Springerlink. He has recently co-edited a special issue of the international journal *Sanglap: Journal of Literary and Cultural Inquiry* on 'Caste in/as Humanities'. His first Bengali monograph on 'Syllabus of Resistance' will be published in early 2020.

Foreword:

Supriya Chaudhuri is a Professor of English (Emerita) at Jadavpur University, Kolkata, India. Her research interests include English and European Renaissance literature, Indian cultural history, travel writing, modernism, critical theory and translation. Her recent publications are *Commodities and Culture in the Colonial World* (co-edited, 2018) and chapters in *The Oxford Handbook of Modernisms* (2010), *The Cambridge Companion to Modern Indian Culture* (2012), *Celebrating Shakespeare: Commemoration and Cultural Memory* (2016), *A Companion to Virginia Woolf* (2016), *The Cambridge History of Travel Writing* (2019), *The University Unthought* (2019), *Blind Spots of Knowledge in Shakespeare and His World* (2019) and *Modernist Communities Across Cultures and Media* (2019). She has translated extensively from Bengali fiction and poetry.

Preface:

Tathagata Bhattacharya is the only son of Nabarun Bhattacharya and Pranati Bhattacharya. He lives and works as a senior journalist in Delhi.

Translators:

Malini Bhattacharya studied English literature at Jadavpur University, Kolkata. She has worked as a writer, editor and translator in publishing houses and at start-ups in Delhi, Mumbai and Kolkata. She is mainly a writer of narrative non-fiction, but also writes the odd short story, flash fiction piece and, rarely, poetry. She has been published (among others) in *Coldnoon: Travel Poetics* and *Litro* magazines. As a reader, she takes a special interest in contemporary literary fiction by women, especially working with a strong gender focus. Malini lives in Kolkata, India, and enjoys travel, cooking and photography.

Debadrita Bose had started her career as a writer, translator and literary editor. She has two books of Bengali poetry. She is also a filmmaker. In cinema, she sought a more dynamic way of expression. She is passionate about issues of gender and sexuality. Her films have toured national and international festivals. She has just finished her latest film, *Goodbye Beautiful*, in which, for the first time, a transgender woman plays a cis character. Debadrita believes that no kind of marginalisation process can work on its own, and other forms of power-play always come into work. This is what she tries to express in her works.

Atindriya Chakraborty is currently a Kolkata-based writer, translator and lawyer. He has written and published extensively using various genres, such as poetry, short stories, history of literature, indigenous mythology, the bhakti movement and human rights abuses. As a lawyer, human rights activist and travelling writer, he has worked in various states of India, such as West Bengal, Assam, Jharkhand, Odisha, Chhattisgarh, Kashmir and Karnataka. One of his primary areas of passion lies in translating selections from Bangla literature from ancient, medieval, modern and postmodern times into English.

Rijula Das is a recipient of the 2019 Micheal King Writer's Centre Residency in Auckland and the 2016 Dastaan Award for her short story 'Notes from a Passing'. Her debut novel *A Death in Shonagachhi* will be published in 2020 by Picador India. Her English translation of Nabarun Bhattacharya's novel, *Kangal Malshat,* is forthcoming from Seagull Books in Fall of 2020. Her short fiction has appeared in *Newsroom* and *The Hindu*. She holds a PhD in Creative Writing, and her research examines the relationship between public space and sexual violence in urban India. She lives and works in New Zealand.

V. Ramaswamy lives in Kolkata, India. He is currently concluding a long-term project of translating the short fiction of Subimal Misra, the anti-establishment Bengali writer. His Subimal Misra translations include *Golden Gandhi Statue from America*, *Wild Animals Prohibited* and *This Could Be Ramayan Chamar's Tale: Two Anti-Novels*, all published by HarperCollins Publishers India.

Partha Pratim Roy Chowdhury teaches English at Sammilani Mahavidyalaya, Kolkata. As an editor and translator, he has been closely associated for years with *Puran Kosh*—an encyclopaedic dictionary of the Ramayana, the Mahabharata and the Puranas—under the supervision of one of the world's leading Indologists. He has presented his papers in national and international conferences on authors, including Nabarun Bhattacharya, Arundhati Roy, Atin Bandyopadhyay, as well as on topics like Planetary futures, the posthuman and others. His maiden monograph deals with the writings of activist–author Mahasweta Devi. Currently, he is working on philosophical horror and psychoanalysis.

Essays:

Arnab Banerji is an Assistant Professor of Theatre History and Dramatic Literature at Loyola Marymount University, Los Angeles. He is currently working on a monograph on Bengali Group Theatre to be published by Routledge. Arnab's essays and reviews have been published in *Theatre Journal*, *Theatre Topics*, *Asian Theatre Journal*, *TDR*, *BOOM California*, *Ecumenica*, *Theatre Symposium*, *Sanglap*, *Cerebration*, *SERAS* and *Virginia Review of Asian Studies*. His current research is on performances by the Indian diaspora, translations of Indian vernacular plays and contemporary Bengali theatre.

Anustup Basu is an Associate Professor at the University of Illinois at Urbana-Champaign. He is the author of *Hindutva As Political Monotheism* (2020), *Bollywood in the Age of New Media* (2010) and the co-editor of *InterMedia in South Asia* (2012) and *Figurations in Indian Film* (2013). His essays on film, media, culture, philosophy and politics have appeared in journals like *boundary 2, Semiotic Inquiry, Journal of Human Rights, Postscript, PostModern Culture and Critical Quarterly.*

He was also the executive producer of *Herbert* (2005), the national award-winning film based on Nabarun Bhattacharya's novel.

Priyanka Basu received her PhD in South Asian Studies from the Department of South Asia, SOAS, University of London. Her research interests include folklore, theatre, film histories, gender and dance studies. She is the curator of 'Two Centuries of Indian Print' project at the British Library, and as part of it runs the South Asia Seminar series. Her current research focuses on the history of *Shakespeareana* in India. Her recent publications have appeared in *Journal of South Asian History and Culture*, *Emerging Dance Studies*, *Sanglap*, and in edited books, such as *The Moving Space* (2017), *Film Studies* (2020), *South Asian Performers and Crafts* (forthcoming), etc. Her monograph based on her doctoral research on the cultural politics of Kobigaan will be published soon.

Aritra Chakraborti did his doctoral research on chapbooks, pamphlets and printed mass-media in colonial Bengal. Digital archives created by him, on early 20th-century printed ephemera and contemporary printed Bengali pornography, are available at The School of Cultural Texts and Records and The British Library, respectively. His research interests include science fiction and fantasy, history of the book and the social history of pornography. He currently works as a Technical Editor in an information technology company.

Carola E. Lorea is a Research Fellow at ARI, National University of Singapore. She works on Bengali literature, sound cultures, folklore and oral literature in relation to esoteric religious movements and Tantric traditions. Her monograph *Folklore, Religion and the Songs of a Bengali Madman: A Journey Between Performance and the Politics of Cultural Representation* (2016) is the result of a four-year travel-along ethnography with Baul performers in West Bengal. She has received research fellowships from IIAS, Gonda Foundation (Leiden) and SAI (Heidelberg) to study travelling archives of songs in India, Bangladesh and Andaman Islands. She has authored several articles on folklore and sacred songs, translated the works of Bengali poets and novelists, such as Jibanananda Das and Nabarun Bhattacharya, and has been socially engaged as an interpreter for Bangladeshi refugees for several years.

Anuparna Mukherjee is an Assistant Professor of English in the Department of Humanities and Social Sciences at IISER, Bhopal. She holds a PhD degree in literature from the Australian National University and had completed her graduation from Presidency College. She had convened a conference under the auspice of the Humanities Research Centre at ANU on 'strangers and strangeness in urban literature'. Anuparna has guest-edited a special issue on 'City, Space and Literature' with Arunima Bhattacharya in 2017. Her recent article 'After the Empire: Narratives of Haunting in the Postcolonial Spectropolis' was published in *South Asian Review*.

Anindya Sekhar Purakayastha is a Professor in the Department of English at Kazi Nazrul University, India. He was a Fulbright Nehru Academic and Professional Excellence Fellow 2018–2019 in the University of Massachusetts, Amherst. He has also been a Fellow in the Institute for Critical Social Inquiry, New School for Social Research, New York in 2017. His current area of research focuses on postcolonial political violence, citizenship rights and governmentality crisis. His co-edited volumes include *Violence in South Asia: Contemporary Perspectives* (2019). He co-edits *Kairos, A Journal of Critical Symposium* and is one of the founding members of the Postcolonial Studies Association of the Global South (PSAGS).

Dibyakusum Ray teaches English, Philosophy and Cultural Studies at the Indian Institute of Technology, Ropar, Punjab. He has worked on the archaeology of 'Other' and 'Liminality' and its absorption in Bengali 'radical' literature. He also frequently writes about speculative fiction, especially the theme of 'horror', in modern global literature. Ray is currently heading a centrally funded project on the archiving of lost media elements during the Indian National Emergency, 1975–1977, in collaboration with the Royal Holloway London. He is the co-editor of an ongoing anthology on *Horror and South Asian Popular Culture*, and has published work in *Palgrave Communications* (Nature), *Economic and Political Weekly* and others.